A biography of Agnes Macphail

a biography
of Agnes Macphail

Ask no quarter

Margaret Stewart

Doris French

published by

Longmans, Green and Company

Toronto 1959

Longmans, Green and Company
20 Cranfield Road, Toronto 16

Longmans Green & Co. Inc.,
119 West 40th Street, New York 18

Longmans Green & Co. Ltd.,
6–7 Clifford Street, London W.1

First Edition, 1959

Designed by
Arnold Rockman, M.T.D.C.

Printed and bound by
Hazell Watson and Viney Ltd.
Aylesbury and Slough, England

Contents

Foreword, 7

Chapter 1 : "Madam ; fellow members . . .", 13

Chapter 2 : Scottish pioneers : the Campbells and
Macphails, 19

Chapter 3 : Pupil and teacher, 28

Chapter 4 : A new career—farmers on the march, 42

Chapter 5 : "We have made history in South-East Grey !", 49

Chapter 6 : 1922—Ottawa, 61

Chapter 7 : A dash of ginger, 76

Chapter 8 : New causes, 85

Chapter 9 : Riding relations, 94

Chapter 10 : The devil and the deep, 102

Chapter 11 : Another election, a new protégé, 120

Chapter 12 : Before the great depression, 127

Chapter 13 : Tours and travels, 137

Chapter 14 : R. B. B.—and hard times, 152

Chapter 15 : Formation of the C.C.F., 157

Chapter 16 : The C.C.F. in Ontario—the U.F.O. in
and out, 171

Chapter 17 : The Baynes incident, 182

Chapter 18 : The dark prison house, 200

Chapter 19 : The cause of labour too, 215

Chapter 20 : On the crest, 223

Chapter 21 : Colleagues and other people, 231

Chapter 22 : 1940 : defeat, 245

Chapter 23 : No safe harbour, 257

Chapter 24 : A change of pace, 266

Chapter 25 : Defeat and recovery, 275

Chapter 26 : The last battle, 289

Chapter 27 : Finale, 296

Index, 305

Foreword

The writing of this book has been a happy experience for its authors. Everyone agreed that the biography of Agnes Macphail must be written, and no one was rude enough to suggest that some one else should write it. This encouragement was continuous as the work progressed. Help came readily from many quarters. The Dominion and Ontario Archives and the Library of Parliament were open to us; the newspaper libraries, especially in Toronto, supplied valuable clippings. Notes and letters came from Agnes Macphail's family and friends. One of her lifelong admirers sent us his entire file of her columns from the *Globe and Mail*. The International League for Peace and Friendship sent along their files concerning her work with them. Editors of weekly newspapers to which she had once contributed dug into the dusty past for us. The National and Ontario offices of the C.C.F. party were most generous in giving us access to minutes of proceedings. Research that involved travel was made possible through funds supplied by the Ontario Woodsworth Foundation and Les Recherches Sociales.

Individuals—Lilla Bell, E. B. Jolliffe, M. J. Coldwell, Angus and Grace MacInnis, D. M. LeBourdais, Elmore Philpott, and a great many others—supplied us with information and reminiscences. Acknowledgement is made to books on the period : *Woman Suffrage in Canada,* Catherine Lyle Cleverdon; *The Progressive Party in Canada,* W. L. Morton ; *Canada, a Political and Social History,* Edgar MacInnes ; *The Royal Power of Dissolution of Parliament,* Eugene Forsey ; *Report of the Royal Commission to Investigate the Penal*

System of Canada, Joseph Archambault; *The Incredible Canadian,* Bruce Hutchison; and an unpublished M.A. thesis by George Hougham describing the minor political parties in Canada.

In response to an appeal to a number of women's organizations, which was helpfully picked up and broadcast by press and radio, we received hundreds of letters from friends and acquaintances all across the country. Our trips to Grey County were rewarding indeed.

When we say our helpers have been too numerous to mention, it is literally true. We ask pardon, therefore, for singling out two names—Miller Stewart and Rob French.

Agnes Macphail herself was most anxious that this book be written. Some time before her death she spent five afternoons a week for six weeks, talking to Margaret Stewart, to whom she also gave her files (now in the Dominion Archives) and an autobiography that she had begun and abandoned.

As a consequence of those talks, this book came close to being called *The Two Live of Agnes Macphail.* It was apparent that the separation between her public life and her private life was very complete. She was so accustomed to maintaining that separation that it was difficult for her to talk frankly, even though absolute frankness was her aim. It required a real effort to hold open the door of communication. Agnes was always so open and at ease in her public statements that it was surprising to find this barrier. She overcame it very deliberately, because she wanted the story of her life to be full and accurate, not a eulogy. "I don't want to go down in history as a frustrated old maid," she said.

We have been as accurate as possible. We have checked dates and facts, and have learned the fallibility of human memory including that of our subject. We have omitted one of the best known anecdotes about Agnes. It seems that she was in the midst of a speech when suddenly a male heckler shouted at her, "Don't you wish you were a man?" Quick as a flash, Agnes retorted, "Yes. Don't you?"

This story is said to have happened in Parliament, at a

meeting here, there, and several other places. It has become a legend. But because we were unable to pin it down to a time and place, we have omitted it. Countless other anecdotes, well documented, have been left out because we did not wish to make this book simply a collection of incidents, however amusing they might be. Dozens of people will be disappointed that the little story they sent us is not in the book. The little story they sent us was one more ray of light to illuminate our subject, and most gratefully received.

Margaret Stewart and Doris French.

"To open the blind eyes,
to bring out the prisoners from the prison,
and them that sit in darkness
out of the prison house."

ISAIAH, 42 : 7

Ask no quarter

One

"Madam; fellow members . . ."

The opening of the Fourteenth Parliament of Canada, in March, 1922, was packed with the stuff of drama. Openings are always somewhat breathless affairs, but seldom has there been one so significant as this.

Parliament, like the theatre, is its own world. As the theatre has its devoted following, so those who live closely with parliaments breathe in their heady atmosphere and are spoiled, afterwards, for ordinary ozone.

The analogy is strong. Someone, disgusted, said that Parliament is "a theatre magnificently lit, for dull acting, undeserved applause." But it is only when parliamentarians overact—when a too-handy Union Jack is ostentatiously flung over the empty desk of a Member ejected by the Speaker—that the performance rings hollow. When members, as they sometimes do, ignore the temptation to play to the galleries, and honestly and bravely treat the issues of their times, to nudge on history this way or that—then Parliament does have a dramatic power and excitement beyond the highest moments of the theatre.

Each session, like a play, must start with fanfare and an opening. The press is there in strength to laud the stars, speculate on the length of the run, and sort newcomers over into those who seem promising and those who can be either ignored or disposed of in a neat and telling phrase.

So in the early spring of 1922 they waited again on Parliament Hill for the curtain to go up on the old pageantry, with a new cast, a new play—and some other rather startling innovations.

To begin at the highest point, there was a new governor-general. Not that governors-general were supposed to have an effect on the political fortunes of Canadians; they had been taught their place before Confederation. This one's vice-regal bearing, his voice as he read the Throne Speech text were duly noted, but nobody in the galleries put him down as a real participant. This time the observers were wrong. The new governor-general was General The Lord Byng of Vimy, who within a few years would be the centre of a political battle that would decide another election, and is still refought at intervals by students of the affair.

Ennobling this Parliament was an addition to the buildings themselves. The members of the House of Commons passed through an arched centre entrance and a stately Hall of Fame that had just been officially opened. (Oddly, the Governor-General, when he arrived with an escort from the Princess Louise Dragoon Guards, had to go in by the Senate entrance, because the main door had been ruled within the precincts of the Commons!) The base of a central tower over the entrance was there, and soon the tall bell tower would add Gothic grace to the rebuilt Centre Block. Inside would be a Memorial Chamber beautifully designed to honour the war dead, and the entire structure would be known, of course, as the Peace Tower. For if there was anything Canada was agreed on, in the spring of 1922, it was what this tower would stand for—a nation at peace with the world.

This was the post-war Parliament of Canada. The convulsions and the agony were now past; the national wounds could begin to heal. The previous Parliament had been elected in 1917: its Government had been called Unionist but was in fact Conservative; and its Opposition had been a dissenting part of the Liberal party. Its life had been marked by a series of the bitterest and most disruptive issues: conscription; the Ontario separate-school question, which exploded racial antagonisms; tariff "betrayals"; a bungled and painful demobilization; a plunge into economic depression. The country had rid itself of the old Parliament in decisive fashion; the Conservative force

"Madam; fellow members ..."

had been cut to fifty, their smallest number since Confederation.

This was the great question behind the others : how was the new Parliament going to meet the challenge of far-reaching changes in the country itself, changes brought about partly by war and partly by the end of an economic era? The period of agricultural expansion was over, the period of industrial growth had begun. The pressures were enormous : from immigrant labour, from fledgling business enterprise, from outworn and outgrown constitutional forms—and most of all from that group that usually is heard from least, the Canadian farmer. The most disturbing feature of the national scene was that farmers' children no longer stayed on farms, and from this change arose a host of others that were the items of business before Parliament in 1922. The only international demand was a negative one : at any cost, keep us out of another war.

All eyes turned therefore on the key figures in the House of Commons, and the make-up of that assembly was never more closely scrutinized. Who were the people here who would last, who would stand forth as leaders and strong public servants in the days ahead?

There was a new Prime Minister, Mackenzie King. He was a disappointment to the eye—a round-faced, proper little man in his mid-forties, who had worked for Rockefeller in the United States a good part of the war years. He hadn't associated himself closely with the sweeping promises of the Liberals' 1919 convention platform. He spoke of it as merely a chart, and during the election campaign he had gone about making soft, conciliatory speeches without much wit or spice to them. He called himself obsequiously "the servant of all". It was rather astonishing that such a man should turn up at this time, when the country was straining toward its brave new future : but he probably wouldn't last long.

There was a new Opposition leader—roughly the same age as King, but far more impressive in person and reputation, and obviously enraged by the reversal of position. The Right Honourable Arthur Meighen was already noted for his brilliant mind and political fire. He had taken over the reins of government briefly at the close of the last session, when ill health forced Borden to resign. His election campaign had been bold and eye-catching. If there was betting on political futures in the galleries that day, the odds must have favoured Meighen.

But the truly extraordinary thing about the new House of Commons was that the Government party and the Opposition party were not all. It had never happened in Canada before; but in 1922, it happened—a third group and, indeed, even a fragment of a fourth group took seats in Parliament and refused to fall into line as either Liberals or Conservatives. The big third group called itself "Progressive", and the separate pair of men in the extreme left corner of the chamber called themselves "Labour". The speculation in the galleries grew warmest over these dissident, duly elected members, for they were present in numbers that could not be ignored. The outlandish outcome of the past election had been success at the polls for sixty-five Progressives, nearly all of them farmers from Ontario and the Western provinces.

It is amusing to note that the same tones of moral reproach that are heard today on the subject of third parties, were voiced in 1922 by editors and newsmen. They talked to the errant Progressives like schoolmasters, reminding them of the neatness and fittingness, not to mention the sanctity, of the two-party system of government. However, three months after the election, there was already reason to believe that the awkward state of affairs might not last. T. A. Crerar, leader of the Progressives, had talked with King. Almost from the moment the election results were known there had been reports of meetings between Liberal leaders and Crerar and his followers—though "followers" was not an accurate term, because everyone in the Progressive group seemed to be there on his own, and the very name of "party" was anathema to some of them. A swift return to the pattern of two parties, the pattern of "ins" and "outs", could be clearly foreseen; just as it is still so clearly foreseen in 1958.

But if, because of its size, the Progressive group could not be ignored in the composition of this Parliament, no such consideration applied to the Labour pair. The one in the lead was a

"Madam; fellow members..."

slight, bearded man recently confined to a Winnipeg jail for his part in the general strike in that city. He was a former minister of the gospel who had broken with his church. Who, in looking over the Commons in March, 1922, would not have dismissed J. S. Woodsworth out of hand? Yet here was where the galleries were most wrong.

It looked like the kind of parliament that is bound to make news, even though many of its exciting elements were still unguessed. The press gallery was crowded and alert.

And there was one thing more. To the gayer sort of reporter it was something of a joke. To the long-established member of the press gallery who had become indistinguishable from a veteran M.P., it was a shocking disturbance of the accepted order, and something he would do his utmost to ignore.

As the House of Commons met, every eye strayed, as soon as dignity would permit, to a desk far down on the left side, beyond the Conservatives, in the front row of Progressives. For seated at that desk among the lawmakers of Canada *was a woman.*

Now women had always—pretty things—graced the galleries and even the Senate chamber, for a brief, fashionable flutter on opening day. But what was this woman doing here, where men got down to business and fought their hard political wars and handled the complex affairs of state?

A woman in a dark-blue serge dress, prim and long-sleeved. She did not wear a hat; her brown hair was set in the corrugated waves of the current style. Her face was ruddy, her eyes sharp behind steel-rimmed glasses. Her name was Agnes Campbell Macphail, and she came from Grey County in south-western Ontario.

The 1918 woman-suffrage law had been followed in 1919 with an act permitting women to sit in Parliament, and four daring females had entered the 1921 contest. Agnes Macphail had been *elected* in the rural riding of South-East Grey! The aberration was surely proof that rural unrest must be viewed seriously.

Newspaper women had been assigned to cover this strange

"first". Most newspaper women wrote for the social page; and they reported that the dark serge dress had been worn more than fifty times—in fact, on every public platform during her election campaign. They disclosed that advice had been delicately offered: "Our kind of lady would prefer to see you wear a hat"; but Miss Macphail had retorted that she "couldn't think as well with a hat on".

And this was all that most people had learned, so far, about the first Canadian woman elected to the House of Commons—beyond the fact that she was what she appeared to be, a strong-minded country school-teacher. Her age was a matter of record, too. She was thirty-one.

"Surely," said the political pundits, "only the oddest mixture of circumstance could have brought her *here*. Surely she will escape with relief, in the briefest possible time, to the obscurity of a school in the back concessions."

The first act of the first session of the fourteenth Parliament of Canada, on March 8th, 1922, was to elect a Speaker of the House. He was chosen, the Honourable Rodolphe Lemieux.

Ascending to his chair to assume his office, Speaker Lemieux addressed the House of Commons to thank them for this honour. His first word reverberated; the incredible new thing had happened.

"Madam; Fellow Members of the House of Commons . . ."

Agnes Macphail was on stage.

"Madam; fellow members . . ."

Two

Scottish pioneers: the Campbells and Macphails

Agnes Campbell Macphail was born on March 24, 1890, in Proton Township in Grey County, which runs south from Georgian Bay in Ontario. It is typical of the choice so many Scots made in picking homesteads out of the wilderness. They seemed to suffer a deep nostalgia, so that they chose rocky, hilly land that reminded them of the homeland of their ancestors— the homeland that was left because they could not make a living on the same kind of rocky, hilly land. There are good farms in Grey County, but there are many stretches of swamp and thin-soiled uplands.

Proton Township is known for its black swamps. Once cleared and drained, the land is excellent growing soil, but the work of preparation is heart-breaking and back-breaking. It is not as hilly as the rest of the county, possessing one long esker, or ridge, full of gravel. Here are the headwaters of six Ontario rivers, the Humber, the Credit, the Grand, the Beaver, the Nottawasaga, and the Saugeen—the last the most important locally. A visitor to Grey can still see, on many farms, the progression of prosperity and higher standards of living. There are log cabins, the original dwellings, now abandoned or used for sheds. Then there are frame houses, larger than the cabins, now demoted to storing implements, or used as cottages for the help or for the married son; and, finally, the brick or stone farm-houses that are still in use. Here in Proton Township the Macphails and the Campbells settled and farmed and produced many children, among them Agnes.

After a visit to Scotland a few years before she died, she

wrote an account of her family which she called *My Ain Folk*.
In it she said :

> A few miles north of Oban, looking out over the Firth of
> Lorne, with Ben Cruachan lifting his hoary head far in-
> land, lies the little village of Kilmartin. Progress has passed
> it by. The little stone church is still lit by the great hanging
> sconces of oil lamps. A quarter of the gravestones are moss-
> grown and scoured by the sea to illegibility. But inside the
> building the brass plaques commemorating the famous
> dead are kept gleaming, and the stained-glass windows
> throw rainbows on the pavement. My Macphail ancestors
> came from Kilmartin, and standing in the doorway which
> they must so often have entered, I thought how like the
> church is the family tradition. No one generation built that
> church or gave all that stained glass or put up all those
> plaques. But each had its part in something which by its
> very age and continuity became more than the sum of all
> of them.
>
> The country around Oban is very beautiful. The Mac-
> phails must have hated to leave it. They must have been
> driven by economic desperation. My great-grandfather
> was head shepherd on a large estate with thousands of
> sheep. He lived with his wife and twelve children in a small
> stone cottage at the foot of the mountain. His eldest son,
> my grandfather, helped him, but there was no future for
> the others in Kilmartin, no way for the family to keep
> together, for the land was not their own. About 1846 the
> Macphails decided to emigrate. One daughter, Sara, who
> had married very young, stayed in Scotland. The rest of
> the children emigrated with their parents.
>
> (One son emigrated to Jamaica, where he made a for-
> tune in rum, and became Sir John Macphail.)
>
> Grandfather Macphail was sixteen when the family
> settled between Galt and Guelph in Ontario. But when
> young Alexander, turned twenty and ready to settle down,
> came to look for a farm, he walked up to what is now

Mount Forest and east to Proton with his bundle in a bandanna, to squat on land which he later acquired legally. It was the twelfth concession of the township, just over from the Campbells, who were on the fourteenth.

His wife's people, the Jacks, walked into the same township from Hamilton, a journey of almost 100 miles, and carried with them all their belongings. Grandmother used to say she wondered why they walked so far, since by doing so they settled on poorer land than they passed, and came into virgin forest where they were the only settlers so far as they knew.

Tragedy soon befell the Jacks family, for when [grandmother] Jean was twelve years of age, her mother died, leaving her the awful task of keeping house for her father and brothers, the youngest a baby of one year. Such was the stuff of which our ancestors were made that she managed to do it. At twenty-one she helped found her own home, and after raising her own twelve children lived to the ripe old age of eighty-five.

The first product these early families in Proton had to market was maple sugar. They carried it strapped to their backs nearly twenty miles to Mount Forest. And sometimes, Grandmother Jean Macphail said, the walking was such hot work that the sugar was melted a little when they got there. Butter was not easy to make at first. The cows ate leeks in the bush which tainted the butter. And then, too, they had no proper place to ripen the cream. The earthen rooms called milk-houses came later. I have heard my grandparents' generation tell of getting only ten cents a pound for butter, and paying a dollar a pound for tea. The load coming home from the market place wouldn't be so heavy.

After a time the second house and barn were built. The timber was hewn on the farm, and the lumber made from their own logs. The cost was just what the stonemason and farmer charged—possibly not over $200 in all. When the same barn was re-roofed a few years ago, it cost more than the original structure.

Alexander Macphail was a man who took his duties as a citizen very seriously. He became the second Reeve of Proton, and it was said in his family that he looked after all the widows and orphans in the neighbourhood, and had not time for his own twelve children. Township reeves and deputy reeves constituted the County Council from the formation of Grey County in 1852. This necessitated a periodic trip to Sydenham, now Owen Sound, for the council meetings. After the first year the Council passed a by-law, which has not been rescinded, making their meeting date a Tuesday instead of a Monday, so that their members would not have to travel on the Sabbath to attend.

Alexander Macphail built a Sunday school for the Presbyterian children—to which all denominations were invited—before he got around to enlarging his own home. The result was that Dougal, his eldest son and Agnes' father, had to act as head of the family, looking after his younger brothers and sisters, and going out at seventeen to earn money at custom threshing. He was resentful of the situation, and grew up with a determination to see that when he married, his family would come first. At twenty-five he married Henrietta Campbell. The Campbells had little use for orthodox churches, but Henrietta went with Dougal to the Esplen Presbyterian manse to be married in 1889. Of her Campbell ancestors, Agnes wrote:

The Campbell history can be traced back more readily than the Macphail, because the Campbells were to all intents and purposes landowners. My grandfather Campbell's great-great-grandfather, James, and his two brothers broke away from the clan at the time of the "Fifteen" Rebellion. James became a wealthy farmer down in Ayrshire, having married a daughter of a chief of the Stewarts of Appin.

James Campbell's descendants might still be living in Ayrshire if they had not decided to grow potatoes. The

Scottish pioneers: the Campbells and Macphails

Presbyterian Church then regarded these "imports from heathendom", sponsored by Catholic clergy and nobles, as the cause of palsy, scurvy, leprosy and so on. The Campbells grew fat and healthy on the forbidden diet, and made money selling the "devil's tubers" to the nearby garrison. When the parson refused to baptize James' grandson, the parents took little Tommy to the garrison chaplain, and stopped contributing to the church. Tommy's family, when he was grown and married, continued the potato-growing; bad relations with the church resulted in a village fight. A distrust of sanctimonious intolerance became a family heritage, and no doubt persuaded the Campbells of later days to accept the simple evangelical doctrine of the Latter Day Saints, when missionaries brought it, purged of its undesirable Mormon features, to the neglected pioneers in the Canadian bush.

My great-uncle, Tam Campbell, is said to have been the first commoner in Scotland to take an aristocrat to court and the first tenant to sue a landlord. Lady Boswell, whose husband, Sir James, Tam's landlord, was serving in Malta, decided she wanted Tam to cancel his leases. When he demanded a high premium for doing so she doubled his rent. The bailiff refused to accept rent at the old rate, seized a quantity of Tam's goods, and quartered a man at his farm at Tam's expense. Tam sued Lady Boswell and won his case. She had to accept rent at the old rate and pay damages and costs.

At the age of thirteen, my grandfather, John Campbell, won a steel pen for the best letter about a plan of life:

"Dear Teacher: In a few years I will go to America where there are no landlords and no rent and no queen. I will get a house of my own there and a farm, maybe two farms. I will have a home of my own and a farm before I am thirty years old, and a wife too!"

A typical stubborn Scot, he made good every promise. His wife was Jean Black, the sonsy, merry farm dairymaid, with whom his elder brother was also in love. They travelled to Canada in the *Heather Bell* on a voyage which lasted for ten miserable weeks, and their infant son died of a "bloody flux" and was buried at sea. The work in the new world was hard too; seamen and stewardess on the voyage; brickmaker, sawmill operator and fencer, or laundress and cook on land. But by 1855 they had completed their contracts, homesteaded and bought a claim, with a house of sorts already put up. In that very year he was joined by his brothers Tam and Geordie, and they settled near each other and near the Macphails in Proton. . . .

In this gallery of my ain folk, perhaps one figure stands out particularly. My Grandmother Campbell was brave and bonny. She could work in the slash with the men and rush home a few minutes early to prepare the bannocks and bacon. She several times drove off bears which were threatening the stock, and she never shed a tear when a gang of fifteen "swamp angels" took all her food, turned her and Great-Uncle Geordie's wife and their children out of their painstakingly built log homes, and burned the little dwellings. Grandmother said she couldn't cry, she was so angry.

Grandmother often told us stories of her youth. The daughter of a coal miner, who died when his five children were almost infants, Jean Black had few worldly advantages, but she had an indomitable spirit. She learned to read by standing behind her uncle's chair and following the finger with which he kept his place as he read aloud the weekly newspaper. At twelve she became one of the family breadwinners, learning wherever she went, and winning all hearts by her eagerness and industry. In her day writing was a frivolous accomplishment for a young farm woman, and she did not learn to write until her daughter Maggie married and moved away. At sixty-seven she became an accomplished penwoman.

Scottish pioneers: the Campbells and Macphails

Her grandmother Campbell was the guiding spirit of Agnes Macphail's life. There was a bond of love and respect between them that never weakened. Agnes was always fond of attributing her various qualities and virtues—and weaknesses—to her parents and grandparents, but spiritually and emotionally she was the child of Grandma Campbell. She remarked: "She could do everything a woman is supposed to do and do it better than most women, and she could do most things a man is supposed to do and do them as well as most men. That's not unusual in a farm woman, but I idolized her for it."

Jean Campbell was far ahead of her times in her thinking and in her interests. She had definite ideas about a welfare state. She had a horror of any kind of discrimination or prejudice against people of a different creed or colour. She taught Agnes that the duty of the strong is to protect and champion the weak.

John Campbell's determination and independence were the death of him. As an old man, he decided one day to help with the reaping. He said nothing to his wife or to his sons, but went out on his own. He made a mistake in the fastening of the reaper. The horses ran away, and John was badly injured. He lingered for some months, lying in the fine stone house he had built, and nursed by his wife until he died. Agnes was about ten at that time. Her grandfather Macphail died about the same time.

When Dougal Macphail married Etta Campbell, they had very little to set up married life on—"$800, a few sticks of furniture and a team of oxen". They were given a farm in the neighbourhood, with a mortgage on it, a log barn and a house. It was low-lying and poor land. Mrs. Macphail hated it, but it gave Agnes the opportunity, which she cherished, of saying truthfully that she had been born in a log cabin like a true pioneer. It was hard to heat in winter, and the water in the kettle used to freeze overnight. One of the things Mrs. Macphail disliked most was the impossibility of keeping house plants alive over the winter. She was a passionate gardener.

Dougal built a new barn, but he never did get a new house

25

on the place. They lived there until Agnes was twelve, and two sisters completed the family. Her memories of it were very happy. It had a big, hospitable kitchen, the centre of family life. Agnes always remembered the shining look of the cabin on Saturdays when the floor and all the furniture were scrubbed to gleaming whiteness. Mrs. Macphail was a "demon house-keeper" no matter what the difficulties. There was still plenty of bush in the area at that time, and squared timber was being taken off. The logging crews had to be fed two substantial meals every day. Mrs. Macphail was a very industrious and con-scientious woman, and she had neither the time nor the temperament for gaiety and relaxation. It is not surprising that she was impatient of holidays and celebrations. If Christmas happened to fall on Monday, it was not allowed to interfere with washday. For years Agnes firmly believed that Santa Claus simply did not know where she lived. It was Grandma Camp-bell who supplied the emotional warmth and party atmosphere that Agnes craved. It was not until she was grown up that Agnes understood and appreciated the strength of character and endurance, the staunch moral fibre that drove her mother to severity towards her family. She was a very strict disciplinarian —another contrast to Grandma Campbell. The little girls were expected to take their knocks and tumbles without tears or sympathy. And later, when the hurts were not physical, they were expected to endure without whining. The only time Mrs. Macphail ever expressed sympathy with Agnes was when she was being berated and slandered during her battle for penal reform. Agnes said of her, "Perhaps if I owed my father the ability to get into Parliament, I owed her the ability to stand it when I got there."

These, then, were the people who produced Canada's first woman Member of Parliament. All her life Agnes Macphail identified herself absolutely with her background. She was proud of being farm bred. She was proud of coming from pioneer stock. And she was proud of her Scotch blood. She considered her people—the farmers from the British Isles, and

Scottish pioneers: the Campbells and Macphails

particularly from Scotland—to be the backbone of Canada in a perfectly literal sense.

Her ancestry, the determined and rebellious Scotch forbears, and her environment, the sturdy, hard-working farm community, may explain many of her actions and attitudes. The people who influenced her, the currents of her time, swept her into political life. But none of these things explain her personal magnetism, the charm and warmth that attracted people to her. The camera slandered her, making her face look flat, and hiding the good modelling of her bones, giving her an appearance of gravity and severity that misled the people who knew her only through her pictures. Still, she was not a pretty girl, or a pretty woman. But her personality drew men and women alike, singly and in crowds. Her flashing wit and amusing phrases kept her audiences in roars of laughter, while her serious purpose crept into their minds. She had scores of deadly enemies and thousands of enthusiastic admirers. She was impatient and persistent, sincere and devastatingly forthright, impulsive in some fields and painstaking in others. She was so sensitive that she suffered from every slight, so courageous that she could not be halted by the most vicious attack. She was a great admirer of thrift, and an extravagant spender. And she was a very beloved woman.

Three

Pupil and teacher

When Agnes Macphail was five years old, she trudged off to the little country school, S.S.No.4, Proton. She was a pupil there until she was twelve, when her father bought another farm near Ceylon, not far away, and the family moved there.

The new house lacked the picturesque quality of the log cabin, but it was much more comfortable—a conventional brick farm-house that could be heated all during the cold weather. Moreover, Dougal became an auctioneer and his fortunes improved. He was a very quick-witted man, famous in the countryside for his flashes of humour. Sometimes his tongue got ahead of his sympathies, and he made slashing remarks that really cut. He always felt very badly after one of these episodes, just as he did after losing his temper. But, as his wife remarked on one occasion: "If he doesn't mean these things, why does he say them?" He seldom curbed his anger beforehand. Agnes felt she inherited his temper, and she considered it her worst fault; but, like him, she was a little proud of the violence of her rages. On the rare occasions when her mother gave way to anger, Dougal became a very meek and quiet man indeed.

Dougal had great charm and was very popular. He took no part in politics, remembering the price he had paid for his father's absorption in public affairs. Agnes always felt he had great abilities that were never developed, but there were no signs that he mourned for lost opportunities. He seemed to be a happy man, and he produced an affectionate and tightly knit family.

As an auctioneer, he travelled the countryside. Agnes claimed he could "sell haggis to an Englishman on St. George's Day". He knew how to handle hecklers—a trait Agnes inherited. One day Dougal was making his spiel about a young heifer. In the audience was a man who made a hobby of following Dougal around from auction to auction, pointing out to the crowd the weaknesses in whatever Macphail was selling. This fellow shouted, "But Dougal, she's only got three teats!"

Without a pause, Dougal replied: "Well, your mother only had two, and look what a fine calf she raised." That finished the tormenter.

His refusal to take an active part in politics did not mean that Dougal was not interested. He was deeply concerned over public affairs, locally and widely. When World War I broke out, he was terribly depressed, as distressed as if every casualty were one of his own neighbours.

The Macphail farm-house was a social centre, with plenty of company, and the conversation ranged far and wide, so that Agnes grew up in the atmosphere of discussion groups. A farm forum, later on, was nothing new to her. It was the custom for the men to gather in one room, to talk farm and politics and affairs in general; the women in another, to discuss personalities and household and church matters; and the young people in a third, to play games. Agnes invariably drifted into the room where the men gathered, where she listened with absorbed interest. Her sisters would come to the door to try to persuade her to come and take part in the games, but she waved them away.

At other times, of course, she played with the greatest enthusiasm. She and her sisters had plenty of friends. The Muirs were particularly close, and the McLeods had three girls matching in ages the Macphail girls. The Olivers lived nearby, but Farquhar, who was to play such a large part in her political life, was just a baby.

Dougal did not believe in women doing heavy work, and he never used his daughters as field hands. This did not suit Agnes too well, as she was not at all enthusiastic about housework. Her father did let her milk cows, and harness horses, to the admiration of her sisters, who were afraid of the big beasts.

When Agnes was fourteen, she passed her high-school entrance examination. When the news came, she was beside herself with joy. She rushed over to the Olivers' and burst into the house, crying : "I made it, Jim, I made it !" Then she went home and retired to the cellar, where she gloated over her success and made great plans for her future education. She was going to be a teacher.

She was utterly heart-broken when she was informed that her school career was now over. She was needed at home. For a stormy temperament and ambitious nature like hers, it was a crushing blow. The future stretched out before her without hope. She could see the whole picture—several years of helping with housework and cooking at home, and then marriage to some young farmer, and a lifetime of housework and cooking and raising children in a home of her own. It had no appeal whatever. To her, then and forever after, marriage implied submission, constant catering to the whims of a man, and days too full of distasteful tasks to leave time for outside interests. And a farm marriage meant virtual slavery.

Later, in trying to analyze her attitude, Agnes wrote : "In my very early teens I did a lot of thinking on the subject ; men, women and marriage. I saw that men did a job in the world outside their home and women did not. At fourteen I turned it around in my mind this way ; a woman has children, the boys do things and the girls marry and have other children, of which the boys do a job in the world of affairs and the girls do not, but in turn have other children in which family the boys do——, and I asked myself : 'Does this thing never end in a woman being a person and making a contribution, in addition to, or in place of, having children ?'

"At this time I read and re-read *Lives of Famous Men and Women,* by Sarah K. Bolton, a book in the school library. As I read I thought I could learn to do many of the things that these famous men did ; but the women who were philanthropists, musicians and artists, were, I knew, what I could never be. This reading strengthened me in the resolve which I always seem to have had of doing some work as a person."

Pupil and teacher

She was fascinated by the life of Elizabeth Fry, but it seemed that women, in order to accomplish anything, must be either rich or married to rich men. She wrote :

> But I love children and I have always had dear men friends; it was a deep sorrow to me that I couldn't do all that I expect women to do; to be a wife and mother, but also *an untrammelled active person* finding outlet for her ability in the fields of learning, agriculture, industry, business, the arts or government. I was poor, and had I married, the man would not have been rich or even comfortable in a financial sense. In addition, I have never enjoyed housework. I can do it if I must, but it gives me no sense of fulfilment. This I regret, but so it is.
>
> Deciding on such a matter can never be final; the whole question has to be threshed over again and again, according to the success of one's work, the attraction of one's men friends, the lure of children. To have part of life can never be enough, one must have all. That is what I want for women. There are some women who want only a husband, children and home. For them there is no problem. Keeping the home is enough. But for others it is not.
>
> One of the outstanding features of this age is the number of intelligent women who do not marry. Some old-fashioned and stupid people may say they had no chance: any normal woman has had the chance, but for some reason she hasn't married the man she could have married. . . . But I have talked to hundreds of these fine, alert and very capable women in business, the professions and the arts, and their reason was the same as mine : *the person* could not be subjected.

It is curious that her attitude never changed. To her, love was an experience like plunging briefly into a swift current that might sweep her into danger; she never let herself get so far from shore that she couldn't get out at will. Many people loved her, and she responded just so long as no demands were made on her which she might interpret as involving her "submission".

That is why most of her friendships were undying, but her love affairs were transitory.

At fourteen, resignation is extremely difficult even in small things, and the end of Agnes' school career was a very big thing indeed. She had decided to be a teacher, she had decided to escape from the housewife's role, and she did not give up. She yielded, but only for the time being. The persistence that served her and her country so well in her maturity was evident in this situation. She did what she had to do, but she made it plain, persistently and continually, that this was not what she intended to keep on doing. Her parents stuck it out for two years.

This was a hiatus in her life, but by no means a vacuum. She was at home to help her mother, and she did so, performing the household tasks that were duty, helping with the cooking for harvest crews and so on. She had great affection for her sisters and helped them evade the strict family discipline whenever she could. She would take on their chores to let them go off and play. Her youngest sister, Lilly, had a vivid memory of sitting on the doorstep waiting for Agnes to get her breakfast. She had slept late. Grandma Campbell was there, a mild woman and no disciplinarian; but even she said "You're spoiling that child, Aggie, you're just spoiling her!"

Agnes loved the evenings of discussion with the neighbours and friends who dropped in, and she was a frequent visitor at the Olivers' nearby, Farquhar Oliver went to the Old Durham Road school like the rest of them. He was in first grade when Lilly, the youngest Macphail, was in entrance class. The Olivers always invited Agnes over when Uncle John Oliver came to visit from British Columbia. John Oliver was Premier of British Columbia. He had a great, booming voice and a pleasing personality, and Agnes admired him enormously. She was probably influenced by this admiration when she came to choose a political protégé later on; when she decided on Farquhar Oliver.

At sixteen, Agnes won her battle with the family, and went off to high school at Owen Sound. This was the first break in the family, and Dougal felt it very keenly, although it was he who decided she should go there. He said if she was going to a high school it might as well be a good one. It was only thirty miles away, but at that time one travelled by train, and there was no coming home for week-ends; only major holidays were important enough for the trip.

Agnes had never been away from home before. She had never been among strangers. It was the first time she was made to feel different from other people. She discovered that town girls dressed a little differently from farm girls, and were inclined to look down on them. The town girls had cliques, naturally enough, since most of them had come through the public schools together. Agnes was indignant, because she was firmly convinced that there were no finer people than farm folks, and it infuriated her to be treated as odd and slightly inferior. Other young people from her neighbourhood were there too, and they tended to draw together into a country group.

At that time, school activities were confined to classes and an annual Promenade—a real promenade, where the boys and girls paraded around two by two and no dancing was allowed. There were no organized social activities outside of this. The only thing open to people like Agnes was the Literary Society. She promptly joined this, and became quite prominent, giving papers and leading discussions. She was a rather tall, slim girl at that time, with high colouring and bright eyes and, as always, very attractive to boys. As she settled in, her boarding-house became more of a home than the dreary barrack it had seemed to her at first, and she made friends with boys and girls from other districts.

The sixteen-roomed high school served a wide area. The principal, Mr. Murray, was an excellent teacher and a widely respected man. But he had a fault that is common to many teachers; he was inclined to bully his pupils, especially the meek ones. This was the sort of thing Agnes could not stand. She was not one of the victims—far from it. On one occasion, as Mr. Murray passed down the aisle, he tripped over her foot. He stopped and looked at her. "Now, Miss Macphail," he said silkily, "I wonder why I should fall over your feet?"

"Probably because your own are so big," replied Agnes calmly, to the horrified delight of the class.

A rather timid girl named Isabel Roberts was called to the blackboard to demonstrate a geometrical problem one day. Mr. Murray harried her into such a state of nervousness that she was unable to do the problem at all. "I knew this before I came up here," she said miserably.

"Isn't it an odd state of affairs that Miss Roberts should know her problem so well when she was sitting in her seat, and forget it so completely when called to the board?" Mr. Murray remarked.

"There's nothing odd about it," Agnes retorted. "Nobody could know a straight line from a crooked one with you after her!"

Mr. Murray apparently admired both Agnes' brains and her spirit. They got along very well, all through her school career.

As time went on, and she became firmly established at the school, Agnes was astonished to find that the town girls often came to her for help in their studies. She remarked wryly; "I guess I thought that the possession of a bathtub meant the possession of brains too."

Agnes sailed through High School in two years, getting her junior matriculation at eighteen. The normal school at Stratford was the next step. Here she lived with an uncle, who was an enthusiastic member of the Reorganized Church of Latter Day Saints. Agnes' adherence to that faith was, to a large extent, emotional, a desire to be as much like her grandmother Campbell as possible. But even in later days, when she attended and supported the United Church most of the time, she still felt that the Latter Day Saints possessed more social conscience than any other church. While she was a practising member, the only real difficulty she had was over her dancing. She dearly loved to dance, and the Church frowned on it. She made valiant attempts to feel guilty and sinful about her frequent lapses, but never really succeeded.

On the way to write her examination, Agnes passed by the jail at Stratford. The black flag flew, signifying a hanging.

Pupil and teacher

Agnes had a feeling of depression and outrage, a strong emotional rebellion against the forces of law-abiding society conspiring together to take the life of a human being.

Her first school was at Gowanlocks, four miles east of Port Elgin. She was a very happy young woman. She liked teaching, she had attained her primary ambition, she liked the school, and she liked the people she boarded with—the Gowanlocks. Mr. Gowanlocks was called "Old Watty" by everyone in the neighbourhood. There were young people in the family, all interested in community and church activities, and life was very full. The salary was five hundred dollars a year, paid in four instalments.

As Thanksgiving approached, Agnes longed to get home to her family. When she took the train to Walkerton, where she would transfer to the Priceville train, she had the ninety dollars of her first pay in her purse, and she felt like a tycoon going home to be admired and petted. She knew perfectly well that it was not the way of her parents to do anything of the kind, but she felt that the atmosphere would be there even if they said nothing. At Walkerton she had several hours to wait between trains, and that was her downfall. Full of affection and loaded with money, she bought presents for her father, her mother, her sisters Gertha and Lilly. And she bought herself a wonderful hat. It was a wide brown hat with curling feathers around the brim, and Agnes found it irresistible.

Instead of the gratitude and joy she expected, her parents scolded her roundly for her extravagance. Her father pointed out that ninety dollars was no fortune, and it was a long time till next pay day. Her mother reminded her that she had promised to pay back the cost of her year at normal school, so that the money could be used for Lilly when she was ready to go there. Agnes thought this very harsh and unreasonable, as she did all criticism of her spending all her life long.

After the brief disappointment of her reception, she went happily off, driving with one of her boy friends. This particular one drove a white horse, and one of her neighbours found the fact an endless source of amusement, teasing her about white hairs on her clothing. She had two particularly devoted admirers at this time, both medical students. It used to worry her father when they turned up the same evening, but it didn't disturb Agnes one bit. She had a gay holiday and returned to school happy and refreshed.

Agnes found that the teacher was expected to put on a school concert. This was hard for her, as she had no ear for music whatever. She had no difficulty in preparing a play and drilling the smaller children in their "pieces" to recite, but the musical part of the program was beyond her. A friend, Margaret Black, came to the rescue, and undertook to train the children in music. Gertha Macphail came on a visit for the occasion of the concert. She was definitely musical, and intended to make it her career. But at Gowanlocks she met young Meredith Reany, who lived on the next farm, and later on they were married.

At normal school, Agnes' class had been advised to resign at the end of the school year, to leave the school board free to re-hire or to replace each neophyte teacher. Agnes followed this advice. She said bitterly in later years that her adviser knew nothing of the workings of country people's minds. The Gowanlocks School Board was disappointed, but concluded that she was not satisfied there, and advertised for another teacher. Agnes was grieved, but thought perhaps the board had not been pleased with her.

She was essentially a country school-teacher. She felt close to her pupils, and close to their families. A country school in those days was the centre of social life, and Teacher was not only "boarded" at the home of one of the pupils, she was invited out to supper whenever there was anything special to eat, and she was a part of all community activities. Agnes felt perfectly at home. These people were her own kind.

The next year Agnes accepted a school as Kinloss, midway between Walkerton and Kincardine, where she lived with Mr. and Mrs. Sam Braden, the owners of the larger of the two shops in the village. Sam Braden had a very strong influence on Agnes. He had a high opinion of her, and pulled her into the discussions that took place almost nightly in his store. Farmers would drop in to do a little shopping, play a game of cards or crokinole, and talk. They loved to talk politics, and Braden was a strong Liberal, willing to take on all the Conservatives he could find—and there were plenty around. He would often come to the door of the stairs leading to the living quarters above the store, and call : "Come down and help me! These Tories may win this argument if you don't."

Agnes would descend with alacrity and wade into the discussion, sitting on the counter swinging her legs, which greatly disturbed Mrs. Braden. Sam didn't care about her being a lady —he wanted only her interest in public questions. At that time, there were two morning papers in Toronto—the *Globe,* which was Liberal, and the *Mail and Empire,* which was Conservative. Sam Braden insisted that Agnes read both papers and then make up her own mind. It was Sam Braden who first convinced Agnes that "big business" had undue influence on the public policy of Canada.

And at Kinloss it occurred to Agnes for the first time that there might be more for her in life than country school-teaching. Until that time, being a school-teacher had been the height of her ambition. But the local minister asked her one day if there was no possibility of her going on to university. He said she had a fine mind, and it should be trained. The idea of further formal education did not seize her imagination, but the suggestion did make her realize that she had brains and ability beyond her present position.

The arguments in Braden's store were particularly hot in 1911. It was the year when the question of tariffs was to the fore—the year when the general election was fought on the question of reciprocity with the United States. Town and country, East and West, were bitterly divided on the issue. Canada's industries were becoming established, and her industrialists felt the need for protective tariffs to reduce the competition from the more highly industrialized, more heavily populated neighbour to the south. Canada's farmers, particularly in the West, were convinced that only through free trade could they find the markets for their products. The Liberals were sure that only low tariffs could save the country economically. The Conservatives were sure that tariff reduction would break the British connection and make Canada just one more state in the Union. There was a good deal of emotion, and wild stories about the Liberals trampling the Union Jack in the mud. Most of the farmers around Kinloss, however, were loyal Conservatives, with a strong distrust of the Grits.

Election day came in September. There was no telephone in the village, only a telegraph wire—to Sam Braden's store. So it was he alone who knew, by nine o'clock that night, that the Liberals led by Laurier had been defeated, and the farmers' hopes for lower tariffs were shattered. He went up to the living quarters and told Agnes the bad news. "The store is full of Tories," he said, "but I won't tell them until I have to." He did have to, of course, and the crowd went wild. They went up to the other village store, where they bought brooms and soaked them in coaloil to make torches. Then they came down, led by fife and drum, and paraded in front of Braden's store, back and forth. Agnes stood out in front, watching them. "Come and get warm at a good Tory fire, Teacher!" somebody shouted.

"I'd rather freeze!" said Agnes haughtily, disregarding the balmy September evening.

The election made a deep impression on her. She was biased against the Conservatives by family opinion, and as she read and thought about the plight of the farmers, she became more and more convinced that they must take political action of some kind.

It was at this time that the matter of women's votes first came to her attention. Rumours from England were discussed in the store—stories about the fight the English women were putting up to get the franchise. Someone asked Agnes how she felt about it. She would like to vote, she replied, but she didn't think the movement would get anywhere. She never took any part in the battle for votes for women, curiously enough. She was so absorbed in farm problems and co-operatives that the struggle seemed a long way off. She was never a formal feminist, nor even an informal one in the conduct of her life. She blamed

Pupil and teacher

women as much as men for the inferior position of the female citizen.

All work and no play was no part of Agnes' program. She played strenuously. There was a little lake called Silver Lake nearby, and Mr. Braden went sailing there every Sunday. His wife and Sarah Morrison, the helper, refused to go with him— it frightened them too much. So he invited Agnes, and she went, Sunday after Sunday, determined to learn to enjoy sailing. She never succeeded.

But she did love dancing, all her life. And there were dances many times a week. It was the most popular form of entertainment for young people. House dances were held in the farm homes. A couple of sleigh-loads of young people, two fiddlers, and a caller made up a party that went on till all hours of the night. Sometimes Agnes went home just in time to change and breakfast and go to school. It was too strenuous, even for a girl of boundless energy. There was one week when Agnes had taught all day and danced most of every night. By Friday she was tired out. She asked Sarah to let her sleep in on Saturday morning. The waking signal was the noisy sound of the lamp over the dining table being pulled up on its chain out of the way for the day. So Sarah agreed to pull it up at bedtime Friday night and let Agnes sleep in. When Agnes heard the squeak of the lamp, she opened her eyes in some indignation. It was still quite dark. She thought black thoughts about Sarah's broken promise, and tried to go back to sleep. She could not. So finally she dragged herself out of bed and appeared, ready to tell Sarah what she thought of her. She saw the clock just in time. It was suppertime on Saturday night, and the lamp was being pulled *down* to light the table.

Mrs. Braden worried about the pace Agnes was keeping up, and warned her that she was overdoing things. Towards the end of the school year, Agnes became constantly weary, and uncharacteristically prone to tears. The term ended gloriously, with a picnic at Silver Lake. Her fifty-two pupils and their parents put on a bang-up party for her farewell. She was called to the platform, and as she walked toward it, she was showered

39

with rose petals by the children. There were speeches and a presentation. It was an expression of love that kept the memory of Kinloss warm in her heart all her life.

At home, her physical condition became worse. She tried to rest, but could not recover. Finally a doctor was called in and diagnosed the trouble as "inward goitre". Agnes impatiently demanded an operation, but at that time it was a very dangerous thing, and the doctor had recently lost two patients through the operation. He would have none of it. He advised rest, and added that she would never be able to earn her living again.

Agnes was appalled. She had no intention of submitting to such a verdict. After many attempts to rest herself into health, she went to Toronto to a chiropractor. After the first treatment, she slept through the night for the first time in weeks. She had several more treatments, and then decided that a change of air might improve her health. She went west, to an uncle and aunt in Oyen, Alberta, financing the trip by teaching in a summer school there for six months. Only a few miles away lived Bob Gardiner, whose life was to entwine with hers far away in Ottawa, but at the time they had never heard of each other and did not meet.

She had no affection for the Alberta countryside; it did not compare with the Ontario hills she loved. But the experience did widen her horizons. She was strongly attracted by the western people, whom she found more outgoing and breezy than her Ontario neighbours. But she also found that living was a great deal more primitive in a tiny Alberta community than she was used to at home. Ontario farms might be, and were, lacking in plumbing, but there were other amenities that she had taken for granted. Climbing a ladder to go to her room every night was not her idea of convenience, and some of the houses were so badly built that western breeziness came right in from outdoors.

The weather defeated her. She could not read the signs of trouble as the natives could. One day in October she was teaching her class of ten quite unconcerned, but the pupils were

Pupil and teacher

increasingly restless and inattentive. Finally one of the older ones told her they should all start home, or they'd never get there. A blizzard was coming for sure. Just then one of the farmers knocked at the door and advised her to send her class home. He had a sleigh and would take all the children going his way. Every child in school, and teacher too, rode ponies or horses, but the children could ride in the sleigh and lead the animals.

Agnes and two of the children were going in the opposite direction from the rest, so the farmer instructed Agnes to let the eldest girl lead, and to ride close behind her. He had no high opinion of the eastern teacher's sense of direction. She followed his advice, and they got as far as the Ball homestead where her guide lived. There she stayed the night.

Later, her account of it said: "The wind howled and shrieked and blew snow halfway across the main room of the house, a combined living-room-kitchen. It sounded to my ears as though the house were in danger of being carried away too: to get out of the blowing snow I sat on the arm of a large morris chair which the Ball family had brought from their home in the United States. Looking very forlorn, no doubt. One of the family, a little peeved by my distaste, said, 'Do you never have storms in Ontario?' 'Oh yes,' I said, 'We have bad storms, but then, we have houses too!' For which statement I ought to have been spanked!"

That blizzard finished her with the West. She resigned and left for home. She filled a vacancy at Boothville, in Grey County, occasioned by the illness of the regular teacher. There she lived with the Jack Hill family, and became great friends with them and with the Dougal McCannel families. They became her staunch political supporters when she entered public life. Her term at Boothville marked the end of her apprenticeship. When she moved on to the excellent school at Sharon, the door was ajar for her entry into the wide world of public affairs.

Four

A new career—farmers on the march

It was at Pegg's School in the township of East Gwillimbury near Sharon that Agnes Macphail took the first tentative steps into public life, and here that she discovered her gift for speaking, her enormous appeal to audiences. When she first took the school, it did not occur to her that it was just a stepping-stone. It was a good school, the sort of school where a teacher could be very happy. She was allowed plenty of leeway, and she was very popular with both pupils and parents.

Agnes never did separate herself from her pupils. She had too much confidence in herself to feel any necessity for being set apart, as so many teachers must do in order to hold their authority and their position in the pupils' minds as someone above the ordinary adult. And Agnes was too strongly gregarious to allow herself to be put into a different category from the rest of the community. She was known as "Mac" around Sharon, and Mac got invited to everything that was going on. The community was more sophisticated than the areas she had taught in heretofore. There were more cars, the village was closer to the big city of Toronto—forty miles or so; and the atmosphere was more urban. But the girls and boys she taught were still country people, and the problems of their parents were farmers' problems.

Agnes wrote about that period:

> This school section took a great interest in their school, and did all they could to make the school comfortable; it is true that the pupils and their teacher raised part of the

money for the decorating job, and for having screens and window-boxes made to fit the windows. It is sometimes said that school children take no pride in their school after it is decorated and are just as likely as not to deface the walls. The cure for that is, have them work to earn some of the money. If any small child put grimy hands near the walls, some senior bore down on the little offender with ferocity.

We tried a few other things—getting a school magazine and a daily paper, and having a period each day on the news dealing with agriculture, education, or some other topic. If I did not pick a topic the children would fasten on all the horror stories; at least we made an effort to relate the child to the world in which he lived. It is interesting to me that that school has continued to be one of the most progressive rural schools. . . .

Many times afterwards when public criticism of me was severe, I wondered why I left off teaching in the splendid communities I have described. But more and more I was wanting to talk to adults on matters which seemed important to me.

She became engrossed in farm organizations, particularly co-operatives, and in the farmers' move toward political expression. She studied everything she could find on both subjects. She read about the Scandinavian countries and longed to visit them and see co-operative living in action. It was characteristic of her that she so steeped herself in information that when she was called upon to talk she sounded perfectly casual and offhand.

In the *Farmer's Sun,* she read a letter from a country schoolteacher complaining of the hardships of being boarded with farm families. This infuriated Agnes, who had been so happy under the same circumstances. She wrote a very hot and eloquent reply. Shortly afterward she received a letter from Mr. Ross, the editor, suggesting that if she happened to be in Toronto he would like to see her. Agnes "happened" to be in

Toronto as soon as she possibly could, and called on Mr. Ross. The interview resulted in her joining the United Farmers of Ontario and undertaking to do all she could to help them. She was qualified to be a member because she was a rural school-teacher.

It was no new thing to have the farmers organize and take political action, but the wave of agrarian enthusiasm and indignation which was to send Agnes Macphail to Ottawa was an unusually large one.

From the time when Confederation basted the pieces of Canada into the beginnings of a nation, there was conflict between town and country. Farmers complained that they sold in a free market and bought in a controlled one. Tariff reform was the continuing thread that ran through all farm movements. They felt that they were inadequately represented in Parliament. At intervals Canadian farmers organized into pressure groups that evolved into political movements. Some of them were wrecked on religious differences, some died when the economic conditions of the farmer improved briefly and interest wilted with the fading of the urgency for reform.

The Patrons of Industry, originating in the United States, flourished towards the end of the last century, and died. The Grange, apparently a strong farm organization, was demoralized by the defeat of Sir Wilfrid Laurier on the reciprocity issue in 1911. J.J. Morrison had been its secretary. He was one of the most important men in the Ontario farm world, and his influence on Agnes Macphail lasted all her life. She had the greatest respect and affection for him, and when their political paths divided, the friendship remained—they simply avoided the subject of politics.

By 1913, agriculture was once more in a depressed state. A committee was formed to organize a new body founded on the old Grange, the Farmers' Institutes, and so on. Morrison was secretary of the committee, and W. C. Good of Paris, E. C. Drury of Crown Hill, and Colonel J. Z. Fraser of Burford acted on it. On March 19, 1914, three hundred delegates from various farm bodies met at the Labour Temple on Jarvis Street

A new career—farmers on the march

in Toronto. They formed twin organizations—the United Farmers of Ontario, and the United Farmers' Co-operative Company. The motto of the U.F.O. was "Equal opportunity for all—special privilege for none." It was intended to be an educational and social movement. Farmers' wives and daughters were admitted as honorary members, but a few years later the United Farm Women's Organization was formed, and soon they had a real voice in the U.F.O. The Co-operative Company was organized on a joint-stock basis. J. J. Morrison was secretary of the two organizations, and an invaluable link between them.

Morrison was known as a natural leader of strong convictions, who had an ability to express the farmers' problems in a way that they could understand, and to point out solutions that appealed to them. He agreed with Henry Wise Wood of Alberta philosophically. Like the old Grange organization, they believed that political parties as they were constituted were wrong; that, instead of a party in power and another party trying to get in, with party organization, whips, caucuses and patronage, there should be groups in Parliament representing various trades and professions. These groups should co-operate whenever they could find common ground. The Cabinet should be elected from Parliament, and should represent the various interest groups. It should function until it lost the confidence of the House, as expressed in a non-confidence vote.

These people believed, fundamentally, that a Member of Parliament should first of all represent his own constituency; that he should be under its direct control, even to the extent of the power of recall—the riding could reject him if he let them down during a session, and he would lose his seat. They believed in government by referendum. And most firmly, most unbendingly, they believed in tariff reform and the doctrine that farmers must represent farmers at Ottawa and in the legislatures of the provinces. "Elect your man," Morrison said, "and keep him independent."

Under Morrison's tutelage, Agnes Macphail accepted this theory and rags and tatters of it clung to her all her life.

By 1915, the farmers were being urged to produce to the very limit of their ability, to help the war effort. At the same time, recruiting officers were urging all young men to go to war. The farmers resented these mutually exclusive appeals.

By 1917 the country was split over the issue of conscription. Laurier and the Quebec Liberals, Western Liberals, and farmers all across Canada were bitterly opposed. A union Government was formed, dominated by Conservatives, but containing pro-conscription Liberals; and a general election gave it the backing of the nation as a whole. One of the five farmers elected was Thomas Crerar, a Manitoba reform Liberal, and a farm stalwart. He became Minister of Agriculture. The farmers' sons were exempt from conscription. They were reassured, but not for long. The very day Crerar was urging them to still more production, the Prime Minister, Sir Robert Borden, moved to amend by Order-in-Council the Military Service Act. The intent was to raise 50,000 soldiers. The result was the abolition of exemption for farmers' sons.

The farmers, having extended their acreage and bought extra machinery in response to patriotic appeals, were wildly indignant. Over five thousand of them went to Ottawa in May. They met rebuff wrapped in patriotic verbiage from the Government, and indignant contempt from the press. They left the capital convinced that since both Liberals and Conservatives were in the Union Government, since even Crerar was powerless to help them, then neither of the old parties was any use to them. The United Farmers must move into politics.

At first they intended to support any candidate who would subscribe to their platform, whatever his political affiliations. The platform, first issued by the Canadian Council of Agriculture, and later endorsed by Ontario, Alberta, Manitoba and Saskatchewan farm groups, was astonishingly radical for the time. Among many other reforms, it advocated : public ownership and control of railways, water and aerial transportation, telephone, telegraph and express systems, all projects in the development of natural power, and coal mining; reform of the Senate; the admission of women to Parliament; and the de-

A new career—farmers on the march

velopment of the British Empire as a partnership between free and equal nations.

In 1918 the Ontario farmers demonstrated their strength by winning a provincial by-election in Manitoulin Island. In October that year the U.F.O. met and decided to run candidates in any by-elections that turned up. The same month they took over the old *Weekly Sun* (a heritage from the Patrons of Industry) and renaming it the *Farmer's Sun,* made it their official organ. It was a fine forum for political arguments.

Early in 1919, the U.F.O. won another by-election in Northern Ontario, in spite of energetic campaigning by members of the Ontario Conservative government under Sir William Hearst. A general election was surely coming. Under the leadership of E. C. Drury, Manning Doherty and W. C. Good, the U.F.O. prepared their election platform.

In this 1919 election, Ontario women voted for the first time. They had received the provincial franchise in 1917, after thirty years' struggle for it, but had not exercised it, since there had been no general election. And until 1919 they were not eligible to hold either provincial or municipal office. It had been a long fight, conducted in the main in a much more lady-like manner than the same struggle in England, where gentle-women cast their inhibitions aside and deliberately behaved outrageously, with the courage and dedication of martyrs.

The West led in the granting of votes to women in 1916, and in 1917 the first women were elected to the Alberta Legislature. They were Miss Roberta Macadams and Mrs. L. M. McKinney of the Non-Partisan League, supported by the farmers.

The technique in Canada was the tireless annual presentation of petitions to the heads of various governments. This usually resulted in a great many tenderly facetious speeches from the men members, some of whom felt quite free to be offensive. In Ontario Sir James Whitney as Premier had many opportunities, which he took, of turning down Dr. Augusta Stowe-Gullen, president of the Canadian Suffrage Association. Sir James made his refusal very pious—women in the kitchen was the divine order of things. This caused the lady to remark that she had become very suspicious of men who hide their own infirmities behind the Almighty.

In 1917 women whose next of kin were soldiers on active service were given a vote in the federal election. There were about half a million of them. The next year the Borden Government passed a genuine woman-suffrage act which extended the federal franchise to all women who already had a vote in provincial elections. (This meant that in Quebec women did not get the vote until 1940, when Mme. Pierre Casgrain and her helpers prevailed on Premier Godbout and a reluctant Legislature to grant them the vote.) In 1919 women were granted the right to be elected to the Commons. They were not very quick to seize the opportunity that had taken so many weary years to open to them.

A new career—farmers on the march

Five

We have made history in South-East Grey!

Agnes was now enthusiastically committed to the United Farmers of Ontario. She spent many an evening talking late into the night about farm problems with neighbours and friends. She and her close friends, the Wilmotts, attended discussion groups and meetings together. Agnes took a lively part in all these affairs, but she had yet to speak from a public platform.

A provincial election was called in 1919, and the United Farmers went into the campaign determined to make their voices heard in the councils of the province. They did not run candidates in predominantly urban ridings; but in constituencies that were mainly rural but contained towns with organized labour, they accepted labour support—with some misgivings.

One evening, R. W. E. Burnaby of the U.F.O. turned up at Agnes' boarding-house to invite her to go with him to a political meeting in Mount Albert in support of Sam Foote, the U.F.O. provincial candidate. She went along quite happily, ignorant of the fact that she would be called on to speak. When this happened during the meeting, she was in a genuine panic. She wanted to refuse. But as she said later, "Farmers in that day were too reluctant to get on their feet and talk in their own defence, and often I told them that they couldn't expect others to solve their problems; especially those others who made their wealth and gained their power by legally robbing the farmers out of their just portion of the wealth they so abundantly produced."

So she gathered her courage and rose to her feet and spoke for ten minutes. When she finished, the audience cheered. "It must have been my nerve they approved!" she commented.

During the same year there was a federal nomination in York North. Mackenzie King was nominated for the Liberals and R. W. E. Burnaby for the U.F.O. The farmers of North York turned out in great numbers for the U.F.O. nomination meetings. Agnes Macphail, among others, was nominated. The move was not serious; it was done to give her an opportunity to make a speech, at the end of which she declined the nomination with thanks. She was finding her voice.

The provincial election took place on October 20. When the votes were counted, the Conservatives had 25 members, the Liberals 25, Labour 11, Independent 1, and U.F.O. 44. The farmers were suddenly in a position to form the government. They were in the ticklish situation of power without the desire to be a formal political party; with, indeed, the conviction that regular political parties were against their principles.

Through the columns of newspapers, William Irvine of Alberta exhorted them to put into practice their theories of government—to elect from the Legislature a Cabinet that would represent as far as possible under the electoral system a diversity of interests, a co-operative rather than a coalition government.

They did not do so. They formed a conventional cabinet. J. J. Morrison was offered the leadership but declined it, and E. C. Drury became the Premier of Ontario at forty-one years of age. He headed an inexperienced group of farmers who were astonished and in most cases disconcerted by their sudden leap to power. His first act was to cut $3000 off his own salary as an earnest of economies to come.

The U.F.O. was elected in Ontario on federal issues, not on provincial ones. Their gains were mainly from the Conservatives. To the farmers, the Provincial Premier, Sir William Hearst, represented the Ottawa Tories, and certainly the federal Conservatives had spoken for him during the campaign. There was still a soreness left from the conscription fracas, and the

We have made history in South-East Grey!

high cost of living was blamed on the Dominion Government. Daylight saving, a war measure, was a sore point too. The specific provincial issue was prohibition, a measure that won a big majority through a referendum at election time.

The provincial campaign was a thrilling experience for Agnes Macphail, who had been an interested political spectator since childhood, but had never before taken an active part. She enjoyed the meetings and the speeches and relished the success of the people she had been working with and for in the co-operative movement and the U.F.O. She enjoyed being in a group that she considered idealistic and worth-while, and that was obviously marching forward all over the West as well as in Ontario.

The U.F.O. was fated to fall disastrously in 1923, but during the first couple of years an inexperienced person would not recognize its shakiness. Drury wished to make it a genuine political party by widening its base of membership. Morrison and his followers were determined opponents of such a move. Morrison's dictum, "elect your own man as a farmer and keep him independent in the House to voice your interests", expressed the strictly agrarian viewpoint of many U.F.O. members. The organization's high point saw it with 60,000 members and 1600 clubs, and it was in that atmosphere that Agnes Macphail's political career began.

The U.F.O. had a real asset in Agnes as a speaker, and they knew it and used her as much as her work as a school-teacher would allow. Evenings and week-ends were largely devoted to U.F.O. and co-operative meetings. In the hamlet of Queensville, not far from Sharon, H. H. Hannam was teaching school. His family had lived near the Macphails in Grey and Agnes was a friend of the older members of the family. Later on she and Hannam worked closely together in the co-operative movement.

In February, 1920, she went to Orono, a farm community not far from Bowmanville, to make a speech. She was feeling quite ill with a bad headache. She made her speech all right, but became worse during the night, burning with fever and shivering with chill alternately. In the morning she was all for leaving, as she intended to go home to Ceylon for the week-end. Her hostess would not hear of it and called the doctor. Her illness was diagnosed as smallpox. No local nurses were available, and one had to be brought from Toronto. Meanwhile Agnes in all her misery was very concerned to spare her family worry. She managed to write a note, saying she had changed her mind about coming home because she had a bad cold.

This had quite the opposite effect to her intention. Her father flatly refused to believe a word of it. He knew his Aggie too well for that. Since when, he asked, had a cold kept her from going where she wanted to go? And she wanted to come home that particular week-end. Her mother maintained that if Aggie said she had a cold, she had a cold, and there was nothing to worry about. Dougal had been very ill with pneumonia himself, and that was what he feared. He sat down at the telephone and instructed the operator to try every doctor in the Bowmanville area until she found the one who was looking after Miss Agnes Macphail. The first one she called turned out to be the man they were looking for. Dougal talked to him and assured himself that she was making fair progress, had a good nurse and was among kind friends. Then he wrote to her, saying that he certainly had been worried to hear she had such a bad cold, but as long as it turned out to be only smallpox, he would stop worrying about it. At the time, it didn't strike Agnes as the height of humour.

She was quarantined for some weeks, in the home of the secretary of the local U.F.O. club, where she had expected to stay for one night. Agnes was tremendously impressed by the expert care she received, and the cheerful way the nurse did the necessary housekeeping for the two of them as well as her regular duties. But the hours of convalescence were long and dull, in spite of the showers of letters and cards from her pupils at Sharon.

She was also very worried about the unexpected expense. Her salary was $800 a year, which didn't leave much margin for doctors and special nurses. J. J. Morrison, secretary of the

We have made history in South-East Grey!

U.F.O., came to the rescue. He said that since she was among strangers, working for the U.F.O. when she was stricken, the organization would foot the bill.

In her home county, the farmers were organizing rapidly. By 1920 Agnes considered it the best-organized county in Ontario. They were thinking about running a candidate for the federal House. The *Durham Review*, published by Charles Rammage, carried some editorials on the subject. The *Review* suggested that Agnes Macphail would make an excellent candidate, as she was a native daughter of Grey, of pioneer stock, and her father was probably the best-known auctioneer in those parts. Her work for the United Farmers movement had shown her ability. This was the first serious suggestion that she might be a candidate.

It made her shy about taking speaking engagements in her home county. She was determined that if they wanted her, they must come after her. She would not seek the nomination. She would not even put herself forward to further her chances. But she was becoming something of a public figure. She appeared at a public hearing under the chairmanship of Sir Henry Drayton, then federal Finance Minister. Among other things, she informed him that the protective-tariff system kept Canadian farmers in a state of vassalage similar to that in which the Hudson's Bay Company kept the Indians of North America centuries before.

At the end of the school year, she resigned and went to live with her grandmother Campbell in the old stone house on the Campbell homestead. Agnes was a very honest person, but, like many another honest person, she had a fine flair for self-deception. She firmly believed that her move had nothing to do with politics. Shortly after the editorial in the *Durham Review*, she had a remarkably vivid dream. In her own words, "I saw my lovely grandmother as a miniature, being dragged along by the hand of a normal-sized woman; the little lady was protesting that she couldn't go on so fast even when she tried her best. Finally, after what seemed a long walk she turned and looked over her shoulder at me and said : 'Aggie, come and take care of me.' "

This was the motive Agnes admitted to herself. There is no doubt that her love for her grandmother was deep and sincere, no doubt that she knew the old lady had not too many days remaining to her. But it seems highly probable that she would, under ordinary circumstances, simply have spent the summer with her, instead of taking the drastic step of resigning from a school that met most of her requirements, and where she was successful and popular.

Back in Proton, she spent most of her time with Grandma Campbell. But, of course, she had to take part in community events. One of them was a picnic. The speaker was Dr. David Jamieson, the sitting M.L.A., and Speaker of the Ontario Legislature. He was a Conservative. He made a speech that offended the farmers thoroughly. He told them what was wrong with them and their methods, and they resented it very strongly. A small committee of U.F.O. officials came to Agnes and asked her if she could answer him without preparation. She certainly could. And did. The farmers were delighted with her. She was pleased with herself.

She was now a serious candidate for the nomination for the House of Commons. She still refused to go into townships other than Proton to make speeches. We will never know whether this backward campaign was instinct, or inspired understanding of the mentality of her neighbours. In Canada we still have the curious notion that it is somehow sinful for a person to really want public office. Political ambition is not quite nice. It was still less nice for a woman in a country that had never had a woman Member of Parliament, where the women's vote was a new thing. And in a farming community, it was sufficiently startling to think of the possibility of running a woman candidate. If she had shown how very much she wanted it, the farmers would have been shocked and repelled. Her behaviour, however, fulfilled all the requirements of a female candidate— she was modest, retiring, capable, and available for nomination.

The nominating convention was called for September.

We have made history in South-East Grey!

Agnes' parents were very much opposed to her accepting, for they felt that, to a young woman of her temperament, the disappointment of losing would be overwhelming. And the prospect of winning was even worse, in their opinion. She respected them, but her feet were set in the path of her ambition and nobody could have turned her aside then. Hard work did not frighten her. She was confident of her ability to represent the riding well, if they sent her to Ottawa. She had no idea of the hostility she would encounter there, no conception of the picayune traps that would be set for her, or of the slurs that would be cast on her. She had grown up in an atmosphere of affection—critical affection, certainly, but behind her parents' scolding there was love. And in her relations with pupils, parents, and school boards there was affection and respect. In her dealings with the public so far, she had met admiration and approval. She had no armour against unkindness and distrust and ridicule, except her native courage and obstinacy.

Neither her parents nor her ninety-two-year-old grandmother went to the nomination meeting at Durham. Her sisters were there with their husbands. Gertha had married Meredith Reany, whom she had met when Agnes was teaching at Kinloss. Lilly had married Hugh Bailey, one of the young farmers in her school section. Hugh Bailey was a lifelong friend of Agnes', and they worked together for many years in the co-operative movement.

Four hundred people were at the meeting, 125 of them accredited delegates. The men from Proton were there in force. Agnes wrote later : "Ten men and one woman were nominated. I do not remember all the speeches, but two are clear. One man, a farmer, made quite a play on the fact that he had taught Sunday school for many years ; and the other, a high-school-teaching son of a farmer, stressed his scholarship and quoted some Latin for the edification of the farm audience. But it was evident that Latin wasn't their dish—they wanted better prices for farm products and didn't see what good Latin would do."

The balloting took most of the afternoon. Agnes kept out of the hall much of the time, going downtown with her sisters and their husbands for ice-cream. When they returned, they found that Proton Township was swinging the convention, and they were a solid Macphail block. It took until six o'clock, but they finally won.

When the sun came over the barns the next morning, the farmers looked at what they had done, and it seemed to many of them that they must have been hypnotized. The riding executive was besieged by protests. As Agnes reported, "One old farmer in Osprey township voiced the thoughts of many when he said : 'A woman as candidate! Are there no men left in South-East Grey?' " The pressure increased until the executive called a meeting in Flesherton and asked Agnes to attend. The meeting was attended by the losing candidates as well, and some of them took the opportunity to stir up all the trouble possible; they suggested that Agnes resign and make way for another convention 'in which saner judgment would be possible'. But she had her foothold and she dug in her heels. She refused. She had not campaigned for the nomination; she had been properly chosen by accredited delegates, and she stood her ground.

The election was called for December 6, but Agnes started campaigning early in October. She knew she had a real fight before her, and that she must get started as early as possible. Her good friend, J. J. Morrison, secretary of the U.F.O., promised to help. He attended the first campaign meeting, held in the Durham town hall. It was jammed. Wherever she went, Agnes drew crowds. None of the halls were big enough to hold the people who wanted to get in.

She was very nervous about her meeting in Hanover. That was the home of the sitting M.P., Mr. Ball, and it was new territory to Agnes. By the time of the meeting, the town hall was overflowing, and the extra people were sent to the rink. This meant that Agnes had to make two speeches, and she was delighted to make the extra effort. Of her opponents in this election, she said : "The only thing that needs to be said about Mr. Ball was that he was a silent Member of Parliament. The people were in no mood to be represented by silence. The

We have made history in South-East Grey!

Liberal candidate was Mr. Walter Hastie of Holstein, a kindly and delicate man who should not have been campaigning in the miserable late fall weather. He never had the slightest chance of election."

It was a home-grown election campaign. The money and the talent came from the riding itself. The whole campaign cost less than six hundred dollars. Agnes would not accept more than a dollar from any donor. She always believed that if a candidate received one dollar from each person who intended to support him or her on election day, there would be no necessity for financial appeals or for large donations from any organization; nor would there be any obligation for pressure from special groups on the elected member. She made only one appeal for funds, and that was a general appeal on behalf of all candidates.

There were no imported entertainers, chairmen or speakers, aside from Mr. Morrison at the first meeting. Agnes never did relish big names from outside coming to speak to her constituents. When, later, she had people like Bill Irvine and Elmore Philpott on the platform with her, they were there as guests of equal status. Basically, she felt nobody could express things better than she for that audience.

She had learned to drive at the East Gwillimbury school, where a member of the school board had taught her to run his Model T Ford, but she had no car. The farmers who did own cars were generous both with gasoline and their time. She travelled by rail a great deal. Her usual practice was to stay in various farm homes and move from meeting to meeting, getting back to her own home perhaps once a week.

There was nothing shabby about the campaign, although so little money was spent. Town halls and schools were available for meetings, which were conducted with dignity. Public interest was very high. She found hospitality and goodwill in most places she visited. Writing about the physical aspects of the campaign, she said : "It was then that I took a fancy to small farm homes; the spare rooms in the big brick structures were ice-houses, but in the little ones the guest bedroom would probably

57

open off the kitchen and be heated by the kitchen stove. I looked for small homes for the overnight stops, and sometimes had the good fortune to stay several nights in the same home."

One of her most enthusiastic and hard-working supporters in this campaign, as in all those that followed until her defeat in 1940, was Farquhar Oliver, the son of her family's good friends and neighbours. He was a very large, handsome, curly-headed young man, unmistakably a farm boy, with boundless energy and great admiration for Agnes Macphail. One of the mental pictures she kept all her life was that of Farquhar walking up the driveway to the Macphail home in overalls and a big straw hat, carrying a full-sized typewriter as if it had been a small parcel. Dougal was standing at the window with his daughter, watching the big boy. Agnes remarked that she thought Farquhar might have a future in politics. Dougal said, "Aggie, if you can make a politician out of that boy, you're a real wonder!"

There was plenty of opposition to Agnes, especially in the towns. In Durham, the Protestant ministers by a strange coincidence preached a series of sermons on various religions, Sunday after Sunday. The series finished close to election day with a strong attack on the Church of the Latter Day Saints, which they labelled Mormon, with all the sinfulness of polygamy implied. Agnes certainly did not get the women's votes in that first election. She not only belonged to the wrong church but she gallivanted around the country with men just like one of them. At that time the "mannish Miss Macphail" had little appeal for the housewives who did not know her personally.

Agnes made fifty-four speeches during that campaign. Her subjects were mainly the drop in farm prices (almost 50 per cent), tariffs, trade, and the autocratic behaviour of the Conservative Government, which had been in power through the first World War, led first by Sir Robert Borden and later by Arthur Meighen.

She was obliquely grateful to Mr. Boyd, an elderly man at the boarding-house where she had lived near Sharon. When she first became seriously interested in the U.F.O., she re-

We have made history in South-East Grey!

marked after a meeting one evening that she must learn more about tariffs. Boyd snorted. A woman couldn't understand tariffs, he informed her. Agnes was on her way to bed. She paused on the stairway and turned back to him. "In one year," she told him, "I'll know more about tariffs than you ever will!" She studied and learned.

At the end of the campaign she didn't care much who got elected as long as the campaign finished and she could get a rest from speaking. "I ached from the effort and strain. The last meeting was in Acton and in the midst of the speech I felt I could not finish, but knowing it was the very last I had a silent argument with myself to buck me up, and continued on to the end. I never again was so completely exhausted."

Election day, December 6, 1921, was the beginning of winter that year. After that day the cars could no longer use the township roads. Nature co-operated with Agnes Macphail on that occasion (just as nature helped to defeat her in 1940, when the roads were clogged by a March snowstorm and blizzard on election day). She described the scene of the election returns:

"In our farm home, which lay between Priceville and Ceylon, all the neighbours gathered to await the returns by telephone—everyone excited. The same Muir who had teased about the white horse driven by the boy friend of my youth, was taking down the returns at first, but soon he said, 'Some of you do it, my hand is shaking too much to write.' When we had heard enough to know that the townships were giving us such great majorities that the towns couldn't overtake our lead, Donald Stewart, one of our good neighbours, said in a serious manner, 'Friends, we have made history in South-East Grey; we have elected the first woman to the Parliament of Canada!'

"Everyone was as delighted as if he or she had been elected. We were a closely knit group in our farm kitchen that night."

They went in to Durham to make whoopee—"unassisted," she says, "by any artificial stimulant."

Agnes Macphail was thirty-one years old when she was elected. The event caused quite a furore in the country. Some of the comment was facetious. The *Flesherton Advance* said: "It was an Agganizing defeat for the two old-line candidates in South-East Grey. The lady wears skirts, but they do not appear to be much of an impediment when she takes a notion to run."

The *Toronto Star* wrote characteristically: "A former school-teacher in North York at Sharon, Miss Macphail is the aggressive lady who enlivened the proceedings of the tariff commission in Toronto last December when she announced herself to be a plain farmer's daughter, and playfully told Sir Henry Drayton, the chairman of the commission, that never before had she stood in the presence of a real knight. She then proceeded to castigate protection and all its works in a spirit of mingled raillery and indignation, declaring that the exactions of the present tariff make matrimony with farmers an unalluring adventure, which she herself declined to embark on."

The *Woodstock Sentinel Review* commented: "If oratory consists in being able to attract and to hold the intense interest of an audience, in being able to sway its emotions as she plays upon the strings of humour and pathos, and in being able to convince them that her viewpoint is right and that her ideas are sound, then Miss Macphail is one of the finest orators in the Dominion of Canada today."

Agnes herself said: "I found myself often sorry for my opponents; the uprising of the people was like a tidal wave and they were impotent to do anything about it. Any candidate who had been the choice of the United Farmers in that campaign would have won in South-East Grey. The fact that I could give a clear voice to their desires may have added to the majority but it did not determine the election."

This comment on her election was true on that one occasion. But when, later, the U.F.O. and the Progressive Party crumbled under her feet, she was so firmly entrenched in her constituency that she was able to survive as an independent.

We have made history in South-East Grey!

_____

Six

1922—Ottawa

_____

Agnes had never been to Ottawa before her election, but one of several speaking engagements during the interval between December 6th and the opening of Parliament in March brought her near the capital. With R. H. Halbert, another U.F.O. member-elect from the riding of Ontario, she went into the city to see the Parliament Buildings.

"They were all I had imagined, and more," she wrote later. "My devotion to Canada was so great, and my nerves so taut at that time, that tears sprang to my eyes."

The Hall of Fame, the high-domed Library, and the Commons chamber impressed her deeply, as did the moving inscription cut in stone over the main entrance : "The wholesome sea is at her gates, her gates both east and west."

"Just walking into the empty and silent Commons struck terror in my heart," she recalled afterwards.

Her fears were well concealed, for the same visit was described ten years later by Lt.-Col. H. W. Bowie, then Sergeant-at-Arms :

"Sitting in my office on the afternoon of January 27, 1922, I was told that Miss Agnes Macphail, member-elect for the riding of South-East Grey, wished to see me. . . . It is said that first impressions are often the best, and in recalling this visit I remember that I was very favourably impressed by her evident sincerity of manner, and the frank fearlessness of her conversation."

The dignified colonel also relates : "She told me she was inclined to think the interior accommodation rather lavish, and expressed the wish that all others as well as Members of Parliament could be provided with as comfortable quarters." She also found occasion to inform him that her majority had been the largest Progressive one in Ontario, although she had fought a three-cornered battle.

Yet her blunt manner does not appear to have given offence here. The same account continues :

"During her first session the novelty of her surroundings and her loneliness amongst her fellow Members, all of the other sex, at times seemed to be almost more than she could stand and it was very difficult for her to maintain her composure. Although she never complained I could see that this was so, and felt deeply for her. . . .

"As time went by . . . she moved about the chamber conversing with Ministers and Members without embarrassment, and the chair adjoining hers was frequently occupied by the Prime Minister; the Leader of the Opposition; Mr. Bennett; and other leading Ministers and members of the House. I occasionally had the pleasure of sitting down for a few minutes' talk with her, which I always enjoyed."

So reminisced the Sergeant-at-Arms, when Agnes Macphail's arrival in Parliament had become part of the country's history.

A sense of history was close to Agnes as she moved in, with other members of the new Parliament, in March, 1922. She resolved to accept no special privilege because of sex; everything she did set a precedent, and all she wanted for future women members was *equality*. The Government offered her an office suite, similar to those occupied by Cabinet Ministers. She refused, but was grateful to be assigned a single office, without the doubling up which is the general thing for private members. She was given the office on the sixth floor nearest the dining-room, a pleasant, airy place that she immediately liked. To a legion of people, it was "Agnes' office" for the next eighteen years.

She had her moment of humility. Perhaps, she thought, the honour should have come to one of the resolute women who had fought for female suffrage, as she had not done. Yet she would lead the way to the best of her ability, and down the great corridor she walked behind the Gentleman Usher of the Black Rod, toward the Red Chamber where the Governor-General waited to instruct the Commoners in the duties of the session. Behind her sounded the heavier tread of men, but she thought of the women who would surely walk this corridor too. "I could almost hear them coming," she said later. Her ear must have been tuned to a still remote time, for in the next quarter century only four other Canadian women were elected to the federal House of Commons.

The attention paid her in the first few days was overwhelming. The mover of the Address in Reply to the Speech from the Throne, E. J. Murray of North Winnipeg, paid tribute in flowery phrases:

"The poet has said, 'The old order changeth giving place to the new,' and we have in this House for the first time a lady member. I am sure that when I say we all appreciate her presence here my words find an echo in the hearts of all."

And the sentiment was re-embroidered by each succeeding speaker. Meighen, of course, was at pains to point out that woman suffrage had been introduced by his government in the session just past, whereupon King added that the original Conservative bill, in 1917, had aroused such a howl of protest from suffragists that the government had been compelled to broaden it. Crerar, too, got in a political thrust when he declared it "fitting" that the progressive move of permitting women to enter Parliament had resulted in the election of a Progressive woman. C. H. Dickie of Nanaimo hoped piously that "she will find political life pleasant and will exercise a refining influence on our assembly".

There were red roses on her desk as she took her seat. Most of Mr. King's Cabinet crossed to her desk, one by one, to speak a personal word of welcome. Of course, Agnes was flattered and pleased, though she tried not to seem so. She knew that men like Sir Lomer Gouin from Montreal stood for everything she and her people were fighting; he was St. James Street

63

and high tariffs and reaction at its most rigid. But chivalry, just the same, was very nice.

In a way, this extravagant reception was what she expected. She was totally inexperienced, and she preened her feathers happily. Up to this time she had encountered no serious hostility in her world. As a schoolgirl, as a school-teacher, as a budding political speaker in a popular movement, she had been petted, praised and admired.

But she had occupied her seat only a few days before all this suddenly changed. She ran head on into hostility for which she was quite unprepared. In a series of successive shocks she discovered in many quarters a cold, implacable opposition to her presence in Ottawa. She was treated to outright derision. She was a freak. She had overstepped the bounds of proper female behaviour. The Parliament of 1922 was by no means unanimously ready to accept a woman member, no matter what was said for Hansard to record.

She was informed, for example, that the roses which she had received on the first day were a cheap prank. Someone was paying off an election bet; he had sworn she wouldn't get in in South-East Grey and somebody dared him to send her a bouquet. There were subtle indications everywhere that the men thought she should have stayed at home.

Her reaction was peculiarly her own. She felt the offence deeply, and she fought back. Her tongue took on an edge. She behaved with more asperity than grace. In those first weeks and months the many eyes watching her saw a cantankerous spinster—and to the end of her parliamentary career this reputation dogged her.

A change came gradually. Presently she discovered which men in the old parties could be counted as personal friends, despite political differences. She formed lasting friendships with such men as Ernest Lapointe, the great burly master of Liberal fortunes in Quebec province, and George P. Graham, the gentle, much beloved Ontario Member who had been a strong contender for the Liberal leadership. Agnes grew fond of George Graham during the years she faced him across the House, and when he was elevated to the Senate in 1926, she believed he was desperately unhappy; she said it was as though he had been "buried alive".

Jean-François Pouliot, the unpredictable member for Témiscouata, showed her many kindnesses and never failed to acknowledge her birthday with a rose placed on her desk in the Commons chamber. Much later, when he also had taken a Senate seat, he said of her gravely, with obvious conviction, "She was a great lady."

Her own colleagues in the Progressive group were, of course, strangers at the outset, and a little in awe of her. They had their problems of adjustment too. Their leader, T. A. Crerar, who had been a Liberal and wartime Minister of Agriculture, was a practised parliamentarian. But most of the others were as new to their tasks as Agnes was.

They were, in the main, rather innocent radicals, farm men with social consciences sharpened a little keener than those of their neighbours, and imaginations stirred, perhaps for the first time, by a large public question that directly concerned themselves and their kind. They were very unlike the party addicted to "Socialistic, Bolshevistic and Soviet nonsense", which Arthur Meighen had made them out to be. The Winnipeg *Free Press* proclaimed in alarm, "This is class war." But this biggest rural uprising was remarkably unwarlike, even though its leadership put forward some revolutionary ideas, and its staunchest supporters throughout the country were "revolutionaries" in varying degree.

The Canadian farm revolutionary was a rather special type of rebel. He was a man who took time to read a book all the way through, and write comments up and down its margins, and think about it perhaps for several weeks (without coming up against any opposing line of argument, written or spoken). By this time, if the message had hit hard enough, he was ready to do or die for it. Nowhere else was the call of Utopia so sweet and clear, the right way so obvious, as to the men who read alone in the absolute quiet of a country kitchen.

Inspired by this kind of pipe-dream revolution, the Progressives had been sent to Ottawa to fight political corruption, and to give the farmers of Canada their fair voice in framing the nation's laws. The theories of "group government", "recall" and "direct referendum" were to be tested out on the actual fighting ground of Parliament.

The first Member of Parliament actually to sign a "recall" commitment and put it in the hands of his constituency organization was a high-minded young Alberta farmer, Robert Gardiner, who made newspaper headlines in June, 1921, by winning a by-election in Medicine Hat with a thumping 9,765 majority over his Conservative opponent. He was back again after the general election, an emerging leader in the Alberta section of the Progressives.

How pure the spirit of crusade was among them is most eloquently told in the words of J. S. Woodsworth, who wrote in his *Grain Growers' Guide* column, "Sermons for the Unsatisfied" : "So the walls between creeds and callings are breaking down. There are dangers : all may become secular; there are wonderful possibilities : all may become sacred."

But the leading geniuses of this revolution were not to see their hopes realized by the large band of Progressives who reached Ottawa. Of their members only a handful were to remain in any sense crusaders, and probably only one, Woodsworth himself, ever achieved the ideal of welding political endeavour and social principle into one sacred effort.

Soon Agnes, quite naturally, was drawn to the United Farmers of Alberta members of the group. The passion and determination which thrust her into political life had placed her inevitably on the side of J. J. Morrison, the doctrinaire, as against Drury, the compromiser. In Ottawa she quickly found herself in the company of George Coote, Henry Spencer, Ted Garland, Robert Gardiner, and the two Labour members, Irvine and Woodsworth.

Agnes accepted the theory of group government to a degree; she expounded it sometimes on public platforms. What she did accept whole-heartedly was the principle of direct relationship between an elected member and the people who sent that member to parliament. She carried this conviction with her throughout her career, and it was her strongest political asset. The best interests of the people of South-East Grey were her first concern, and she kept in constant touch with those people so that she always knew what their problems were.

As the 1922 session got under way, headlines were mainly concerned with the jousting of Meighen and King (a diversion which was scorned by the Progressives as "childish"). Crerar set forth his party's platform, asking the re-establishment of the Wheat Board, encouragement to co-operatives, reciprocity with the United States, removal of duty on farm implements, lower freight rates, public ownership of railways, and proportional representation.

The Speech from the Throne had referred briefly to "the misfortune of unemployment and the decline of farm prices" during the current "world-wide economic disturbance", but had added, "Keen observers of the business barometer feel that the worst is about over." Certainly none of the earlier speakers seemed unduly disturbed. But the House was disturbed within a few days by a lashing speech from J. S. Woodsworth, his first but by no means his last, in which he denounced the "callousness" of those in high places and set on record, in contrast, the plight of Canada's less fortunate men and women.

There were 200,000 unemployed—speaking of markets, how about this home market for the products of our farms and factories? Relief camps sheltered thousands of war veterans, many of them skilled workers. The families of the unemployed were often destitute, what was to be done for them? In the annual statement of the Bank of Montreal, the general manager had stated that "unemployment is a natural corrective."

"I claim," cried J. S. Woodsworth, "that we have come to a period in our history when we must decide once and for all which shall prevail, profits or human welfare."

The man next him, William Irvine, a rich-voiced Celt, brought a delighted laugh from the assembly when he spoke a little later :

"I wish to state that the honourable member for Centre

67

Winnipeg is the leader of the Labour group—and I am the group."

All the new Progressive members found speaking in the Commons a formidable assignment, a sentiment which has been shared by the most distinguished M.P.'s. Sir Charles Tupper at the close of his career confessed to a fledgling Maritime member, "My dear sir, the last time I spoke in that House my knees shook under me."

But within a month Agnes Macphail took the plunge and rose to her feet. She asked a modest question; the House was considering estimates for the Department of Civil Re-establishment, and it occurred to her to wonder why special bonuses being paid to civil servants should be $500 to a well-paid man, and a mere $40 to a lesser employee.

The Minister, H. S. Beland, drowned his vague answer in a deluge of chivalry: "It will be to me eternal honour that some explanations of mine have drawn into the discussion in this committee the first lady member of the House. I hope that I shall be successful in answering the question which she has so gracefully asked."

Then, on March 29th, she made her first speech. The House was debating a change in the Elections Act, which would permit foreign-born women married to Canadian men to vote, without having to make special application for the privilege. Agnes in effect spoke *against* this extension of woman franchise, for she took the position that women ought not to receive automatically the citizenship of their husbands.

"I think women just want to be individuals, no more and no less," she proclaimed.

This maiden speech included a thrust at the man who was to become her bitterest opponent in the Commons, Hugh Guthrie. As Acting Solicitor General in the previous Conservative regime, Guthrie had been responsible for the former alterations in the Elections Act. And Agnes noted caustically that he had distinguished between United States "foreign-born" and other "foreign-born"; she said she found it hard to understand why he considered American women more fit to receive the blessings of Canadian citizenship than women from Paris or Rome.

It was not, in fact, a particularly gentle or ladylike speech. If Guthrie had had a taste of her tongue, it was a promise of other blistering comments to come.

It came as a shock to Agnes and her friends in the Progressive party to discover how ineffective their best efforts were to win in Parliament the reforms they wanted. Their finest eloquence echoed and died in the green chamber. *Why* didn't the Prime Minister take action when things were so clearly wrong with the country?

Within a month of Parliament's opening, William Irvine moved that the House adjourn its regular business to debate a matter of "urgent public importance"—the plight of Glace Bay coal miners who were faced with a drastic wage cut by the British Empire Steel Corporation. Irvine and some Progressives urged an investigation. Agnes had the temerity to throw King's own weighty volume, *Industry and Humanity,* into the debate, reading to the Prime Minister pages of his own argument in support of organized labour. She protested against special government concessions to the mining company, and the sorry living conditions of the miners' families.

Mackenzie King rose to speak after her. He "agreed with much that she had said". But: "There are times and seasons for all things. There is a proper time for a government to grant a commission; there is a proper time for a government to withhold a commission."

Words calculated to leave the Progressives seething! There were social affairs presently at which Mackenzie King always assured Agnes in private conversation that he was at heart a "radical". The government measures, he pointed out, were always "a step in the right direction." Said Agnes later, "What very *mincing* steps!"

Before the first session ended she had stated her position in regard to immigration—a somewhat narrow view based strictly on the attitude of her farm constituents: "Rather than spend any lavish sum of money to bring other people to Canada, it would be well for this Parliament to bend every energy it has toward making farming conditions liveable for its own citizens."

When she rose to speak on the budget she was obviously in much better command of the situation; she was rapidly finding herself in her new surroundings. She began, "I am not disappointed in the budget because I did not look for anything from it."

She protested rural depopulation: "My own riding has lost 14·22 per cent of its people since 1911."

And high tariffs: "I am alarmed at the artificial stimulating of the secondary industries at the expense of the basic industries."

And she ended somewhat righteously with a demand, befitting a good Scotch country-woman, for frugality in government spending. She said, "People would be much better off if they paid their taxes *directly*; and when they are educated up to the true idea of taxation, where the money goes and where it comes from, I think anyone would be willing to have direct taxation. . . . When people know that they have paid the money out of their own pockets, they are going to watch carefully how it is spent."

Outside the House, this first session was a terrifying experience. She was continually stared at by the curious: eating in the parliamentary restaurant was such an ordeal that she began to lose weight rapidly, and took to eating at a small café in downtown Ottawa. She took a room with an Ottawa housewife, Mrs. Quay, through the kind offices of Mrs. Albert Horton, wife of the editor of *Senate Debates*, who was sympathetic to the Progressives.

Mrs. Quay did her best to help Agnes meet the demands of her new position. There was her first Drawing-Room at Rideau Hall, with Mrs. Quay and a neighbour woman summoned to help Agnes dress for the event, and Agnes angry and disturbed at the prospect of having to "bend the knee" to a representative of royalty. She reported later that she did make a curtsey to Lady Byng, but a most reluctant one. When she went to her first dinner-party at Mackenzie King's home, Mrs. Quay attended with her, and that lady thought it very fine and proper of the Prime Minister to take Agnes in to dinner on his arm. Agnes was somewhat less impressed.

She was impatient with the avid interest in clothes, when newspaper women interviewed her. The national interest in her blue serge dress was a real humiliation. Agnes always maintained stoutly that it was a good dress; she had paid forty-five dollars for it, and she had chosen it because it seemed to her a suitable costume to wear in a man's world. Of course, she had worn it on public platforms throughout her election campaign, but it was still, she said, a good dress!

Her relations with the female section of the press could not have been worse. One reporter recalled a tea when Agnes was entertained by the members of the Women's Press Club. Her manner was severe and stiff, almost hostile, and the hostesses all concluded that she still suffered from a sense of "country" inferiority.

She was far too sensitive about press stories. An early experience with two women reporters hurt her deeply. They called on her in her office together, having asked for an interview— representatives of the Toronto *Telegram* and the *Ottawa Journal*. Agnes received them in friendly fashion, or so she believed, chatted with them freely, and was appalled at the garbled versions that appeared in print. Agnes was bewildered; she felt that she had been made to look ridiculous when she had acted in a kindly, human fashion.

A similar incident happened when Lady Astor, the first woman member of the British House of Commons, visited Ottawa. A reception was held for her in the Speaker's chambers, and Agnes' fellow U.F.O. members gave her a corsage of three roses to pin on her plain dark suit as they left the Commons to attend the function.

When Agnes was in conversation with Lady Astor, she took one of her roses in a typically impulsive gesture and gave it to the guest. That night Lady Astor spoke to a large meeting in the old Russell theatre, and wore the little rose as her only ornament, to Agnes' delight.

But the *Ottawa Journal*'s reporter gave the incident a malicious twist: "Agnes Macphail, who attended the reception for Lady Astor yesterday, was the proud possessor of a dozen American Beauty roses, and *generously* gave Lady Astor one."

Agnes told the story herself, at a later time, and she added, "It seemed strange to me then and it does still, that women who had a pen in their hands or who had the public ear in any way, used it in those early days to make my life more difficult. They didn't know me; it couldn't have been any personal dislike. What was it then? Even if I did things they were displeased with, I at least had opened a door which had always until then been closed to all women. Surely that fact alone should have arrested their criticism and called out their sympathy. In the women of the farms it did."

The gentlemen of the press were just as hostile. Charles Bishop, a leading journalist of the *Ottawa Citizen*, wrote with an almost discernible shudder his fear of "descending hordes" of female politicians. Wilfrid Eggleston said that from the press gallery in those days she looked "bleak and severe, her features strong rather than attractive . . . not exactly lovable." But the liberties taken by some large dailies were inexcusable. One of them sneered: "Progressives have no love for Grits or Tories, dramatically declares Miss Agnes Macphail in Toronto. Does Agnes know what love is?"

Just as objectionable were some press stories intended to flatter her! A certain R. E. Knowles set a new record for this kind of article after he interviewed her at a U.F.O. convention:

"With large, but pleasing form, erect as an Indian, fine shapely hands, mouth mobile and delicate and capable of much; gaze straightforward and steady as if done in oils, and a wealth of hair black as the raven's wing and fixed into gleaming regularity like a head-plate of shining steel; pink of cheek, and serene of bearing as a statue of Boadicea, Miss Macphail is indeed an interesting type of what I am sure is a Highland lady some generations removed."

He asked Boadicea some astonishing questions and got some blunt replies.

"Do you think it is possible to go into political life and yet keep radiant and untarnished the inner shrine of a woman's modesty, delicacy, sensitiveness?"

"I surely do. Public life broadens, not blunts, a woman's make-up."

"Do they [the male members] ever give you to understand you're only a woman after all—and have no right there?"

"Yes, they sometimes imply it. But outside the Chamber they are comradely and courteous. I may add that I value their comradeship more than their courtesy."

"Do you think your presence in parliament goes far to temper the asperity of political life?"

"Not much. I'm not much on tempering. I'm no Gulf Stream in the cold ocean of political life?"

To Agnes this sort of publicity was so much twaddle. When an American woman editor wrote her for material for an article, she answered with a brief biographical sketch : "There is nothing about me to tell . . ." and then added a full paragraph outlining her sympathies for the farm people of her country.

". . . In seeking for a solution I began to study economics, trade conditions, etc., which landed me here on Parliament Hill, but I have not yet found the solutions. . . . I can say with John Bright, 'My sympathies are naturally with the class with which I am connected, and I would infinitely prefer to raise the class of which I am one than by any means whatever to creep above it or out of it.' "

Whether the American lady editor was satisfied with this material, or would have preferred a description of her hat, is not recorded.

She began her work at Ottawa with a very stern view of Members' duties, which had to be relaxed as time went on. She believed at first that Members should sit in their places in the chamber as long as the House was in session; but very soon she exclaimed, "One would be a physical wreck within a few months!" She heaped scorn on the Senate : "I should certainly hate to see a good woman wasted there. It is a useless institution, and appointment to it would be like being placed on a shelf, prior to burial."

She worked very hard. Her mail was always heavy, and she tried to answer it all. In 1922 the effects of economic depression were widespread, and Agnes was distressed over the personal requests for help that flooded her desk. She had hoped to find time to study French, but that proved out of the question. She wrote often to her U.F.O. executive in South-East Grey, informing them of her actions in Parliament and asking advice on questions of policy.

But above all her recollections of her first session were that it was "a miserable time". In her own words : "I was intensely unhappy. Some members resented my intrusion, others jeered at me, while a very few were genuinely glad to see a woman in the House. Most of the members made me painfully conscious of my sex by standing up every time I entered the lobby, until I told them I would feel obliged to keep away, unless they treated me as one of themselves." In committee meetings too she was embarrassed because members hastily discarded pipes, cigarettes and cigars as soon as she entered, and once again she threatened to boycott committee meetings, if her presence put such a restraint on her colleagues. During her first session she lamented, "A spirit of awe and timidity hangs over the House. I have addressed thousands of people without increasing my heart action one beat; yet when I get up in the House to ask the Minister of Health one simple question, I am afraid my heart will go out of my mouth. If you are picking a candidate, pick a strong one, who is able to go up against that wall of steel."

In the midst of her very real distress at this time, one person stood out as a friend, and gave her invaluable comfort and encouragement. It was J. S. Woodsworth, the gentle, scholarly, dedicated "saint in politics". For Woodsworth she came to feel something akin to worship.

And so in the early summer of 1922, Parliament adjourned. Leaving Ottawa for the quiet of her Ceylon home, Agnes may well have wondered whether she really wanted to come back again in a few months' time. And the movement of which she was a part was crumbling; there had been two defections from the Progressive ranks as J. A. Binette and W. J. Hammell, both elected by the U.F.O., moved in with the Liberals. The press buzzed with reports of a complete break-up. The Canadian Council of Agriculture had become lukewarm toward its political "arm". There seemed little doubt that the Progressive leader, T. A. Crerar, would soon resign to return to his Liberal home, and in fact he did so in November.

It was a far from auspicious beginning. It seemed that all Agnes Macphail had at that moment was the inheritance from her Scotch mother—the will to hold on.

Seven

A dash of ginger

A country school-teacher is not transformed overnight into a Commons member without a backward look. The problems of rural education were still important to Agnes Macphail, and in addition to her heavy parliamentary duties during her first term, she took on the task of doing all she could, single-handed, to help Ontario teachers demonstrate in their schools the lessons of democracy and government. She made up a booklet describing how ideas became laws, and distributed it widely in the schools. She arranged for photos of Parliament and sent them out to teachers, largely at her own expense. She entertained, out of her own pocket, the entire enrolment of the Ottawa Normal School on several successive years.

Those young Normal School ladies can still recall the event vividly. They gathered on Parliament Hill and were met by the very severe, tall young woman, dressed in plain, almost dowdy black, who was Canada's first female M.P. She ushered them into the visitors' gallery, explaining everything as they went along. After a short stay gazing down on the heads of honourable Members, they were shepherded to the imposing parliamentary dining-room and given tea, and afterwards Agnes Macphail made a little speech and handed each of them the portfolio of parliamentary pictures.

Her rather grim sense of duty was obvious in her early speeches. Her first speech in the 1923 session was during a debate on immigration, when a remark about "common labourers" irked her.

She said : "We do not sufficiently respect those who toil with their hands. I am truly amazed at the sentiments that are expressed by some of our well-groomed luxuriously living friends. They evidently have not had their brow wet with sweat for some time, or if they have, their hands were not soiled with work on that occasion. . . .

"In connection with this immigration scheme one honourable Member recommended bringing in servant girls to Canada to work in homes, to do the work that the woman of the house would do if she did not have a servant. But that girl is not considered the social equal of those for whom she works. Why not? If her character and her brains are as good, is she not the equal in every way of the woman of the house who hires a servant simply because her husband is in a financial position to enable her to do so?"

J. S. Woodsworth could be excused for including her in his own political category. "We socialists . . ." he said to her, and Agnes protested, "I'm not a socialist!"

"I am only judging you by your speeches," J. S. said with a twinkle.

A few weeks later she brought the plight of farm women to the attention of the assembly in vivid fashion.

"It is true that the farmers work hard; it is true their days are long and their pay is poor. But it is also infinitely true that the farm woman's day is longer and her pay poorer. With all due deference to the superior wisdom of men, one mistake that I think the men continually make in this House is that of treating the problem of rural depopulation as a man's problem and a man's problem only. Honourable members talk about the boy getting an education, as if when you have talked about the man and the boy you have finished the family—but you have not. . . . The girls leave the farms first, and that is a pretty sure indication that the boys will leave later."

In the course of this speech she informed Trade and Commerce Minister Robb that she had sent out a letter containing eight questions about their present circumstances to 900 soldier settlers in the province. "If the minister would like to have a pleasant Sunday afternoon I will lend him my 400 answers."

Agnes had not come to Parliament Hill to admire the view. She had said nothing about an M.P.'s duty to his constituents that she did not ardently believe.

Her voice was well suited to Commons debate. Many a male voice was lost in the far corners of the chamber, but hers was strong and deep-toned, and members listened. They did not always like what they heard, and as the caustic jibes flicked sensitive spots to right and left, there were some who began to strike back.

She coined names for the House of Commons and for the Senate : one was the House of Temptation, the other the House of Refuge.

"Temptation?" cried a Member in pretended bewilderment. "I have noticed no temptation here—unless it is the Member for South-East Grey."

The hearty male laughter filled her with confusion. At home, with Mrs. Quay to comfort her, she gave way to tears over the incident.

The House of Commons was an exhausting business in those days, before a strict time limit was imposed on the working day. As the session neared completion the members were anxious, as always, to be finished and get away from Ottawa. Sessions that lasted far into the night were not uncommon.

So Agnes picked a poor time to introduce her first motion in the House of Commons. The 1923 session had only nine days to go. The members' nerves were frayed, their chivalry somewhat tattered. Late in the evening on June 21st Agnes moved an amendment to the Senate and House of Commons Act, on the subject of sessional allowances paid to members.

She herself had been true to her pledge in the election campaign. She had not approved when in 1920 the salary of an M.P. was raised to $4000. She insisted that *no one* needed more than $2500 to live on, and during each of the first two years in Parliament she had gone to considerable trouble, since there was no precedent for such behaviour, to turn back into the public treasury $1500 of her salary. Now she proposed that as a gesture of good faith, since the Government was always advising the

A dash of ginger

people to practise thrift and economy, the members reverse the 1920 decision and put the salary figure back $500. (She now acknowledged that heads of families might need a little more than she did.)

She said, "I am led to move this amendment because I know a great many people have been forced this year to do without telephones and daily papers."

Members were irritable, annoyed, in no mood to be preached at.

She went on, "Another one of the chief pleas that was put up by the members of the Government of 1920, when this increase was made, was that it would do away with the party fund— that if the members were given $4000 a year they would not be slaves to the party or the party fund. The best proof that that is not true is the voting as we have witnessed it in this House. . . ."

At that point the ceiling seemed to fall about her head.

A half dozen Quebec members roared their dissatisfaction with her statement. It was unparliamentary to insinuate that honourable members were prejudiced, when they voted in the House, by consideration for someone who paid money to help them get elected.

"Withdraw!" they shouted at her.

"I would like to know how much my honourable friend received herself . . ."

"The honourable gentleman doth protest too much," Agnes retorted, but the cries of "Withdraw!" grew noisier, and the new leader of the Progressive party, Robert Forke, advised her to withdraw in a hesitant speech as he sought to justify his own personal need for $4000 a year.

Agnes said, "I have no desire to reflect on the honour of any member of this House."

But this customary formula went unnoticed as the six M.P.'s, their tempers thoroughly ruffled, went on for several minutes to protest her allegation. Finally one member pointed out that she *had* withdrawn, and Agnes got in a final word :

"I will withdraw the statement if it is unparliamentary and beg everybody's pardon. The thing I want to say, if I may be allowed to do so, is this: when some of the good party men have declared their views outside on certain questions and we see them come in and vote in the opposite way, what are we to think?"

The Speaker quickly put the question, which was emphatically voted down.

The Progressive Party crumbled and broke before the end of their first term in Parliament. T. A. Crerar completed only one session as their leader, then resigned to devote his time to the United Grain Growers Company, of which he was president. He was re-elected as a Liberal. The Progressives named Robert Forke their leader at the 1923 session, and he held leadership until 1926. But his sympathies also were close to the Liberal party, and he returned to the fold. A majority of the others followed a similar course. W. L. Morton, in *The Progressive Party in Canada*, described "the fraternity of the corridors, the courtesies of the Liberal whip, the insidious sense of acceptance" that undermined the Progressives as a separate force with a reform programme.

Agnes Macphail said bitterly, "Mackenzie King just had to crook his little finger!" And there is no doubt that King did personally, though most discreetly, invite the Progressives one by one to break ranks and join the Liberals.

Agnes herself received overtures, which she bluntly rejected. Between her election in 1921 and her eventual defeat in 1940, she was approached by Mackenzie King on two occasions, with the offer of a seat in his cabinet if she would resign in her constituency and run as a Liberal. She showed not a moment's hesitation in turning down this bargain. While the wily Liberal leader was not one to be caught making such offers openly, it was known to several leading Liberals of the time. Agnes discussed it with Mrs. Quay (who is now Mrs. Frank Tinker of Owen Sound) and with her secretary and close confidante, Miss Lilla Bell.

King was more successful elsewhere. In the summer of 1924 he was able to say confidently, while on a tour of the West, that

A dash of ginger

there was no longer a place in the political life of Canada for the Progressive Party.

The agricultural body that had backed the Progressives in the beginning, the Canadian Council of Agriculture, withdrew its support in March, 1923. The onus for political action was thrown back on the provincial United Farmers organizations. And in some provinces, notably Ontario, the United Farmers had run into rough weather. The Ontario U.F.O. government under Drury was defeated in 1923. There was a general rush to get out of politics, a rapid ebb of the tide that had launched the Progressives a few years earlier.

In 1924 the split came in Ottawa. J. S. Woodsworth moved an amendment to the budget; fourteen Progressives supported him and the rest did not.

It was another all-night session on the Hill. At seven o'clock in the morning of May 16th, the vote was taken. Agnes spoke just before the vote was called. She said, "Mr. Speaker, I put human values too high to impose on this weary House the thirty-five-minute speech which I had carefully prepared. . . . I will support the amendment . . . which is part of the goal toward which we are working, and working the Government ahead of us as we go." She threw in her lot with Woodsworth and the others who held loyally to their early purpose.

Next month, in the final stages of the 1924 session, six Progressives, who could not tolerate the defection of their group to the Liberals, formally parted company with the rest. They were M. M. Campbell, Robert Gardiner, E. J. Garland, D. M. Kennedy, H. E. Spencer, and Agnes Macphail. All were Alberta members except Agnes. They made public a letter to Forke, saying simply that they desired to "give effect in the political field to that co-operative philosophy which has not only constituted an outstanding characteristic of farmers' movements, but which is the world's best hope of saving civilization."

Somebody called them "The Ginger Group", and the name stuck. Very soon four others joined them: C. G. Coote of Alberta, Preston Elliott and W. C. Good of Ontario, and W. J. Ward of Manitoba.

These ten now shunned the other Progressives, and held caucus meetings of their own, usually with J. S. Woodsworth and William Irvine. What political future was there for the splinter group from a splinter group? But this was the live, able, aggressive core of the farmers' "revolution", and Agnes Macphail was among them.

There was a comradeship in the Ginger Group that lightened the heavy parliamentary load. Outside the Commons Chamber they drew together for company. Friendship among them was warm and deep.

In this group, inevitably, the young Agnes Macphail found not only friends but suitors. It was assumed for a time that she and Preston Elliott were engaged to be married, and Elliott certainly had this event in mind. But Agnes drew back from marriage. Her good friend, George Coote, who was her desk-mate and chief confidant for several sessions, heard her side of the story. Was marriage possible, even marriage to a fellow member of Parliament, so long as she herself remained a member? Where would they live, in his riding or hers? She *belonged* in South-East Grey; she would have to give it up if she moved elsewhere. And marriage, even to a fine person who shared her major interest in life, was no substitute for her own political career. No substitute at all.

Preston Elliott was defeated when the next election came around, and dropped out of political life. Agnes had made the right decision, the only possible decision for her.

A more serious choice had to be made when Robert Gardiner fell in love with her. Gardiner was a silent-mannered man, resolute and of the highest integrity, respected by his fellows. He was anything but a ladies' man. Agnes Macphail was probably the only woman he ever loved. For a time they were together constantly. But the basic choice was the same: *her* life, *her* work—or the wifely role as helpmate to a man? Agnes had to give the same answer.

Agnes had in her first years in Parliament created such a reputation as a grim and militant spinster that many could scarcely credit that men would pursue her ardently and, when

A dash of ginger

rejected, go wifeless all their days. Or the different reaction of a Newmarket man who finally broke with her violently when he could not persuade her to marry him saying, "When I do marry, don't phone and don't wire; I want to forget I ever knew you!"

The contrast between the sharp-tongued female whom Wilfrid Eggleston saw from the press gallery as "not exactly lovable", and the young woman who glowed and laughed and danced with her friends in private, is astonishing.

The Agnes Macphail whom the country was beginning to know, as press and radio reported her public speeches, was a woman warrior in a man-made world, and either admirable or ludicrous according to one's opinion on the role of women. The Agnes Macphail her friends describe, with a warmth and loyalty that years have not lessened, was a woman who loved easy talk and a small, gay party, a woman not always happy, certainly, but capable of immense enjoyment and high spirits. It was she who brought the room alive when she walked in; she who suggested the Chinese supper, the place to go and dance.

One of her dearest friends in Ottawa was a school-teacher, Miss Muriel Kerr, whom she met soon after she arrived in the capital. A quick, impatient Agnes, "who would stand and ring a doorbell four times while a sensible person would ring once and wait"; an Agnes who liked wearing capes, "because they swing when you walk"; an impulsive, generous Agnes, who "bought lovely, special gifts, out-of-season, but seldom bothered with Christmas or birthdays"—this was the friend seen through Miss Kerr's eyes.

The first time Agnes stayed overnight at Muriel Kerr's apartment on Cooper Street, as she was to do many a time through later years, the hostess took pains to provide for her comfort. She showed Agnes the room where she was to sleep, found her a nice plump pillow, and brought in the clock to place next her bed. They had no sooner said good-night than Miss Macphail darted out of the room.

"I think you should keep this pillow, and your clock!"

"Not at all! You have them!"

This polite shilly-shally lasted several minutes, till both suspected the truth. Neither could sleep on a big pillow, and both hated clocks ticking near them as they slept. The discovery was uproariously funny, and the two girls burst into peals of laughter. Their staunch and happy friendship lasted for the next thirty years of their lives.

It is surprising, too, that her intimate friends are unanimous in insisting that Agnes Macphail was a fine-looking young woman, with an excellent figure, beautiful colouring, and shapely, expressive hands. She seemed transformed in their company, and only much later did poise and better grooming carry this impression into the public eye. Muriel Kerr and others mention a certain taste for elegance, for tea in fine china, for a touch of glittering beadwork on a dark dress. It took a few years in the capital to form her tastes, but the handsomely turned-out woman of later years was at least hinted at to those who knew her best.

She never did enter fully into the social life of Ottawa. She was never at pains to cultivate those who would have assisted her socially. On the contrary, she constantly offended ladies, by ignoring or rebuffing their overtures. Perhaps she was still at heart the young country girl at Owen Sound Collegiate, squaring off at authority, and determined to "show" the city girls, who had bathtubs but not too many brains. And, as seems to be always the case with those who behave this way, she was not free from a streak of snobbishness, which cropped up on occasion as she rubbed shoulders with the great.

A dash of ginger

Eight

New causes

From her first term Agnes Macphail held a unique position, not only as the first woman but as an independent member of the Commons. Her associates drifted into politically congenial groups, or became the nuclei for groups that were built around them. She found herself unable to do either. She was elected by the U.F.O. only to find, before another election, that the U.F.O.'s political venture had fallen to pieces, leaving her stranded on the rock of South-East Grey. As a farm representative and a non-socialist, she could not enter freely into the left-wing labour group that was centred in Woodsworth and Irvine, although in the early 1930's she was to make a strong bid to bring her U.F.O. with her into such an alliance. Except for a short period when the C.C.F. was formed, she was a member of no party during her years in Ottawa.

And so her place in Canada's history depends on her measure of personal greatness. No one was there to cushion the shocks for her—or hold a ladder to her pedestal. If she could have foreseen how political parties today court and coax their lady members she might have been envious. Or perhaps she liked it better as it was—the strong challenge, the sense of complete responsibility for her own achievements and her own mistakes.

She spoke philosophically to the graduates of Ottawa Ladies' College at a dinner in 1924. She laid down rules for a good life, and ended : "Do not rely completely on any other human being, however dear. We meet all life's greatest tests alone."

Her first measure of fame came from an appreciation of her quick tongue, her ability to lash out vigorously in the House of

Commons and give pause to any man who dared assume that a woman would back down before him.

A certain Quebec member, Vien from Lotbinière, had the temerity to attack on a few occasions, and was promptly and definitely worsted.

During the 1924 session, when Agnes repeated her opposition to large-scale immigration so long as farm conditions remained unimproved, Vien rose to protest her remarks about farm life. He eulogized the farmers of Lotbinière :

". . . sturdy sons of the old stock . . . who live, it is true, in log cabins, but . . . I do not believe there is any happier group in the country. . . . Of course they do not ride in Rolls Royce cars or in automobiles of any kind ; they have one horse or a pair of oxen ; they live modestly and they practise thrift. They are satisfied with very little—indeed, sometimes with almost nothing at all."

Agnes rose and shot a deliberate question : "Does the honourable member live as his constituents do in order that he may accurately interpret their thought ?"

Laughter rose in the House, and Vien cried, "My honourable friends laugh, but wait a minute . . ."

More laughter cut him short, and Agnes turned to advise the minister of immigration, wryly, to let Vien be the man to give prospective immigrants an accurate picture of farming in Canada.

When the Commons was considering a change in the Divorce Bill, always a hotly contentious subject, Agnes supported the move to make grounds for divorce equal between men and women. She added :

"When I hear men talk about women being the angel of the home I always, mentally at least, shrug my shoulders in doubt. I do not want to be the angel of any home ; I want for myself what I want for other women, absolute equality. After that is secured then men and women can take turns at being angels."

But to her reputation for this kind of speech there soon was added a respect for Agnes Macphail as a tenacious fighter, in dead earnest, for causes that roused her interest and concern.

New causes

Her choice of issues was prompted first of all by a deep and passionate pity, a pity that moved her over and over again to weep, as her parliamentary secretaries affirm, having seen her many times in the privacy of her office give way to tears because of the suffering and indignities borne by those who sought her aid. And she was prompted, secondly, to fight whenever she was annoyed by high-handed authority, with a stubborn Scotch dislike for ceremonious humbug.

Three such issues arose during the last two years of her first term in Parliament, each making her name more widely known, and marking her future course in public life. None of them had to do with farmers, even though this farmer's daughter had come to Ottawa pledged to champion her "class" against all comers. She was not the person to let that kind of pledge become a safe wall against new demands and wider fields of interest.

In 1924 there was still current a military jingoism that seems archaic in Canada today. Much of it pre-dated 1918, but there were still men who prated of war's "glory", and the joys of dying for one's flag. But following 1918 there was released a flood of atrocity stories, of the suffering of men in the trenches and civilians in occupied areas, and on top of this there came a wave of "debunking" by some military and political leaders as well as by intellectuals. J. S. Woodsworth was an ardent pacifist. And Agnes Macphail could not fail to be influenced by one of the strongest, most emotional trends in public sentiment of that period.

The particular issue that roused Agnes, as a former schoolteacher, was militarism in the schools. For, as usual, the wave of "debunking" reached the educational system last of all, and Canadian children went on reciting, "And, smiling, his Chief beside, the boy fell dead," and "Theirs not to reason why . . ." long after their elders had heaped ridicule on these poetic lines.

Education was, of course, a provincial matter, but Agnes seized on the system of cadet training as a fair target, since the federal Government provided an annual grant for this purpose.

Her first motion protesting cadet training in the schools was introduced in 1924, and quickly ruled out of order because she proposed an amendment that would have eliminated the $400,000 grant entirely. No amendment can do this; it may only change or reduce the amount named in the bill. It would seem apparent that Agnes drafted her motion entirely on her own initiative, since any experienced person whom she might have consulted would probably have been aware of this basic rule.

But before the Speaker intervened to rule her amendment out of order, Agnes got in a bitter little speech: "Why should we take young boys, dress them in uniforms and teach them to strut along to martial strains with their foolish little guns and swords at their sides? . . . We teach these poor boys to get ready to defend us at some future time. It is a cowardly thing; it is not a brave thing at all."

Angry insults were hurled at her.

"You had better go to Russia."

"Soviet Russian nonsense . . ."

"If you are a fair example of Canadian womanhood . . ."

"I think I am," interjected Agnes.

"I do not think so."

But in 1925 Agnes was back, much better prepared to press the issue.

She presented a logical case. She had read articles on the subject of military drill and was prepared to support her view that it was not an effective form of gymnastic exercise, and she argued that cadet training and physical education ought not to be confused in the public mind. In a constructive vein she urged a substitute "colourful" gymnastic program for both boys and girls:

> Such a system would result in very much improving the health of our school children, and would leave Canada in a perfectly safe position, because if our future citizens have strong, well-developed bodies and unprejudiced and open minds, then Canada need not fear the future.
>
> It is a much more difficult but a much greater thing to call upon the resources of mind and spirit than it is to bash

one another's noses when we do not agree with each other's opinions, and that is what we have not learned to do internationally. . . . I am not concerned for the old men, but . . . I am tremendously concerned that the old men before they pass on do not leave firmly imprinted in the mind of youth the impression that this is the highest and best way of settling things. . . .

We must never forget that the spirit of the thing is the grinning demon of war. . . . Newspapers have glorified the "gentleman cadet". This is a disastrous thing. We hold up a natty-looking boy, full of life and adventure and beauty, a splendid fellow *who knows nothing about war,* and we *who do know* sit here and let the children who see that nattily dressed cadet think that there is ideal manhood.

And she moved that the appropriation of $400,000 be reduced by $399,999.

Unfortunately for Agnes, she could not restrain her passionate dislike of militarism, and into her speech she also threw words about Empire Day and war memorials:

Empire Day is made the occasion for nothing but a strutty, silly, pompous, bombastic performance by military men and those who are backing them. Do you know— possibly the Government does not know—that the common people of Canada laugh heartily, though they know it is a dreadful thing, a tragedy, but they are moved to mirth by the speeches and performances they hear and see on such a day as Empire Day. . . . Mistakenly we stick up silly war memorials all over this country.

Not surprisingly, the press reports were far from laudatory. She was immediately branded as a rabid anti-militarist. She thought the press was unfair to her.

She thought she had good grounds also for seeking to reduce the government appropriation for the Royal Military College, arguing that sons usually of well-to-do families were being educated at public expense, and that Canada could do without the luxury of a privileged military group such as the R.M.C. graduates.

The cadet at the Royal Military College was provided, she noted, with the cheapest, yet most exclusive, education in the country. The state "gives him horses, boats, canoes, skis and a swagger stick."

> In view of the fact that we are suffering from great economic stress, in view of the further fact that the chief object at the Royal Military College, with some exceptions, is to produce a class of snobs, whose chief duty it is to carry the swagger stick with which the state provides them—in view of the further fact that the vote on tuberculosis has been cut, and there is a threat of cutting out altogether the vote for venereal disease, in view of the further fact that the question of rural credits has not been taken up this year on account of the cost, and the further fact that the Pensions Bill was killed in the Senate, . . . I move . . .

She did not hesitate to hurl a phrase like "A class of snobs" at the R.M.C. Yet she insisted that the press interpretation of her attack was unfair. Hadn't she said, "With some exceptions"?

Outside the Commons, on speaking engagements that were becoming increasingly frequent, Agnes followed up this theme. She tried to defend her position against the newspapers, which had accused her of lack of patriotism :

"I would not have you forsake love of country. I am a Canadian. I love Canada. I have been accused of advocating a system by which one would not love one's country. I never did. I never have." She threw up her hands. "But what's the use? It is no good trying to explain things like that."

Often, throughout the country, her speeches against military expenditure found a sympathetic response. Back home in South-East Grey she spoke to a hushed and solemn audience: "I would say to the gun makers and the cadet trainers, I would say to the people of Canada, 'Whom do you want to kill?'"

New causes

On March 18, 1925, Agnes Macphail introduced a resolution to the Commons on Private Members' Day : "It is desirable in the administration of the penitentiaries to provide : (1) sufficient productive work to keep the inmates employed; (2) that a share of the proceeds go to provide for dependents; and in case of no dependents, such share should be held in trust until release."

She quoted in support of this plan a report made in 1921 by the Superintendent of Penitentiaries in Canada, Brigadier-General Hughes. She noted that organized labour had been consulted about the project, to meet any possible objection to the production of cheap goods by this method. Tom Moore, president of the Trades and Labour Council of Canada, had made plain his sympathy with the idea.

The resolution was "talked out" in a few desultory speeches; it did not come to a vote.

But in this resolution Agnes had got her teeth into something which was to claim a major part of her energy and effort during the next dozen years; penal reform.

Then, at the end of March, 1925, an entirely new and different issue arose.

In Glace Bay, Nova Scotia, another wage cut was in prospect for the coal miners employed by the British Empire Steel Corporation. The men believed they were being pressured by the company, through continual lay-offs and the stoppage of credit at company stores, to accept the cut. They struck. Almost immediately pitiful tales of the hard conditions endured by their families were circulated, and promptly discredited as Red propaganda. A delegation of ladies from a prominent benevolent society made an investigation and reported that the tales were grossly exaggerated; their delegation had visited well-furnished homes and discovered a miner's wife who owned an evening gown.

Agnes Macphail decided that it was her business to go to Glace Bay. She went. She spent several days in the strike area, and returned to devote her forty-minute speech in the budget debate to the coal miners' strike.

It was the longest and by far the best speech of her first years in the House. As she began there was whispering inattention, and the Speaker had to call order. As she continued there was silence. She commanded the Commons, she spoke with the authority of one who had just been deeply moved and must share that experience.

"I wondered why people after just three weeks' unemployment should find themselves on the hunger line—before I went to Glace Bay and the towns in the vicinity of Glace Bay where the strike occurred at mines Nos. 2, 4 and 6. I found that for four years these men had not had regular work; for one and a half years they had had almost no work."

She described what she had seen. "I visited the central relief station and some sub-stations, the hospitals, and all the rooms of the school; and I met 2000 miners at a meeting in the Savoy Theatre in Glace Bay. I met the moderates and the Reds, and by the time I had spent two days in Glace Bay nobody looked Red to me. I think if I lived there very long I would be a lot redder than anything I saw."

She described the homes she went into—small, dilapidated, bare. She reported with astonishment that these people were *Scotch*—on the relief rolls were the McDonalds, the Munroes and the McGillivrays. Their stoic pride won her complete sympathy.

"They feel," she accused the Commons, "that they have not got justice anywhere."

She told of the sick child covered with one quilt on a bare mattress, of the child dressed only in a coat and home-made stockings; she told of empty cupboards.

"These places were not chosen for me, because many times when they would want to go into one house, I would want to go into another; and I went into the one I wanted to go into." There was appreciative laughter.

"I could not help but be struck by the tragedy of womankind *in that place*. Their youth is brief. Some young women are hotly resentful . . . but for the most part, especially if they have many children, their attitude is subdued and apathetic."

New causes

She reminded the government that they had "pampered" the company that was in dispute with these men. The British Empire Steel Corporation "have received almost everything— subsidy, bonuses, protection by tariff and militia . . . An example of the pampering of industry and the neglect of humanity."

Agnes Macphail was welcomed to Halifax on a visit in 1933 by an editorial in the Halifax *Herald,* which said, "Miss Macphail in other years proved herself a good friend of Nova Scotia, and particularly the workers of Nova Scotia, and our own people do not forget."

Nor did the Commons members who heard her speak on behalf of those miners quickly forget. The straightforward sincerity of her words had a compelling effect. Her voice when she was deeply moved was a rich instrument, vibrant and strong, dropping into the lower register with dramatic power. The stark facts she presented, and the challenge to the conscience of the nation's legislators, could not be denied.

With this speech she claimed for herself a place among the builders of a new kind of society, based on the concept of public responsibility for private misfortune. All the major social welfare legislation was still in the future. Canada had no old-age pensions, unemployment insurance, or family allowances. The Beveridge "cradle to the grave" welfare programme for Britain, with its effect on Canadian thinking, was still unheard of. The idea that in times of economic depression the government should act to provide employment by heavy expenditure on public works, was heresy to those who preached thrift and a balanced budget. That the nation as a whole should use its collective wealth to look after its people in childhood and old age, in illness and extreme poverty, was only a vision held by a handful of radicals. Within a relatively short period of time it has become the popular and approved view. But not by accident —rather by the strenuous effort of a few who cared very deeply, and insisted that others must share their concern. Agnes Macphail must be counted among those few.

Nine

Riding relations

Agnes Macphail always said she was no politician. She based this remarkable statement on two things. First, she did not have enough political sense to spend a little money to get a good photograph taken early in her career. She was a difficult subject photographically, and certainly the pictures of her that appeared in the press were the limit in unattractiveness until late in her life, when first-class photographers showed the public what she really looked like.

Her second conviction was that she had no election organization.

She could not be bothered with details, she said. One can only conclude that she never took a look at other riding organizations.

Years of teaching school had left their imprint. Agnes automatically organized in terms of schools and school sections. She aimed at a public meeting in each school section at least once a year, and to achieve this it was necessary to have a group of workers in each section. Her riding executive was formed of representatives from each township group, with the usual officers : president, vice-president, secretary-treasurer.

Each year the South Grey U.F.O. put on a big picnic, the favourite form of recreation for the farmers. Agnes arranged this personally, hiring the performers, planning the programme, and so on. In addition, Agnes sponsored dances and smaller picnics for the young people. She was convinced that children and young people were the most important members of the community—the citizens of the future—and they must be made aware of how the country was governed, and how it should be governed. In the habit of instructing, she set about teaching her constituents. She wrote chatty letters to the school children in the riding, letters which were distributed to the teachers to be read aloud in class. These letters were intended to teach the children in detail how, as Agnes said, an idea in the mind of a Member of Parliament eventually became a law in Canada. They also dealt with current events. She provided every school with a picture of the Parliament Buildings. She sponsored public speaking and essay contests, with the main prize a trip to Ottawa at her expense, complete with a conducted tour of the Parliament Buildings and introductions to prominent politicians of all parties.

These were all public-school events. She felt that while it might be more valuable to instruct high-school pupils, at that time a very small proportion of farm youngsters went on to high school, and she had better get them interested in government while she could get hold of them.

She wrote a weekly report to the riding, which was published eventually in twenty different papers. These reports were very popular, and made less industrious M.P.'s quite unhappy. They made her secretaries quite unhappy, too, because they meant many hours of extra work for them. It was necessary for her secretary to clip newspaper items, to mark daily copies of Hansard for her use, and to work all Saturday afternoon, helping to compile, and then typing, the weekly report. But they were widely read. Agnes remarked later that she was often quoted to herself when she visited the riding.

She organized the "Holdfast" Clubs—U.F.O. women's organizations much like the Women's Institutes. The members met in each others' homes and had speakers and discussion on current affairs, followed by a really stupendous "tea"—a meal that a city dweller could not distinguish from a very large supper. These clubs kept Agnes in continual contact with the farm women in her riding and gave them a feeling of participation in public affairs through her. She did not think of them as a political manœuvre. She was genuinely concerned that women, particularly country-women, should be interested in the outside world, and that their dealings with their own local problems should be the fruit of intelligent discussion.

She organized clubs for young farm people as well. These were the United Farmers Young People's Organization, and they were, in a measure, rivals of the Junior Farmers, although the two groups co-operated in an annual festival, with athletic events, and public speaking and debates. The Junior Farmers were government sponsored and, to some extent, government controlled, with the Agricultural Representative in the district a moving spirit in them. The "Ag Rep" was naturally inclined to feel something less than friendship for the rival group, who were distinctly critical of government policy. They were also articulate—Agnes saw to that. An important part of their activity was public speaking in the form of debates, addresses, and forum discussions. It was in this group that Agnes looked for young people of promise to go on with political and co-operative work. It was this group that she expected to plunge into adult education with enthusiasm. She took a strong personal interest in many of the members and she was inclined to disapprove when they got married, fearing that their interest would turn to private rather than public affairs.

It was from this group that Farquhar Oliver was selected when Agnes was asked by her riding executive to pick out a "likely fellow" to run provincially for the U.F.O. She had difficulty deciding between Oliver and another large and handsome farm lad named Joe Crutchley, a boy of attractive personality and real ability. In later years she felt she had made the wrong choice. Crutchley kept out of politics except as a trusted helper of both Agnes and Oliver, and became an important figure in the co-operative movement and the Federation of Agriculture.

To Agnes, going back to her riding was very much like going home from her teaching jobs, and she had the same impulse toward generosity and present-giving that had betrayed her in the past. She was as thrilled at receiving her first indemnity as she had been at receiving her first pay as a teacher, and her reaction was much the same. She wanted to do something wonderful for her parents.

They were still living in the brick farm-house near Ceylon. Agnes bought, very secretly, a really handsome sleigh. She had it driven in style up to the farm, looking very smart, complete even to a warm lap-robe thrown over the back of the seat. She and her father stood in the window, watching it come up the driveway. Her father was impressed and admiring. But when he discovered that it was his, a present from Agnes, he exploded. She must be crazy, he roared—what use was such a thing going to be? He and her mother would be leaving the farm in a couple of years, and they'd get very little for it if it was sold second-hand. There was an angry scene and he stamped out of the house.

Hours later, her own anger spent and her tears dried, she went to look for him. She found him in the feed room of the chicken house, sitting with his head in his hands, bitterly contrite over having hurt her so. Even years later, Agnes could not speak of the incident without tears. But it had no more effect on her extravagance than the earlier experience had had.

Her generosity was very welcome in her riding. People liked being taken out to dinner, as she treated her executive on her visits home. They liked the picnics and dances she provided for them. It was traditional to ask the M.P. for donations for every fund-raising campaign, church, farm groups, women's clubs, schools. She donated prizes for small events, as well as the big trip-to-Ottawa prize given every year. When she found herself with two engagements for the same time, she went to one meeting and consoled the other by hiring a band to give a concert for them. Individuals wrote to her for help and received it. People borrowed money from her. Whenever anyone visited Ottawa she took him or her—or a group—to luncheon or dinner in the parliamentary dining-room.

Much of this spending she thoroughly enjoyed. Some of it she resented, because she wanted to be generous on her own terms. She was caught in the net, not only of her own warm-heartedness, but also in the convention that a Member of Parlia-

97

ment was a pretty wealthy person and could well afford to donate money. Being an independent Member, part of a minority group, she had none of the local patronage to dispense that members and candidates of the long-established parties had. Her election could mean nothing in the way of a "gravy train" for her followers; they could expect nothing more than good representation in Parliament.

By 1924, she had realized that she had made a serious mistake in turning back $1500 from her indemnity. It would have been easy enough to say nothing, and then, when she was re-elected, simply to accept the whole sum. But Agnes felt she had a real responsibility to account for her actions to her people. So, at her nomination meeting at Durham, on September 15, she announced that she intended from that time on to accept the indemnity of $4000 like everyone else. No other name was brought forward in nomination.

During the campaign, she spoke at forty-one meetings—two as many as she had attended during the 1921 campaign. But between elections she had held eighty-three meetings in her riding. The pattern of her relations with her constituents was established. She was their Member of Parliament, who was particularly a spokesman for the farm interests. What she did besides that really did not concern them as long as she did not make them uncomfortable by trying to involve them too deeply in her other interests.

In the Federal election of October, 1925, Agnes won against Dr. Campbell of Markdale, Conservative, by 3100 votes. She and J. H. King of North Huron were the only survivors of the Progressive group returned in Ontario. Agnes declared herself free of any party, responsible only to the United Farmers in her own riding. She told newsmen she would support, or fight against, bills on their own merit. She spoke of the ideals that animated men like J. S. Woodsworth of Winnipeg, and W. C. Good, who had been defeated in Brant:

"The consuming love of members representing economic groups (labour and farm groups) for the people is the light flickering in the darkness of Ottawa representation." But she was very caustic about the majority of Progressives. She accused them of "doing as little as they could, taking the comfortable course and being interested mainly in getting along comfortably." She felt that most of them richly deserved to be defeated, particularly some of the Members from Ontario. As early as 1922 she had written to J. M. Murray, editor of the *Sunday Leader* in Halifax :

"In all groups of the House I find people of valour, and in all groups their opposite. For those who come to the House of Commons enthused with the idea of changes coming immediately because they are so necessary and so sensible, the sensation is very much like attempting to batter down a wall by hitting it with your head. This, of course, will either produce unconsciousness or sense enough to use a more sensible tactic, such as very carefully cutting out in this wall enough space to let the reform through."

Regarding the commission set up to investigate the coal strike, she said :

> The debate that we had in the House regarding the coal miners was to me the turning point in this new Parliament and the most encouraging thing that has happened, because it proves that if we have courage enough we can do things even after the Government have decided that they should not be done. . . .
>
> I sometimes marvel that we who are so decided in our opinions and so vigorous in the presenting of them outside of the House are so much milder in the House, and I concluded that there is no need to fear radical action in Parliament because the whole tendency is away from it, and the real fear is that there will be no action. You see the broader one gets the flatter one gets, until finally there is nothing left but a large expanse of polished surface.

Agnes Macphail made it very plain to her constituents that she had no intention of being a large expanse of polished surface.

After the 1925 election the Toronto *Star Weekly* of November 14 published a double-page spread with a special article by Fred Griffin entitled "How Aggie Did It". There was a cartoon depicting Agnes "Driving Her Own Car"—a reference to the break-up of the Progressive and United Farmer political movements, and her survival as an independent. The cartoon showed a very grim-looking Agnes, in a car with side-curtains (she did have an old Starr so equipped). There was a photograph of her parents, looking very rustic; and a photograph of her. It was a friendly article. Griffin quoted her father about the hard work she did in her constituency between elections as well as in the campaign. And he quoted Tom Gilchrist, the blacksmith who also handled the Ceylon mail. Gilchrist subscribed to Hansard because "you can't trust the papers".

"She's an awful good mixer," he said. "She's one of the few women who would drop into the shop here for a chat, yes, long before she ever thought of running for Parliament—she was always like that. If she went into your house and felt hungry, she'd say she was, and if she felt like it, ask you right out for a piece of pie. Not like some women who'd drop with starvation before they'd admit they were even hungry. . . . If this term of Aggie's was for four years instead of only a few months as now seems likely—and suppose on top of that she was elected for another term, then the devil himself wouldn't beat her after that in this riding."

It was an indication of her magnetism and prestige that people were flattered rather than critical when she made herself very much at home in their houses. Another woman would have been considered rude and forward under the same circumstances in that area. But not Agnes. Besides, she never made the housewife feel uncomfortable—it was perfectly obvious that she was not making a mental survey for dust. Everyone knew she was an important person in the outside world, but around the riding she behaved like a combination of a beloved relative and a popular school-mistress.

Most people called her Miss Macphail. This was not because she was a particularly formal person, but simply in keeping with

Riding relations

local custom. In many rural districts it is still the custom to address a woman as Miss or Mrs. when at the same time the men are called by their first names. People certainly called her "Aggie" behind her back. She disliked the name but tolerated it from her family and intimate friends. It was in this year, 1925, that her spelling of her surname became established. The telegraph editor of the *Star* wrote her about it, and she replied :

Ceylon, Ontario
July 8, 1925.

Dear Mr. McGeary,

Regarding the business of my name—it is puzzling even to me. My people spell it MacPhail, but I write it Macphail, so, without intending to, I have changed it to one word with a small p—and I like it better that way. It is easier written and looks better. So Be It.

Yours sincerely,
Agnes Macphail.

She was becoming conscious of what photographs did to her and wrote a note asking the editor, "If you must print my picture, please use the enclosed."

In an interview after the election, Agnes spoke very highly of Farquhar Oliver, who had been immensely helpful to her in the campaign. He was just twenty-one at the time, and she had high hopes for him. He had come up through the young people's group, making short speeches at first, and then learning to make longer ones, and gaining a reputation for excellent oratory. He had left school at the end of the eighth grade, but Agnes claimed he was a great reader and student, as well as a "modest and a hard worker". She had her eye on him for the provincial nomination, but, of course, did not confide this to the reporter at the time.

Ten

1926—the devil and the deep

A Member of the Canadian House of Commons who survived the chaotic session of 1926—while two governments, one after the other, fought to survive—must feel entitled to a special badge of merit. For those not aligned with either government party it was a time of extreme mental strain, as charges and challenges, ugly rumour and wide-open scandal, were hurled about the chamber, and the heavy decision of maintaining Canada's constitutional freedoms fell on the House at last like a final blow. Even the hardened politician must have felt disgust at the raw battle for power. But one as sensitive as Agnes could not fail to respond, as well, to the packed excitement of those weeks, the dramatic interplay of personal careers and the true welfare, even the survival, of the state. Somewhere in the midst of it a vivid, almost sensual love of Parliament entered Agnes' bones and blood. She gave herself completely to it. She came back to Ottawa from her second campaign a seasoned politician. She came through the turbulent session a devoted member of the House, so much a part of it that electoral defeat, when it came to her at last, would be almost like death.

Nothing was farther from Mackenzie King's mind than defeat in the 1925 election. Things had rolled along smoothly, the Progressives were slipping back one by one into the Liberal fold, he thought he had only to call an election to consolidate his forces and head a comfortable majority for another full term of office. Instead, the Conservatives under Meighen made great gains, electing 117 members, while the Liberals slipped to 101 and the Progressives to 24.

Despite their reduced numbers, the Progressives were in a better strategic position than before. Following the election King approached Forke. He then felt sufficiently confident of Progressive support to inform the Governor-General, Lord Byng, that he was prepared to meet Parliament and continue in office with the expectation that he could muster a majority in the Commons to back his Government. However, he must accomplish this feat by proxy, since he had personally failed to get elected, along with eight of his ministers. He was, of course, fighting for his political future, and Mackenzie King when he had this end in view was an unusually dedicated man. If he had resigned, as might seem to ordinary citizens the obvious thing to do when defeated in an election, he would almost certainly have been ousted from the leadership of the Liberal party.

When King's decision was made public on November 5th, there were cries of agony from the Conservatives. What position was Agnes to take? She had campaigned against both Liberals and Conservatives, with an emphatic "plague on both your houses". As a matter of personal taste, she probably hated the Liberals a little less, and the "Tories" (she seldom deigned to call them "Conservatives") a little more.

She trusted Mackenzie King's attitude in foreign affairs, his efforts to gain for Canada independent status within the Commonwealth, and she shuddered at Meighen's "Ready, aye, ready!" approach to the British connection.

On the other hand she felt obliged to make very plain her independence of the Liberals, because of the defection of U.F.O. members provincially and Progressives federally. No one must accuse her of selling out to King.

The Progressives met in caucus before Parliament opened. They drafted fourteen points of legislation which they submitted to King and to Meighen. Chief items were a reduced tariff, a Hudson's Bay railway, rural credit, transfer of natural resources to the prairie provinces. On the basis of the replies they received, the Progressives voted in caucus to support King's government. Forke informed them that King was also offering three Cabinet seats, but United Farmers of Alberta members rejected this proposal.

Agnes, when she spoke in the House, put her own position plainly, and it was also the position of the U.F.A. members of the group :

"During the last Parliament, the King Government gave us only crumbs of reform, and those grudgingly. The King Government could have put through any reform which we favoured, but instead of that they chose of their own free will to mark time and to appeal to the country on the plea that they had not a sufficient majority ! And now, weakened in numbers and in prestige, the same Government comes back and promises everything. . . . I want to say quite plainly that I have absolutely no confidence in the King Government. I could not possibly give blanket support to either party but . . . shall deal with each piece of legislation on its merits."

It sounded frank and clear-cut enough. But what did it mean in practice, in the actual day-by-day proceedings of the House ? It meant that Agnes and the other Progressives, trapped by the party system of Cabinet responsibility that they had always vigorously condemned, must vote for King at every turn, no matter what the motion before the House, since to vote against him would defeat the Government before it had an opportunity to put through the promised legislation. And the Conservatives wasted no time in putting motion after motion of criticism, of non-confidence, as Meighen hurled every weapon he could command against the man he felt was a usurper as Prime Minister of Canada.

Agnes appeared to despise King in his desperate clinging to office (she chortled when a Conservative called the Liberal Government "a decapitated chicken with wings still flapping"), and to feel a certain respect for Meighen, whose speeches in the House were brilliant and caustic. Yet her sound judgement told her that the reform measures she had come to Parliament to win were more likely to happen through King than through Meighen. She wrote, in a letter to her South-East Grey executive on January 23rd, "We evidently have to decide between a strong party with a poor policy or a weak party with a good policy."

She was also afraid that the hard-fighting manœuvres of the Conservatives, who had the added advantage of a majority in the Senate, would in the end block the legislation they wanted passed, and the Progressives would find that they had thrown their support behind King, and thereby lost face in the country, to no practical purpose.

The non-confidence amendment of Mr. Meighen that had been introduced the first day of the session, condemning King for remaining in office following the adverse election results, came to a vote on January 18th. The Liberals and Progressives outvoted the Conservatives by *three*. Agnes wrote to the members of her executive back home: "Messrs. Woodsworth, Gardiner, Garland, etc., in whom I have very great confidence, could not understand why I so reluctantly voted against Meighen's amendment, but you who know how Ontario has suffered from too close friendship with Liberalism, will understand I am sure."

The fact that Meighen had based his want-of-confidence on King's right to meet Parliament while leading a minority group gave the Progressives their justification for voting him down. They contended that King had the constitutional right to try to govern with the combined support of several small groups. Agnes said in a letter which appeared on the front page of *The Farmer's Sun*, January 21st:

"No group had a majority. It seems logical that the Government should meet Parliament before advising His Excellency to call on the leader of any other group. In spite of all the up-roar, we only said that the Government was constitutionally right in meeting Parliament."

And now, as the Throne Speech debate began, Meighen moved another amendment, ostensibly concerned with the Government failure to provide greater employment and to assist primary producers. Meighen was making it hard for the Progressives to vote against this one.

The Conservative section of the press was in a frenzy. Said the Muskoka *Herald* of January 21st :

"Never in the history of Canada has there been such disgraceful dickering as has been going on between the followers of Mr. Mackenzie King and the Progressives. . . . No less than three portfolios are said to have been offered to the Progressives to induce them to support the Government. About an hour before the vote Miss Agnes Macphail, who spoke against the Government, was heard to say that she would not vote for King. Shortly after that, Hon. Vincent Massey sent for her and had an interview lasting an hour or more ; when she returned to the House of Commons to vote for King, carrying it is said the portfolio of Minister of Labour in her handbag."

Agnes denied this.

"The newspapers must have their little joke," she said.

Appealing to her constituency executive for advice, she concluded, "With me the arguments of each side are about evenly balanced, which is the cause of my sleepless nights, and now I am handing the burden over to my Executive. I want to hear from every one of you at the earliest possible moment, but not later than Wednesday, January 27th. It is an exceedingly difficult session and yet a very interesting one."

That extraordinary man, J. S. Woodsworth, pursued his single course through the turmoil with unerring purpose and a manner apparently serene. In the struggle for power between Meighen and King he saw only a lucky break for the old people of Canada. On January 29th he rose to tell the House with complete candour what he had done behind the scenes.

He had sent identical letters to Mackenzie King and Arthur Meighen, requesting the enactment of an old-age pension. He could promise either man the support of enough Progressives to help achieve this legislation. King's letter of January 28th, agreeing to bring down this legislation, has become a treasure in C.C.F. archives. King had agreed ; Meighen had stalled. Therefore King, with J. S. Woodsworth gently propelling him, would continue in office until the Old Age Pension Act was passed.

"It seems to me that we must be very grateful indeed that the peculiar combination of circumstances which we find existing in the House at this time has seemingly made it possible to place upon the statute books long overdue legislation in the interests of some of the most needy but least influential elements of our population," said Woodsworth.

The Government bill appeared on the order paper, and on March 18th the Government introduced the Act, which would pay $20 a month to every Canadian over seventy years of age who passed a means test. What this little monthly sum, increased several times since, has meant in the lives of thousands of elderly men and women since that time can hardly be calculated. To J. S. Woodsworth the obvious and direct good which such a measure could bring was sufficient motive; he would proceed to ignore all the clever devices of Meighen to topple King. "So long as the Government is prepared to bring down legislation which commends itself to our judgement we must continue to support it," he said.

No doubt Agnes Macphail and others were persuaded by his logic. What replies she received from her Executive are not on record, but their attitude probably would be support for King. The second Meighen amendment followed the fate of the first; it was defeated 125 to 115, with Agnes Macphail and most Progressives voting against it.

Outside the House, Agnes had moved into new quarters of her own, for her former landlady, Mrs. Quay, had remarried and left Ottawa. But Agnes had little leisure to spend in her small flat. All-night sittings were again a familiar occurrence on the Hill. Her mail was prodigious, and like every M.P. she must read a selection of the newspapers, which were violently concerned with the unprecedented political happenings. And there were countless meetings in corridors and offices as Progressives tried to thresh out their problems, and emissaries from the Liberals and Conservatives came a-courting. In 1926 every private member's vote was worth a fortune—either King's fortune or Meighen's.

Suddenly what had been an exciting see-saw gave way to

much graver and more shocking developments. Ernest Lapointe who had been standing in for Mackenzie King as House Leader, brought forward a motion that the House adjourn as soon as the Throne Speech debate was finished, until March 15th, when the by-election in Prince Albert would be over, and the Prime Minister presumably returned.

It was February 3rd, after the dinner recess. The Conservatives quickly moved an adjournment of the debate until next day, to give them time to consider their strategy. They were voted down; the House continued to sit through what turned out to be one of the longest and surely one of the blackest nights on Parliament Hill.

H. H. Stevens, Conservative from Vancouver, rose to protest Mr. Lapointe's attempt to adjourn the House to accommodate Mr. Mackenzie King. It turned out that he was afraid that such a procedure would prevent investigation by a committee, notice of which he had previously placed on the order paper, of scandal and misconduct on a vast scale in the Customs department. Fearing that he might otherwise lose his opportunity, Mr. Stevens let go with an incredible blast of accusation, charging the Government administration with bare-faced graft and corruption, while Liberal members sat numbly in their places and the Progressives looked on amazed.

> The Government is . . . exceedingly anxious to escape the risk of certain things coming to light . . . which . . . will complete the utter discrediting of this Government. . . . Let the House judge whether or not we should allow this Government a lengthy period of adjournment for the purpose of deleting from the files the evidence of their maladministration. . . . I wish to say right now that already nine filing cabinets filled with records containing damaging evidence have been removed. . . .
>
> Anywhere from $50,000,000 to $100,000,000 a year is being lost through smuggling operations. . . .
>
> The Montreal Customs House is the greatest clearing-house for stolen goods in Canada. . . . J. E. Bisaillon, Chief

of the Preventive Staff of the Customs District of Quebec
. . . the intimate of ministers . . . the recipient of a modest
salary, he rolls in wealth and opulence, debauched and
debauching. . . . He had a farm on the boundary, a
rendezvous of noted crooks and smugglers. . . . He had
been known to offer a bribe of $100 *a week* (a steady
salary) to secure a coveted appointment, yet following this
the Government had appointed him to his present high
post. . . . He received moneys of the Crown to the extent
of tens of thousands of dollars, deposited them to his own
account, and . . . never remitted those moneys to the
account of the Receiver General.

This villain, Bisaillon, had clearly been mixed up with nar-
cotics smugglers, gangsters and murderers, yet retained his
government position. Nor was the villainy limited to the Montreal area. Across the country large orders of cotton and silks
were coming in to Canadian firms without the payment of duty,
while the illegal traffic in liquor (aggravated by prohibition)
was wide-open and on a prodigious scale.

Boivin, Customs minister newly appointed by the Liberal
government, rose to speak after Mr. Stevens. His only defence
was personal innocence and a professed determination to press
the investigation even farther than Mr. Stevens demanded.

Long past midnight, the Conservatives again moved that the
House adjourn. A motion which must surely have seemed
desirable to punch-drunk members, it might still be interpreted
as a "want-of-confidence" vote—to vote for it might mean the
defeat of the Liberal Administration, the end of their legislative
session.

At this moment in history Agnes Macphail was given the
dubious distinction of deciding the fate of King, of Meighen,
of the Old Age Pension bill, of the Customs investigation.

The vote gave the Liberals a majority of *one*.

Now obviously any one of the negative votes might be said to
be the deciding one, but the peculiar circumstances were these :
Five Progressives, persuaded by Mr. Stevens' black charges,

now switched their support to the Opposition. This was exactly half the majority of ten that had saved Mr. King's skin on the earlier motion to adjourn. At that time Agnes had withdrawn from the chamber and had not voted. She was back in the chamber for part of the grueling debate that followed. If she had been persuaded, as her five colleagues were, to vote with the Opposition, the King Government would have gone down to defeat. But she rose in her place to support the Liberals, giving them 119 votes this time to 118 for the Conservatives.

Such at least was the interpretation of several Canadian newspapers next day. An editorial in the Montreal *Gazette* was headed "The Failure of Miss Macphail". It said that the King Government, holding office by mere "squatters' sovereignty", had been placed under debt to her by reason of this saving vote. It was all especially disgraceful (to a paper with a strong Tory bias) because she was a *lady* member, "and to her conduct the public must necessarily look for evidence of that finer influence which the participation of women is expected to exert on public affairs."

As far away as Cleveland a banner headline in the *News* proclaimed "Woman Again Saves Premier" : "On a Conservative motion to adjourn for twelve hours at the close of a session lasting until 3 a.m., five Progressives supported the motion and only the arrival of Miss Macphail, who had been absent from the House earlier in the evening, gave the Government a majority of one vote in the division."

On February 5th the Government set up a special committee to investigate the Customs department. There were two other close votes before the House passed the Lapointe motion for a temporary recess, and again Agnes voted in support of the Liberals. Then the Throne Speech debate was resumed, with yet another Conservative amendment, this time protesting a trade treaty with Australia that affected Canadian dairy farmers, in another attempt to woo Progressive support.

Meighen's method of "wooing" was the opposite of King's. Speaking to this amendment, he lashed out at the Progressives in cutting style. The Hudson's Bay railway and the other fine promises had been put in the Throne Speech "just to offer an alluring berry patch to honourable gentlemen on my left"; and he deplored "a practice hitherto unknown, that Members of this House who ran against Government policy and the Government record should be induced in Parliament to vote for the Government on the faith of new promises made." He adjured the Progressives, although "purchased by promises", not to fail "to do justice to their position as members of a British Parliament."

Other Conservative speakers singled out Agnes, quoting her firm statement of "no confidence in King".

But most Progressives, with the Labour members, J. S. Woodsworth and A. A. Heaps, doggedly gave their support to the Liberals. The Throne Speech debate ended at last and the House adjourned, until it could begin anew on March 15th, with Prime Minister Mackenzie King seated on his precarious throne.

On March 31st, Agnes had her brief moment of triumph. The resolution that she had brought forward the previous year, calling on the Government to set up a full programme of gainful employment in the penitentiaries, came up again, received the stamp of approval from Justice Minister Lapointe, and was passed by the House. She was to spend the next several sessions reminding the House that the resolution had been passed, and urging its implementation, but at least the Government had committed itself to carry out her proposal. She felt at last the glow of a positive accomplishment.

With hard fighting all along the line, the session continued through April, May and June.

On June 10th a news item appeared in the Durham *Chronicle* in South-East Grey, informing its readers that their Aggie would soon be off to Europe. She was travelling, it said, to attend a conference of the Women's International League for Peace and Freedom in Dublin, Ireland. She would go on from there to Denmark, to see the rural school system as a guest of the Danish government.

But Agnes did not go to Europe that summer. Hearing of her

proposed departure after she had actually booked passage, Mackenzie King took alarm and approached her personally at her home to request that she stay in Ottawa to give her support to the Government until the session ended. Agnes recounted later her perverse joy in giving him no definite answer. King turned to Woodsworth, appealing to him to use his influence to persuade her. (One story has it that she got as far as Montreal, and was only prevented from boarding ship by a long-distance call from Ernest Lapointe!) She cancelled her passage and stayed on in Ottawa.

On June 15th Mackenzie King began talking boldly of dissolution. He revealed his clear intention, if the House out-voted his Government, of requesting the Governor-General to dissolve Parliament, and proceeding, still as Prime Minister, to hold another election. The occasion was a want-of-confidence motion on the question of transferring Alberta's natural resources to the province. King said, "If this Administration does not enjoy the confidence of this House of Commons, the sooner we know it the better, and we will carry our appeal from Parliament to the country."

But his position was immediately challenged by the Conservative member for Calgary, R. B. Bennett, a rich and successful lawyer. Bennett retorted, with spirit, that King had no right at all to assume that asking for a dissolution meant that he would get one. Asked to explain further, he asserted that it was quite possible that the Governor-General would ask Meighen, who after all had a larger group of Members than King, to try his hand at forming a government.

Bennett's retort may have given King pause. At least it is clear evidence that the final test of the 1926 session was already being given shrewd consideration in the minds of the chief combatants.

King survived that particular want-of-confidence vote, and several more.

On June 22nd his greatest hurdle presented itself: the tabling of the report of the committee investigating the Customs scandal. The report laid bare the shocking corruption which

Stevens had revealed to the House on February 3rd. The only question remaining was the severity of censure of the Government itself. The committee blamed the laxity of the Administration, but H. H. Stevens was not satisfied, and presented in the House an amendment censuring the Minister, the Government, and senior officers of the department.

Debate on Mr. Stevens' amendment was violent and vitriolic. A particularly damaging fact was that Bureau, the Minister in charge of the Customs department during the period of most of the scandalous proceedings, had been removed from office and *appointed to the Senate* !

On June 23rd, J. S. Woodsworth observed : "This House of Commons, which is primarily a legislative body, is these days turned into a court. . . . In the general outside atmosphere as well as in the political conditions which prevail in this House we cannot hope to assure that impartiality and independence of view which will give us real justice. . . . I suggest that it is not altogether an edifying spectacle, when charges of moral turpitude are advanced against members of the Government, that there should be such vociferous applause. It seems strange that we should rejoice not in truth but in iniquity."

Woodsworth refused to make the mistake of whitewashing the Conservatives because they had revealed the blackness of the Liberals. He pointed out that one bit of sworn evidence before the investigating committee had been the heavy contributions paid by leading liquor interests to the campaign funds of *both* Liberals and Conservatives.

Musing on the strange scale of public morals, he told the Commons, "According to our law, the penalty for ruining a life (knowingly communicating venereal disease) is six months with the option of a fine ; for stealing an automobile, two years ; for criticizing a government (sedition), twenty years. . . . What is the penalty for debauching a government department? A senatorship."

Woodsworth had been trying, he said, "to see daylight through this problem, and I think many men have been worrying a great deal . . ."

He was interrupted.

"And one woman," said Agnes Macphail.

Woodsworth accepted the "amendment". Many men and one woman had been worrying about the right course of action. He anticipated that to vote the Liberals out would "presumably" put the Conservatives in. But the Conservatives had shown themselves not sympathetic to his Old Age Pension. "Do you suppose I could vote on any question in this House without recognizing the possibility of placing in the seats of power men who defeat legislation of this nature!" Woodsworth attempted to keep the session alive with a milder amendment, which would take the censure out of Stevens' amendment, and would go on to set up a judicial commission, outside Parliament, to pursue a more complete investigation.

But Woodsworth's effort to preserve the King administration a little longer failed. The Conservatives worked feverishly behind the scenes to persuade the Progressives to censure the Government. They felt that George Coote and Agnes Macphail were perhaps the two most deeply shocked by the scandal, and they pleaded with them so strongly that Coote was forced to leave Ottawa briefly to escape the mental strain.

Agnes divulged in later years that the Conservatives resorted to outright bribery. Robert Manion was the emissary. She was promised any Cabinet portfolio she wanted, except that of Prime Minister or Minister of Finance, if she would join the Conservative forces. She had not hesitated earlier to say no to King; she refused Meighen with even greater alacrity.

They were frenzied times. T. W. Bird, Progressive from Nelson, B.C., protested to the House that he had received an anonymous letter on House of Commons stationery, saying, "If you continue to allow yourself to be bought and sold much longer, the hope for your entry into heaven is small."

The Woodsworth sub-amendment, which had been accepted by the Liberals, was voted down on June 25th by a vote of 117–115. King had lost his majority in the House.

Torn too profoundly to reach a decision, Agnes did not vote. Neither alternative was acceptable to her. She did not want to vote the Conservatives in; she did not want to condone the Customs scandal.

Still another last-ditch effort was made, a sub-amendment drafted this time by two Progressives, Fansher and Coote, which repeated Woodsworth's motion with a qualified censure added. The Speaker ruled this one out of order. The Conservatives appealed against the Speaker's ruling. They won the vote 118–116. This time Agnes voted, with the Liberals.

And a third time the vote went against King, on a Conservative motion to adjourn. Agnes voted with the Liberals but the Meighen forces were *one* vote ahead on the final count.

The House staggered on. An effort was made to consolidate the Fansher sub-amendment with the Stevens amendment. Then C. G. Power moved adjournment, and this time the motion carried, 115–114.

It was 5:17 a.m. on Saturday, June 26th. King's Government was overthrown.

Agnes slept late next day, but there was probably no sleep for Mackenzie King. He had an audience with Lord Byng, and afterwards called twice more, before he could bring himself to accept Lord Byng's decision. The Governor-General decreed that dissolution would not be granted at this time, and at King's request. The Conservatives were to be given a chance to form a government and carry on the business of the session.

It was a haggard King who rose to face Parliament on Monday afternoon, on June 28th.

"His Excellency having declined to accept my advice to grant a dissolution, to which I believe I am entitled, I immediately tendered my resignation. . . . At the present time there is no government."

His tone was petulant, injured. "Some other adviser must assume responsibility for His Excellency's refusal . . ."

What did it mean for Parliament, for Canada?

The House adjourned.

Twenty-four hours later they met again. The House had a new Prime Minister, Arthur Meighen. He had been asked if he believed himself capable of forming a government, had given a positive answer, and had been that morning sworn into office.

It was a strange form of government. As the session had opened without Mackenzie King, so this short final act began without Meighen. For the law, since changed, required that ministers of the Crown, when appointed, must resign their seats and run again for Parliament in a by-election. Meighen had accordingly resigned his seat, and was Prime Minister in absentia.

And what of his cabinet? If he had sworn in a number of ministers they must also have resigned, leaving the Conservative seats dangerously emptied. He chose instead to make seven men his Acting Ministers, in receipt of no ministerial salaries, to carry on the business of the House and complete the work of the session. Standing in for Meighen as Leader of the House, as Ernest Lapointe had acted for King, was Sir Henry Drayton. Another notable absence was R. B. Bennett, who had been summoned to return with all speed from a trip to Calgary, to serve as one of the Acting Ministers.

The tables had been turned. What was Miss Agnes Macphail to do now?

As she had begun, when the session opened in January, by stating her lack of confidence in King and then had proceeded to lend him her reluctant backing, so she proceeded now to proffer Meighen what was surely the most grudging support in the history of the Commons.

The business of the House must be got through; she had been persuaded, along with other Progressives, to support the new Government to that extent. But:

"I have resented since I came here five years ago, and particularly this session, the self-righteous attitude of the Conservative party members. . . . They are smug and self-righteous . . . My only satisfaction in this change is that they are now sitting [on the right of the Speaker] farther away from me."

For the first time she expressed her heartfelt wish that more women would join her in Parliament, for she was sure that most women would not carry on in the way the Commons had behaved this session. "Rumours and counter-rumours of the past week have almost destroyed my faith in human nature. . . . The things that are being said, the whisperings going on and the members visiting other members in private rooms are not creditable to Members of this House. . . . I have come to the place where I almost wish I had gone to Europe the other morning."

And so Agnes did what she certainly would never have believed she could do when she entered political life : she voted to keep a Conservative Government in office. Three times on June 29th and 30th she rose in the chamber to record her vote for Meighen.

She subscribed to the view expressed by E. J. Garland, who declared that his group had ceased to co-operate with the Liberals when King, by abruptly resigning instead of bringing the session to a proper close, "decided to fly away from his responsibilities, to fly from possible defeat, to fly from the carrying through of his legislation and his estimates . . . From that moment on we were placed in an entirely different relation towards him and his ministry."

The Meighen Government lasted three days.

Mackenzie King rallied from his sulky defeat. In the question of Meighen's constitutional right to govern through a group of Acting Ministers, in the action of the Governor-General in refusing the advice of his Prime Minister, he found his opportunity. Fighting desperately and brilliantly, King charged that the Government was no government at all, and could not be granted the disposal of treasury funds through the departmental estimates.

"I say there is not a single Minister of this Administration sitting in his seat tonight who is entitled to ask this House to vote him a single dollar."

All the next day—and it was by coincidence Dominion Day, July 1st—King built up this argument. His performance was masterly.

He professed in one breath his complete acceptance of the principle that the Crown is above reproach; in the next breath he left no doubt that he did seriously challenge the right of the Governor-General to *interfere,* to take sides, as King made it appear, with the Conservative party, instead of granting King his dissolution when he asked for it. The inference was adroitly presented : the Conservatives stood for the imperial power of the British crown; Canada's hard-won freedom as an independent nation, with the shackles of colonial status thrown off, was now put in jeopardy.

If this "counterfeit government of shadows" could vote itself money through a supine Parliament, "what guarantee have we of future liberty and freedom in this country?" King cried.

Ignominiously, from the gallery, Meighen had to watch his skilful adversary press this advantage to the full. It must have been a very bitter time for him. It was the end, the final defeat, of his political ambition. In this race of hare and tortoise, the unprepossessing tortoise was miles ahead in the last lap. Meighen could not take the floor to defend his constitutional right to be Prime Minister and, Bennett being absent, no other Conservative appeared sufficiently able to make the strong case that has since been expounded in support of both the Governor-General's course of action and Meighen's constitutional position as head of a government.

The Progressives were moved by King's impassioned logic. They had decided to give Meighen a chance to finish the session's business, but if this arrangement was unconstitutional, if Meighen's Government was not legally formed, then they must reconsider. The charge of sending Canada back to colonialism was not to be borne.

As Dominion Day faded into July 2nd, 1926, the vote came on ex-Minister Robb's motion challenging the "shadow government". Agnes voted with the Liberals. So did most of the other Progressives. The Administration was defeated by one vote, on a count of 96–95.

The M.P.'s limped home to fight the next election. Agnes was nominated at a huge meeting of 3,500 in the Durham rink. When her Conservative opponent, R. T. Edwards, inevitably taunted her with being "a Liberal at Ottawa", she re-affirmed her independence in typical Agnes style : if a Liberal whip ever tried to dictate to the Progressives, he "would have his head bashed against the wall." She made her position stick. Her majority in the September election was increased to 1,728.

The Liberals went back into power, and King, as Prime Minister, went to London to the Imperial Conference that fall. And there he helped to frame the Balfour Declaration, which proclaimed the member nations of the Commonwealth "equal in status, in no way subordinate to one another." No doubt he saw the hand of Providence behind it all.

Eleven

Another election, a new protégé

Agnes prided herself on not being a petty politician, in the sense of scrounging things for her riding. But she did get a post office for Durham. Durham decidedly needed a new post office, and had been promised one, off and on, for the past twenty years—it had been election bait over and over. In the tense and ticklish situation at Ottawa, with Mr. King wooing the Progressives, Agnes succeeded in getting that post office. She was extremely pleased with herself.

She announced this victory at a meeting in Durham, but unfortunately it was a much smaller meeting than Agnes liked. She had already developed the foible of scolding people who attended meetings for the people who stayed away, and she cut loose at this one.

The *Durham Chronicle* carried a somewhat plaintive editorial the next day. It thanked Miss Macphail for the post office. It also pointed out that not only were there a number of other meetings in town that night, but her particular meeting had been called to discuss the wheat board, a subject in which the citizens of Durham were something less than passionately interested.

When the post office was near completion Agnes discovered that it was the intention of the Government to send a Cabinet Minister to open it. She made vehement and effective protest. The idea of the Cabinet Minister was dropped. But Mr. King was not going so far as to give Agnes an opportunity to open that post office herself. The postmaster, Hector MacDonald, was instructed to open up for business on a specified date, without ceremony. This he did, and it has functioned ever since, but Agnes could never go past it without a feeling of indignation.

Durham was the centre of political activity for Agnes, though Owen Sound was the county town. One of her most stalwart helpers was Harold McKechnie. He missed her first campaign because he was still in the army after the first World War. And he missed the last one because by 1940 he had become town registrar and was formally out of the political arena. He was an intelligent and useful friend, with an acute political sense. It was McKechnie who, by throwing some printing jobs in the lap of the *Chronicle*, took the edge off the editor's hostility. His attitude allowed Mr. Ball to conclude there were no hard feelings. The *Durham Review*, under Mr. Gammage, was an unswerving partisan of Agnes and the U.F.O., and the Gammage family were personal friends as well as political supporters.

Agnes never did separate the obligations of her helpers into compartments. Her secretaries were expected to be friends, literary assistants, arrangers of domestic affairs, and whatever else she required. If she was assigned a secretary she didn't particularly like, or who was unwilling to do these extra chores, the girl didn't last long. It was the same with her helpers in the riding.

Harold McKechnie, for instance, was requested to investigate a woman who had written Agnes for help. He was horrified at the idea of walking into somebody's house to discover if she were really in need. (The woman was a stranger, and moreover had been known to vote against Agnes Macphail.) However, he loyally made the call, and immediately reported to Agnes that the woman was indeed in dire straits, making clothing out of flour sacks, and with a family of hungry children. Her husband was unable to work—he was a discharged war veteran with a disability which had not been apparent at once. Agnes promptly sent some cash and went to work to secure the man a pension.

She considered the co-ops as much her responsibility as her parliamentary duties. She said, "When all the co-ops in Grey County are out of trouble at the same time, I'll be ready to retire." The co-operative movement was an integral part of her philosophy of life, and she did everything in her power to help and encourage every one of the co-operative organizations she encountered—or instigated. She was immensely proud of the village of Dundalk, which had a flourishing retail store, grain business, abattoir, and fuel oil business, all co-operative. Markdale, Flesherton and Durham had their co-ops, all within fifteen miles of her home. Owen Sound had two, but they were not particularly healthy. Agnes darkly suspected there were too many townspeople in them.

She was unable to avoid involvement in the management problems of these institutions, but it was against her will. What she was interested in was the principle of co-operation, not the mechanics. Much later she served on the board of the co-operative movement provincially.

A meeting was called in July, 1926, to nominate a U.F.O. candidate for the provincial election. The day of the meeting, Agnes wired imperiously from Ottawa, saying the session was at an end, and the riding had better save time and money by nominating the federal candidate at the same time. There was no difficulty about nominating Agnes Macphail, but the provincial candidate was another matter. The Liberals had stayed out of the last federal election in South-East Grey and the former Liberal members of the U.F.O. felt the organization should return the courtesy by keeping out of the provincial election. U.F.O. members who were former Conservatives would have nothing to do with such a proposal. After a stormy session, the provincial nomination went to young Farquhar Oliver, Agnes' protégé.

The two campaigns were run together, with the two candidates working as hard for each other as for themselves. Their meetings were crowded and lively, and they spoke wherever a crowd was gathered, whether it was a political meeting or not. On one occasion they spoke at a barn dance in Proton, with flickering light provided by lanterns, some of the overflow crowd perched on the rafters, and the speakers using a wagon for a platform.

The federal nomination meeting took place in Durham on

Another election, a new protégé

September 9th. There were 3500 people present to hear the candidates. R. T. Edwards was nominated by the Conservatives. There was no Liberal candidate. We will probably never know whether this was a local decision, whether Mr. King, like the Ceylon blacksmith, considered Agnes invincible, or whether he clung to the hope that he would eventually entice her into the Liberal fold.

Mr. Arthur Meighen came into the riding and spoke to a crowd of 2,000 in the Durham rink. The campaign was personal and Agnes declared it "dirty". The Honourable Hugh Guthrie came to speak for Edwards. He accused Agnes of being a King supporter and then changing. He also said, "Miss Macphail harbours some doctrines which can only be called Bolshevik in their character. I suspect that she has absorbed her Bolshevistic principles from Woodsworth of Winnipeg, who is quite a Communist." The farmers of Grey, who harboured the same doctrines, found this slanderous statement quite unlikely.

The Toronto *Telegram* sent a reporter to cover the campaign. He was from a hostile paper, and Agnes was well aware of it. She resented his mission and his attitude, because she was convinced he was there to report her defeat, and his dispatches to the paper certainly sounded hopeful of that result. On election day there was a great deal of challenging of voters at the polls, and Agnes had trouble with the returning officers. She said tartly, "I think it is high time the entire election machinery was taken out of the hands of partisans and some experts permanently engaged who know the election law."

Election night saw the *Telegram* reporter ensconced in the Macphail home, somewhat to his bewilderment. He was an alien, but by that time Agnes was used to him and treated him casually. He was fascinated by her restlessness, her bossiness, and her preoccupation with things like the position of lamps and the presence of draughts and so on, which he apparently did not diagnose as election jitters.

Agnes won the September 14th election by a majority of 1,647. The *Telegram* ran a careful analysis of all the polls where her majority had fallen, and somehow managed to convey the general impression that she had been practically defeated.

Agnes turned energetically to the provincial campaign. It was a high-spirited battle, David against Goliath, with Agnes holding the slingshot. She enlisted help wherever she could, including heaven. She spent a lot of time with her friends the Lawsons. There was grace before every meal in that home, and Agnes and Mrs. Lawson always added to the prayer, "and help us to defeat Dr. Jamieson."

Farquhar Oliver was up against an established professional. Dr. Jamieson had first run for the Commons in 1887, and had been defeated by a small majority. He was elected to the Provincial Legislature in 1898 and was re-elected six times. From 1914 to 1919 he was Speaker of the Legislature. Besides that, he was a large property owner and industrialist and an influential citizen. He definitely considered the riding his bailiwick provincially. Agnes did not revere him. She called him "the Governor-General of Durham", a mockery that caricatured for the citizens Dr. Jamieson's every small pretension.

There were no scruples against a personal campaign, and Agnes and Farquhar Oliver made fun of Dr. Jamieson's girth— a matter of some embarrassment to Oliver in later years when his own girth was impressive.

Oliver's election to the Ontario Legislature on December 1, 1926, caused quite a stir. He was just twenty-two, a real farm boy, with a reputation as a "boy wonder" as a speaker, and the support of Agnes Macphail. She had a very proprietory attitude towards him, naturally enough. He was her political son. They shared the same riding executive and organization— there was very little difference between the provincial and federal riding boundaries at that time.

The federal and provincial members from South-East Grey were to work together on every campaign until after Agnes' defeat in 1940. Indeed when the next provincial election came up, Agnes moved into the Oliver home for five weeks and directed the campaign from there. She succeeded after some argument in convincing Farquhar's parents that he could not

Another election, a new protégé

get up at five in the morning and do his regular chores and farm work all day and then go out and make speeches till all hours of the night!

There had been "understandings" between Liberals and Progressives in forty-eight constituencies in the 1926 federal election. And eleven "Liberal-Progressives" now sat side by side with the 118 Liberal Liberals in the House of Commons. Agnes was one of the nine Independent Progressives who survived, with eleven United Farmers of Alberta members and three Labour men, from the shambles of the previous House.

A discouraging number had turned to smoother, fatter ways after their brief protest had spent itself. Agnes saw the second Progressive leader, Robert Forke, gathered to the Liberal fold and rewarded with a portfolio as Minister of Immigration. In 1957 she would have been saddened but not surprised to hear her first leader, T. A. Crerar, now safe in the Senate haven, speak out crustily against old-age pensions.

Agnes was not tolerant of such tarnished warriors. In the Commons she declared bluntly:

> I should hate to bear upon my shoulders the responsibility which rests today upon the shoulders of the Liberal-Progressives in this House. They have done much to discourage progressive thought in Canada; they have, to my mind, a great deal to answer for.
>
> Indeed I should not care to be the Liberal party. I should not care to bear the responsibility for false friendship such as they have shown towards the new groups in this House, from 1921 to this day. . . . The history of the whole attitude of the Liberal party to the new groups since 1921 has been one of protestations of friendship which, if accepted, have proven to the honest to be the graveyard of their hopes and to the others a fulfilment of their treacherous plans. Speaking for myself, I would rather have the bitter, uncompromising, unfriendly and snobbish attitude of the Conservative party. At least it was honest and we knew where we stood.

Complained Mitchell Hepburn, later the bombastic Liberal Premier of Ontario : "To those of us who were the objects of her attack I am sure that, not even excepting the old-age pensions, the forty-minute rule appeared to be the most humanitarian legislation ever enforced in this House."

Agnes put on record the achievements of the Independents. It was always her claim that, far from being ineffective, the Independent members had a high score to their credit, certainly far beyond that of any old party back-bencher.

> In that awful session of 1926 we were accused every day of being Grits or Tories, although as a matter of fact we were neither. . . . In 1926 we got a legislative programme from the Government which was not their programme, but the programme that had been introduced into this House by the independent group by resolution during the four sessions between 1921 and 1925. . . . We got a reduction in the tariff—the only real reduction the Liberal party has ever been guilty of ; we got rural credits ; we got old-age pensions; we got the Hudson's Bay railway. . . .
>
> I fear the legislative programme of this session will not weary us too much. . . . We have a Government with a very comfortable majority, a majority which unfortunately has been added to by men who should have known better.

Another election, a new protégé

Twelve

Before the great depression

Agnes served her second full term as a Member of Parliament during the halcyon days of the twenties. It was the jazz era, the time of Rudy Vallee and brief chemise-like gowns of lace and crêpe-de-chine, of making whoopee. There was a spontaneous joy in man's inventiveness—the motor car, the aeroplane, the radio—coupled with cheerful faith in man's progress toward a better world. It was a time which can only seem painfully naïve, in the light of what came next in history.

Presiding over this era in Canada was Mackenzie King, at the high plateau of his career, having made himself unquestionably the Liberal Party leader, and his party unquestionably the strongest, most firmly based political body to appear thus far on the national scene. King, adept in platitudes, pronounced all well with the economy, and no one saw reason to doubt him seriously. The socialists in Parliament skirmished for those left out of the general prosperity, for fair labour practices and welfare schemes, and some of them preached of a different social order, but to careless ears.

Agnes lent her support to these fellow radicals, pressed her own perennial objections to military expenditure, and presented an increasingly able brief for Ontario farmers. By this time she ranked among the dozen or so most listened-to members outside the Cabinet itself.

Said the *Ottawa Journal* at this period :

"Agnes has wit, satire, good humour—she has developed a parliamentary manner which would delight a Lloyd George, a manner which would go at Westminster to an extraordinary and surprising degree."

Later the *Journal* was moved again to write :

"Miss Macphail's speech had structure and passion, plus a fine and restrained vein of sarcasm, a dancing wit, some passages of pathos, and a deal of good humour. It was far and away the best speech that has been made in the House this year."

Single-handed, Agnes could often score a point with the Government now, to her own vast pleasure.

The year 1927 was Diamond Jubilee year—Canada's sixtieth birthday. On February 17, Prime Minister King announced in the House the appointment of a national committee to oversee the celebrations. Among the illustrious names was Agnes Macphail. But Agnes objected, tartly. First, she hadn't been consulted beforehand. Second, she was not pleased with the other names on the committee—where was a Labour representative, for instance? What of non-Anglo-Saxon Canadians?

"I ask that my name be withdrawn. . . . Looking over the names here, I see that they do not belong to my class, and unless I can go in as one of my own people I would not care to go in at all."

King hastily asked her to defer her decision until after the six o'clock recess. Would she, after consulting others, bring him several names?

When the House met after dinner, King rose to add six more names to those on the Jubilee committee : Tom Moore, President of the Trades and Labour Congress of Canada ; Michael Luchkowich, M.P. ; M. J. Coldwell, President of the Canadian Teachers' Federation ; Hon. Cyrille F. Delage, President of Public Instruction of Quebec Province ; Henry Wise Wood, President, U.F.A. ; George F. Edwards, President of the Canadian Council of Agriculture.

It was a minor triumph, but a satisfying one.

In the 1920's, the largest international problems looked easy and the answers within reach. Mackenzie King was in Paris in August, 1928, signing for Canada the euphemistic Briand-

Kellogg pact : a "Multilateral Treaty for the Renunciation of War".

The following winter the terms of the pact were ratified by the Canadian Parliament. Agnes spoke in support of this action. Her support was unequivocal, to an embarrassing degree. Since Canada had now renounced war she saw no point in continuing a defence program.

I consider this a great step forward. . . . The fact that fifteen nations that day signed the outlawry-of-war pact, and that this number has now grown to sixty-two of the sixty-four nations of the world is no small thing.

I would subscribe fully to the pact of Paris if for no other reason than that it has hushed the shrill voice of the jingoist. . . . I think in every nation there are two schools of thought . . . one believes in security through armaments . . . one believes that security must be found by new methods . . . conferences, arbitration, conciliation, and so on. . . .

The military estimates in the year 1925 were $11,000,000. The Prime Minister of this country and very many other leading citizens of Canada have been talking peace from that day to this, yet the estimates brought down the other day will require over $20,000,000. . . . My pet cadet vote is standing where it was, at half a million dollars, and we have military colleges and school books reeking with the glorification of war. During our big celebrations we trot out all the military people, possibly because their coats are bright.

This is a most illogical position to take, and the only thing for us to do is to begin to disarm and keep at it until we finish the job. I never wanted to be in the Cabinet, but I would like to be the Minister of National Defence for one year, and by that time there would be no need for that department. . . .

We should as a nation put international concord above everything else and we should shape our policy to that end.

We need to develop a peace technique. . . . It is well for us at times to be idealists, not to be scoffers and doubters, not to be cynical, but to believe that all the people of the world, regardless of colour, regardless of the country in which they live, are fine people, and if we treat them as though they were, they will treat us in the same spirit.

Outspoken in the cause of peace, Agnes found herself in difficulties several times during these years when her patriotism was called in question.

A great stir was created in April, 1927, over a letter that Agnes had circularized among public schools in her riding. It was one of a series of delightful, chatty letters in which she told the children about tea parties in Ottawa, plants blooming in her office window, and the state of affairs in the great world.

On March 28 she had written :

"Dear Teacher and Pupils : Today we will talk about the Chinese war. . . ." She sketched in bald fashion the trouble behind the Boxer Rebellion, the Opium Wars. She did not spare the British imperialists, or the exploitation of Chinese labourers by British factory owners. "We must remember," she added, "that it is only a few very rich people in England who want to do these dreadful things in China."

The Toronto *Globe* got a copy of the letter, and printed it.

Tommy Church, a Toronto Conservative and a bitter opponent of Agnes' anti-cadet campaign, rose in the Commons to protest the letter in unqualified language. Two other Conservatives leaped into the fray. One declared the letter was full of "poisonous untruths or misstatements of facts as to British history and the part Britain has played in international affairs."

She was even accused of dark treachery : "Insidious secret work is being done . . . including the circularization of this letter."

The dinner recess intervened. Agnes turned to J. S. Woodsworth. Happily, the Labour leader had a complete file on the Boxer Rebellion, with clippings and quotations from Gladstone, Lord Elgin, Sir R. Alcock, the British ambassador to Pekin, and Bertrand Russell. Woodsworth stayed with her during the two-hour recess, helping her put together an excellent rebuttal and defence. She returned to the Chamber girded for battle, and heartened by the kind twinkle in the eyes of her friend : "There, Agnes. Now will you be good?"

But newspapers seized on the story, especially when G. Howard Ferguson, Conservative Premier of Ontario, expressed his indignation at this assault on the minds of the young.

There were distant ripples of indignation even as far as the West Coast, where a meeting of the Women's Canadian Club passed a motion of censure against Miss Macphail for attempting to "shake the loyalty of our young Canadians to the British Empire."

(Agnes had criticized H. H. Stevens, then a Conservative M.P., for freely using franking privileges on private mail. Mrs. H. H. Stevens was an executive officer of the Vancouver Canadian Club. This branch of the Club also turned down Agnes as a guest speaker a year or so later—still, of course, for patriotic reasons.)

Dr. R. L. Carefoot of Markdale sent a copy of a school history book to the Toronto *Star*. Promptly two reporters arrived at a rural school in South-East Grey and interviewed a young teacher.

The teacher was both innocent and frank. She liked getting Miss Macphail's letters. The children always enjoyed them. No, she hadn't noticed anything out of the way about the letter on China. As a matter of fact it followed precisely what she had been teaching about the Boxer Rebellion from the text. She showed the reporters the place in the book.

The reporters went back to Toronto. It was too good a joke to keep. They took the school-teacher's comments back to the Ontario Premier.

"Possibly it is time some of the text-books were revised," Ferguson growled.

The newspapers and the Conservative M.P.'s decided not to press their charges of "insidious secret work".

And Agnes was to have the last word. In March, 1931, she

addressed the Commons with her most queenly air. "May I pause," her deep voice boomed, "to thank from the bottom of my heart the Prime Minister, for appointing the Honourable Howard Ferguson as minister plenipotentiary to London. It is rather hard on the Court of St. James's, but it is a great relief to the Province of Ontario."

Agnes was always at war with the bluest sort of Tory. She did not forgive Hugh Guthrie for his speech during the 1926 campaign, when he came into her riding to say, "Miss Macphail harbours some doctrines which can only be called Bolshevik in their character. I suspect that she has absorbed her Bolshevistic principles from Woodsworth of Winnipeg, who is quite a Communist."

In 1929 Guthrie made a traditional Conservative speech urging protective tariffs, with brash optimism attempting to prove to the Canadian farmer that it would be to his advantage if tariffs went higher.

Said Agnes : "It is fashionable to congratulate somebody and I shall therefore congratulate [Guthrie]. Regarding agriculture, he said, 'Let us eat our own products and so make ourselves prosperous.' I am not so sure that it would make us prosperous, but it would certainly make us *full*."

June, 1929, was a time of notable achievement for a small group of other Canadian women, headed by "Janie Canuck", the intrepid Judge Emily Murphy of Alberta. Their attempt to test the wording of the B.N.A. Act, to establish the eligibility of women for appointment to the Senate, had reached the final round before the Privy Council in London. It was the famous "Persons" case, to prove that women are "persons" in the constitution of the state.

Agnes Macphail called attention in the Commons to this important step in the long struggle for women's rights. She drew protestations of polite agreement from the Government benches. Her irrepressible friend Jean-François Pouliot leaped up to say, "I would suggest that the first appointee of the Government, in case the judgment of the Supreme Court is reversed, should be our charming colleague, the Member for South-East Grey."

But these were lighter moments, and they were not the whole picture, even during the "good times" of the 1920's. Agnes Macphail had become the target for hundreds of unhappy people who hoped for sympathetic help from a woman M.P. They always found it. Agnes was endlessly busy assisting people with their pensions, their taxes, their farm mortgages.

A trickle of ex-convicts visiting her office became a continual stream, as it became known that she had taken an interest in penitentiary reform. They told her dreadful tales of severe discipline, dirt and disease, brutal and ignorant guards, demoralizing idleness, and social ostracism on release.

Agnes hesitated a long time. She did not act impulsively to take up the cause of the ex-convicts from Canada's federal prisons. She tried, in fact, to put this burden from her.

Agnes Macphail was *not* a "sob sister", not a typical "do-gooder" who finds a certain relish in saving the fallen. She was always the stout champion of decent, hard-working citizens, of the best farmers who through hard times keep their self-respect and independent turn of mind. These people were the "class" with which she identified herself and whom she most truly represented in the House of Commons. It is indeed significant that her first act on behalf of penitentiary inmates, the resolution which was passed by the House in 1926, was to provide *work* for them to do, with a modest financial reward—the obvious middle-class approach to anybody's problem.

She did not want to fight the convicts' battle. It is to her everlasting credit that she did so, that she could not in good conscience turn away when she was finally convinced of the sorry state of things in our federal penitentiaries. She found herself impressed, believing in spite of all caution, when these men kept coming from many different places across the country with similar stories to tell.

She began to ask questions in the Commons. A man had been killed while at work in a quarry at Stony Mountain penitentiary in Manitoba. Letters had come to Agnes from his relatives,

133

very bitter letters. Had proper safeguards been taken? The convict hadn't thought so; he had written to his family that the work was dangerous. Would there be a further investigation of this man's death?

What, Mr. Minister, does it mean to "paddle" a prisoner? What does it mean to shackle him to a bar?

Forty-one prisoners in 1928 were paddled; 249 had been shackled to the bar.

Ernest Lapointe was Minister of Justice. A big man, a burly, likeable person, a friend. He answered her questions with gentle consideration.

All that shackling meant, he said, was fastening a man in standing position with arms at waist height to the bars of his cell for a little while, actually during work hours, because this was usually done if the man refused to go out and work with the others, and as soon as he gave in and agreed to work he was released.

"Paddling? Well, really just a spanking," Mr. Lapointe said. "There is nothing cruel about it, it is rather the humiliation that hurts."

She was not quite satisfied. A medical man was always present, as a precaution, when a prisoner was paddled. Was he needed if nothing more than humiliation was involved?

"It does not look very good to me. I think it is degrading, both to the prisoner and to the official who spanks him."

Lapointe agreed with her that it was "unpleasant". But still he must leave some discretion in matters of discipline to the prison officials. His tone suggested it would be well if she would leave the unpleasant subject alone, too.

Agnes sat back, growling softly and looking at the papers on her desk. Leave it alone? Accept the Minister's word that nothing very bad really happened? Or pursue this thing?

Agnes was having rather less to say these days about "social butterflies" and "rich, idle women who spend their time at bridge parties".

She was no longer wearing navy serge. She was seen at the Vice-Regal ball during the 1928 season, modishly gowned,

Before the great depression

dancing every number. She was the dinner guest of Governor-General and Viscountess Willingdon.

She and Lady Willingdon had the same birthday. The Governor-General's lady sent her a gift, some early tulips bedded in wet sand. And Agnes was more amused than shocked by the extravagance of Lady Willingdon, whose passion for redecorating Government House had sent the estimates up alarmingly.

On a Sunday evening she dined alone with the Willingdons, and afterwards, together on a couch in the famous Chinese Room, Lady Willingdon gently probed Agnes' attitude to Canadian titles. "Mr. King is at a great disadvantage in Imperial Conferences without a title." Agnes replied in all honesty : "If that's his only disadvantage he'll manage all right."

She compromised nothing of value, and yet how pleasant it was to walk through the Viscountess' lovely rooms! Surely she was even, at last, with the "town" girls of Owen Sound.

Society Notes reported in March, 1928, that she entertained eighteen South-East Grey folk residing in Ottawa at a dinner in the parliamentary dining-room, and that on the occasion she looked charming in a French gown of embroidered georgette over peach crêpe, with a corsage of violets.

"It was the privilege of all too few Grey County folk to see her in a setting that was hers by right of the personal dignity and intellectual grandeur she contributed to it," raved Dorothea Deans, a writer for the Owen Sound *Daily Sun Times*.

But there were still female social strongholds where she was not accepted. The Women's Canadian Club arranged a top-drawer luncheon to honour the Duchess of Atholl, a vivid personality who had resigned from a British Conservative cabinet because she disagreed on foreign policy. The Duchess looked about at her Canadian hostesses and cried, "Now which one is Agnes Macphail?" The silence was thick, for Agnes had not been invited.

This slight offended Prime Minister King's sense of propriety. He arranged to have the Duchess make a return visit to Ottawa, and Agnes was guest at a select luncheon at Laurier

House, where she met the Tory peeress and was enchanted to discover that her conversation "was more radical than that of 95 per cent of the Canadian House of Commons".

Later Agnes appeared on a lecture platform with her, at a meeting sponsored by The League Against War and Fascism. Canadian women could take pride in Agnes that night, for she not only made an equally good speech, but she was stylishly gowned, with a becoming hat, while the good Duchess, arrogantly dowdy, wore a feather boa and nondescript headgear. All things are forgiven the nobility, as Agnes pointed out wickedly to a friend : "The Duchess is really wonderful, considering the way she was brought up."

And if the women of the Canadian Club would not have Agnes Macphail, some Canadian women felt quite differently. She heard with delight that the delegates to a Women's Social and Economic Conference in Calgary rose during their convention to sing a ditty that began :

"God give us more women like Agnes Macphail;
When the miners were hungry, she never did fail."

The light-hearted twenties were drawing to an end. For Agnes the dancing ceased abruptly for a while in January, 1930. Dougal Macphail, aged sixty-five, died at the Ceylon home to which he had moved five years before when he retired from active farm life.

After the funeral Agnes returned to Ottawa. On her office desk were heaped cards, letters and telegrams. In the small prim handwriting of the Prime Minister, a four-page letter expressed his sympathy. It seemed that everyone who knew her had written, not formally, but warmly and in genuine kindness, for those who knew her were aware of the deep family tie that was always a background to her life and work. Her father had been dearer to her than any other member of the family except Grandmother Campbell.

Agnes drew out a sheet of paper and began to list those who had sent condolences. Her pen wandered, and across the page, erratically, she wote, "lonely", "loneliness".

Before the great depression

Thirteen

Tours and travels outside parliament

Agnes Macphail was a great public speaker by instinct, personality, and practice. Early in 1922 she had conscientiously enrolled in an extension course in public speaking at the University of Toronto, but it is extremely doubtful that it had any effect on her. Her rather jerky manner of delivery was her own ; her asides were apt to be lengthy and sometimes quite irrelevant; she interjected personal feelings and experiences into technical passages. She did any number of things that would arouse the disapproval of public-speaking experts. But her audiences loved her just the way she was.

In the twenties and early thirties, there were large, genuinely interested audiences. People would turn out in crowds to hear speakers on a great variety of subjects. With television unknown, there was more incentive to go out and listen in order to learn and to be entertained. Lectures were popular, and Agnes was one of the most popular lecturers in this country and, as time passed, in the United States as well.

Education was one of her favourite topics; she was frequently a guest speaker at the Ontario Educational Association. She once expressed her philosophy of education in this way :

> Real education should be something that builds up character, that teaches the truth that we can get out of life only what we put into it, that liberty is liberty only so long as it does not interfere with other liberties; that teaches the child to strive after the splendid in life ; that

teaches that our lives are only part of a great plan, and that each individual must play his part in relation to the progress of humanity. . . .

History should not be a study of lives of illustrious bigwigs whose most commendable action was that of dying; nor should it be a recital of the wars which have left their bloody stains on the record of humanity. We should teach history in such a way that the child would realize that neither Britain, the United States, nor Canada has a corner on the progress of the human race.

She was passionately convinced that the way history was taught moulded the children into an acceptance of war, taught them that their own country was always right—and, of course, in Canada, that included England; and that somehow Anglo-Saxons were superior to any other race. Since this was a very popular conception in Canada, it made Agnes' loyalty suspect in many quarters.

Her attempts to make people see the virtues and accomplishments of other races, her efforts to persuade people to look on foreigners as people like themselves who happened to live elsewhere, and speak a different language, were interpreted as attacks on Great Britain, and slurs on the patriotic citizens of Canada. She shared the taint of disloyalty with the farmers who were her main supporters; they too were suspect because they had fought conscription, and were accused of wanting to stay home and prosper while other people fought for them. This was an ironical situation for a woman who was so staunchly proud of her Canadian birth.

Naturally she was invited to speak about women to women's groups. She sympathized to some extent with their inferior position—to the extent that she was willing to say cutting and witty things against men. But she was extremely critical of women's inertia and timidity and unwillingness to go out after the things they thought they should have; executive positions in business, high rank in the professions, and seats in legislatures and parliament.

Tours and travels outside parliament

Her speeches to women's groups were not always on feminist subjects. She addressed the Business and Professional Women's Club on citizenship and idealism in public life, and, later, on varied topics.

She had the honour of being the first woman to speak in Hart House—the all-male establishment at the University of Toronto, where she took part in a debate.

She was in demand as a speaker on behalf of the "temperance" movement. She was tied to this movement through the temperance plank in the U.F.O. platform, and she was perfectly sincere in her support at that time. She spoke in Massey Hall for the Canadian Prohibition Bureau in 1926. Later in life she cooled off on the subject to such an extent that she took an occasional drink at parties, and certainly had no objection to other people drinking.

She could and did speak fluently and expertly on farms and farmers and farmers' wives. She had theories about tariffs which were the reflection of her reading and of the Progressive party beliefs. She made innumerable speeches about co-operatives, which were a major interest in her life. She spoke on the evils of the current parliamentary system, with its suppression of the ordinary M.P.'s, and its insistence on party discipline, which, she maintained, could be countered only by plenty of independent Members in the House, to challenge rule by the Cabinet, and the herd voting of both Government and official Opposition members.

And she spoke about international affairs, peace and disarmament. This was a ruling passion through most of her career. The League of Nations was, to her, the symbol of the will to peace, and the means by which international co-operation could be achieved. Her faith in it rested on the same foundation as her faith in the essential goodness and decency of people; and its final failure and dissolution struck so deeply into her heart that it left her with a permanent feeling of disillusionment.

She worked ceaselessly for this cause, and she was able to reach many thousands of people through her speeches and lecture tours. But it infuriated her to find people willing to listen but unwilling to take any positive action.

She was a member of the Women's International League for Peace and Freedom, and made herself available whenever it was possible for her to speak on their behalf. She spoke many times on the theme that mutual trust was essential to peace; that rancour and a revengeful attitude toward a defeated enemy could lead to nothing but resentment and revenge in return. She pointed out that Germany's economic collapse was a tragedy for the whole of Europe, and the nations that fostered the collapse and withheld assistance, indeed bled the country still further by demands for reparations, were, in the long run, destroying themselves, ruining a good customer, aside from the hatred they were cultivating. She advocated trade with Russia, when it was most unfashionable to do so.

She over-simplified issues, and she overstated her case, sometimes to such an extent that she damaged the cause she worked for. One of the incidents that tarnished her prestige in this field was her campaign against cadet training in the schools, which she carried on outside Parliament as well as in. The United Farmers considered cadet training a waste of money and of time, both of which could be better spent on things that did not foster wars. But Agnes painted such a lurid picture, complete with the accusation that the authorities sent school-boys to abattoirs to accustom them to the sight of slaughter and the smell of blood, that there was a genuine outcry from the public, as well as the usual ponderous fulminations from the military.

She took part in a parade for the organization calling it-self the No-More-War Society. In July, 1923, the Toronto *Telegram*—never friendly toward Agnes—carried a vicious and very amusing account of it. The parade marched from the Normal School grounds to Queen's Park, where a number of speakers harangued a somewhat thin crowd. Among the speakers were Rev. Father Minehan, Rev. Dr. Pidgeon, Rabbi Brickner, Rev. E. Henderson, Agnes Macphail, Jimmy Simpson (a labour leader, municipal politician, and at one time

Tours and travels outside parliament

mayor of Toronto), and Rev. G. Stanley Russell of London, England. These serious people found it worth their while to endure such ridicule because they believed that peace was not only desirable but possible if men and women could be persuaded to work for it sincerely. Dr. Pidgeon explained that the movement was not a "peace at any price" organization, but dedicated to the fostering of friendship between former enemies, to beating down animosity between nations before it developed to the danger point.

Unfortunately, some of the banners proclaimed that the Boy Scout and Girl Guide organizations were militaristic, so that some of the speakers found it necessary to disassociate themselves from this extreme view.

Agnes Macphail's speech was not reported, but it was commented on in the editorial columns of the *Telegram* in a rather curious way. Agnes had blasted the school text-books for glorifying war rather than peace and industry and other forms of courage. The *Telegram* editor said, "To human knowledge the bandstand in Queen's Park contributed the tremendous thought of Miss Agnes Macphail that it is wrong and wicked to record in school books the deeds of men and women who have suffered for their country. In the Third Reader there are sixteen references to such shocking conduct, and in the Fourth Reader no less than twenty-four."

After several more paragraphs of sarcasm it ends, "The universe will never get anywhere so long as Mr. 'Jimmy' Simpson and his platform associates merely clap their hands and yet neglect to put their shoulders behind such world-remaking policies as are enunciated by that noteworthy stateswoman, Miss Agnes Macphail."

In May, 1924, Toronto was host to a Pax Special. This was a train carrying a load of women dedicated to peace and disarmament, on a tour after a conference of the International League for Peace and Freedom in Washington. Agnes Macphail had been the official Canadian delegate to the conference. The entire assembly had been greeted by President Coolidge, and lavishly entertained during their Washington stay. Sir Esme

Howard, the British Ambassador, took part in the entertainment.

All this naturally impressed Toronto no end. A list of the more distinguished women among the visitors was published—women from eighteen different countries, including a genuine Lady from England. A garden party was arranged at Government House. They were welcomed by Mrs. Joshua Smith, who carried no stigma of failure in patriotism. She had prepared copy for many of the recruiting posters during the war, and after the armistice had written a memorial booklet, giving in detail the activities of Toronto units in the victory. This reassured the Toronto papers, giving the whole thing an air of solid, loyal respectability. The atmosphere was very different from that around the home-grown demonstrations for peace.

The platform activity kept Agnes very busy, but she added to it by tours with Chautauqua. The name means very little to most Canadians born after 1930. But for years, Chautauqua was a vital part of life in small communities every summer.

Started in 1873, the movement was the first formal attempt at adult education in the United States. It was an outgrowth of Methodist camp meetings, when families would gather and live in tents for a week or so, attending religious meetings. The scope of these affairs was enlarged to include some secular subjects, even some technical instruction and handicrafts. The headquarters, established in a beautiful section of land on Lake Chautauqua in south-west New York State, included living quarters as well as lecture rooms, gymnasiums, and recreational facilities. The sessions were always held in summer, and were extremely well attended. Chautauqua became a place where people gathered in search of "culture".

But an allied movement brought the "culture" to the people. The Chautauqua tours, while commercial, had an aura of uplift, well salted with genteel entertainment. They were tent shows, serving towns and villages, and actively supported by the local churches and schools and service clubs, heralded by advance publicity with its attendant advance subscriptions. A manager and a young woman in charge of junior activities (very

Tours and travels outside parliament

often a school-teacher on holiday) stayed in town all week. These staff members were usually received by the townspeople as welcome visitors, and asked out to supper all around town.

For a week, Chautauqua was the preoccupation of the community. In the mornings, the children whose parents had subscribed gathered to hear stories and play games and learn simple lines and songs and simpler dance or march steps for the religious or patriotic pageant which would be the final event of the week. In the afternoons, the audience would be mainly women and older children, and in the evenings the men came out too, and the crowd sat on hard folding chairs in the big tent, with their palm-leaf or cardboard fans stirring the hot summer air.

There were small concerts, instrumental or vocal, readings and recitations, and some acts which could quite legitimately be called polite vaudeville. But the substance was provided by lecturers, speaking to educate and to uplift the public. One lecture that was very popular was called "Acres of Diamonds". It was straight uplift—the acres of diamonds were the spiritual riches to be found scattered all over everyone's life, to be gathered for the seeking, plus a little digging.

William Jennings Bryan was probably the biggest drawing card Chautauqua ever had. No one was allowed to deliver a political speech, but Bryan was able to present his own version of economics, and to hold forth with great eloquence on the evils of drink and the virtues of prohibition.

The visiting lecturers and performers made single appearances as a rule, and were looked upon with some awe and little attempt at social mingling. This atmosphere of aloofness was deliberately cultivated by the Chautauqua management.

Agnes Macphail was one of the visiting lecturers. In 1928 she made a ten-week tour of Western Canada with Chautauqua. One of the Toronto papers, reporting that Miss Macphail was going to tour the West, published a facetious warning to the western people to behave themselves, and gave an example of the perils of heckling Agnes. At one meeting, the writer said, a man sat in the front row and heckled. He kept saying, "Aw, why don't you get a husband?" Agnes endured it for a while, and then she walked to the edge of the platform and pointed at him. "Get up!" she commanded. The man just sat. "Get up!" she repeated, and the audience echoed her. The man got uncomfortably to his feet and stood there. "I suppose you're married," said Agnes. He muttered agreement. She turned to the audience: "Now, I'd bet he wasn't like this when his wife married him ten years ago." Fixing the man with her finger again, she said, "What guarantee have I that anybody I married now wouldn't turn out like you in ten years?"

The audience loved it, as audiences do enjoy verbal bloodletting. The Toronto writer, of course, knew nothing of Chautauqua, where people came to be edified, not to argue.

Agnes was paid one hundred dollars a week, which was good money, and she enjoyed the work. She did not enjoy the rules, particularly the one that required that all performers must move out of town on the first available train after the performance. This meant, quite often, arriving in some tiny village in the middle of the night or the small hours of the morning, unmet, unwelcomed, unfamiliar with the local facilities. Sometimes there was not even a hotel. The travellers learned that the only place they could depend on was the Chinese restaurant. Every village, no matter how small, seemed equipped with one of them, and the proprietor was always willing and able to feed the tired travellers and find beds for them.

Agnes told about arriving in one town at 4 a.m. "How will we know where to go?" she asked. Someone replied, "It will be the only place in town with a light on."

And he was right. They saw a light. It was upstairs, but that did not stop them. They roused the Chinaman, and he fed them and gave them rooms—"terribly bare", Agnes said, "but perfectly clean."

She made some Chautauqua tours in Eastern Canada too, and apparently had a little more time to meet people, no doubt because the towns were not so far apart. One young woman, travelling through the counties of Eastern Ontario on other business many years later, claimed that every second elderly

Tours and travels outside parliament

man she met told her that he had proposed to Agnes Macphail when she was touring with Chautauqua.

She became very well known as a lecturer in the United States, working first with the Belo Lecture Foundation, and later for the Peate Bureau. This, of course, was in addition to special lectures and meetings. Her travels gave her an opportunity to meet many famous people, and she kept her critical faculties in abeyance on these occasions, and simply enjoyed the personalities.

Early in 1929 she met Henry Ford. He and his wife attended a Peace Conference in Detroit where Agnes spoke. They came up after the lecture to meet her and invite her to his "Village" the following day. "I won't send a Ford for you," he promised. It was a Lincoln that arrived at her door next day to take her to the Village where Ford lived among his workers rather like a feudal lord. She was shown through the establishment and then entertained by square dancers recruited from Ford's office staff. The orchestra next played for the general pleasure of the company, and Agnes had the unique experience of performing a solemn Schottische with Henry Ford on a summer afternoon.

A little later, she was on tour in the southern States when she received a telegram inviting her to attend the League of Nations as a Canadian delegate. She considered this Mr. King's way of thanking her for her 1926 support in Parliament. "Not if it is a Liberal delegation," she replied cautiously. "Interested if all parties are represented." Mr. King sent a delegation including all parties, and Agnes went very happily.

On her way to Geneva for the September meetings, she stopped off in Prague, Czechoslovakia, for an August peace conference of the Women's International League. The founder and president was Miss Jane Addams of Chicago, an early winner of the Nobel Peace Prize, a great humanitarian, and a noble soul. She was nearly seventy at this time, and not well, but was presiding at the meetings.

Agnes' friends, Violet McNaughton and Laura Jamieson, both Canadian newspaperwomen, had been in Prague enjoying the sights for some days before Agnes arrived. Laura Jamieson wrote later :

When Agnes Macphail arrived the afternoon before the conference was to begin, after a journey across Europe by train, we two hailed her as a compatriot in a strange land. But Agnes was short-spoken and almost grumpy. Violet suddenly said : "Let's go out and have an early supper. Then we can talk better." On our way to an outdoor café, to which the Czechs were as much addicted as the French, Violet said to me privately : "You know, Agnes is much like a man in some ways. She may not know she is hungry, but you know it when her humour and good-fellowship dries up; but give her food . . ." Sure enough, once we began to eat Agnes reverted to her usual merry self, and the meal was a jolly one.

Next morning we assembled in the big auditorium of the college. The Mayor of Prague, a short stocky man with stiff upstanding hair, greeted Miss Addams with courtly manners and wished us well. You will remember that Jan Masaryk was President of Czechoslovakia at that time. He also had sent a representative to receive us. He was a tall, fair man, who bowed from the waist and kissed Jane Addams' hand. It was a far cry from Canada, and rather un-American, too; consequently, being women, we adored it.

Now you must remember that at this conference were many women who had only secured the right to vote a short time before. More important, they were not used to taking part in public meetings. They were not familiar with parliamentary procedure. Jane Addams, however, knew these women, or women like them, from her travels, and particularly from work in her settlement, Hull House in Chicago, where immigrant women and their children came to have their self-respect restored after rebuffs in the economic and social life of the new world.

Now, as soon as the preliminaries were over, Miss

Addams welcomed the delegates and read out the agenda for the conference. Immediately a dozen hands were up, a dozen tongues, each in a different language; all talked at once, giving no chance at all for the translators to do their work. The place was pandemonium.

Agnes Macphail had never experienced anything like this before. She was horrified. She tried to speak, but was quickly drowned out. Undaunted she mounted a chair, and, standing on it, called out in her low-pitched, rather gravelly voice: "Fellow delegates, this must not go on. Surely you know that our beloved Miss Addams' health cannot stand this." Her powerful voice and commanding presence silenced them. She waited for the translators to repeat her words in French and German. She added a few more sentences and sat down. There was a tense silence.

Then Jane Addams, a soft smile lighting up the deep sad eyes, said: "Thank you, Agnes Macphail. Those first few minutes must have seemed pretty bad to anyone sharing them for the first time. But we're always like that for the first few minutes of a conference. You see, many of the women here are getting their first chance to speak in public. But we soon settle down, don't we?" smiling at them all.

After that, discussion became almost normal. Agnes entered into it whole-heartedly, and was a very popular delegate. She was also one of the main speakers at a large public meeting held one evening in the centre of the city.

During a break in the first day's session, Agnes caught sight of a new-comer. "Why, there's Ellen Wilkinson," she said; "I'd love to meet her." "Come along then," said I, "I met her in London when I stopped there coming over." When we reached her I said, "Miss Wilkinson, here is someone longing to meet you, Agnes Macphail, only woman member of the House of Commons of Canada." Ellen Wilkinson greeted her warmly, and Agnes, her hero-worship rising to the occasion, said: "I've read every one of your speeches that were printed; I've known for years the colour of your hair and what kind of clothes you wear, and now at last I meet you." While they were chatting, Miss Wilkinson saw a British colleague coming, and said to her, presenting Agnes, "Oh, you must meet Agnes Macphail, only woman member of the Parliament of South Africa."

I cannot describe the look on Agnes' face. Miss Wilkinson realized her mistake in a moment and rectified it. We all moved on. But Agnes could not forget it. "Of South Africa," she would say under her breath. "Oh I know, she's terribly busy and all that. But there are so few of us women in the parliaments of the world; I should think she could remember at least those in the British family and not get them mixed." I tried to point out to her that Ellen Wilkinson had come to public office after a long hard climb in the Labour movement, and then hard, slogging work in the House of Commons on minimum wages and social services, with hardly time for a glimpse at women M.P.'s in other parts of the world. She was mollified at last, but her hero-worship had a dint in it.

Agnes went on to Geneva after the conference in Prague. She travelled by Orient Express, enjoying every moment of the trip, but arriving very tired. She went to bed at once, and fell asleep. She was aroused very soon by a telephone call from David Cliff, secretary to Hon. W. D. Euler. Mr. Cliff was calling his superior—Agnes had been given the wrong room. Wearily she helped gather her belongings and shifted to the room next door. Once more she fell into bed, not bothering to inspect the door connecting with the room she had just left. Before she could get to sleep again, that door opened, and in popped Mr. Euler, in search of his secretary. Agnes found it amusing, but Mr. Euler did not. He had himself and his secretary moved clear over to the other side of the hotel first thing in the morning.

The British delegation arrived, headed by Ramsay MacDonald, the Labour Prime Minister. All the Commonwealth delegates were summoned to his hotel. Canada was becoming a nation, and no one was more conscious of the fact than Agnes Macphail. And apparently no one was less conscious of the fact that a Commonwealth is not an Empire than Ramsay Mac-Donald.

Talking about the first order of business for the following day, the opening of the League meetings, Mr. MacDonald announced, "His Majesty's Government has decided——" He was interrupted by an Irishman ("a little, emaciated Irishman named McGilligan," said Agnes, "with a diplomatic cough.")

"Mr. Prime Minister," McGilligan said, "you probably intended to say the British Government has decided—we have decided quite otherwise."

There was another clash over the election of a new member to the Council, since Canada was stepping out. Again Mac-Donald announced, "His Majesty's Government has decided that Australia should stand, as a member of the British Commonwealth."

McGilligan promptly countered with the statement that Eire had decided to stand, "as a member of the League of Nations." The rest of the Commonwealth rallied to elect Eire. The other members of the British delegation were, on the whole, embarrassed. They apologized privately for Mr. MacDonald, explaining that he was over-tired.

The Canadian delegation to the tenth Assembly of the League of Nations was a large one. There was a great amount of committee work at the League, and it was felt that Canada should be represented on as many committees as possible. The Government was represented by three Cabinet Ministers: Hon. Raoul Dandurand, who was Canadian representative on the League Council; Hon. W. D. Euler, Minister of National Revenue; and Hon. J. C. Elliott, Minister of Public Works. Alternate delegates were Sir George Foster, President of the League of Nations Society in Canada; Hon. Philippe Roy, the Canadian Minister at Paris; Agnes Macphail, M.P., and Malcolm McLean, M.P. (from Melfort, Saskatchewan).

Agnes was particularly pleased at the inclusion of Sir George

Foster, for whom she had great respect. As far as she was concerned, he was the head of the delegation. It was a wonderful experience for her.

She was altogether convinced that only through the League of Nations could world peace become a reality. To be in Geneva, which she found "grippingly beautiful", the centre of the world's efforts to get along together, to be part of the machinery of international debate, was most thrilling. Sitting among the representatives from fifty-three countries, seeing observers sent by non-members, she felt that truly, in spite of all differences, "the world is a unit". She was greatly moved by Aristide Briand's appeal to the women of the world to eradicate militarism.

An attempt to put Agnes Macphail on the Third Committee annoyed her. This committee dealt with welfare, women and children. "Harmless things!" she snorted. "That's the committee where they stow women away." Disarmament was her subject, and Disarmament was the committee she intended to serve on. There had never been a woman on that committee. "Then we may as well make a start," Agnes stated, and got her way.

She spent the Government's money more cautiously than if it had come out of her own purse. She submitted an expense account of twelve hundred dollars. This was embarrassingly low for the other delegates. She was politely requested to submit another account, not too high, just tactfully hoisted. A few years before she would have made an issue of it. By now she had learned to give way in small matters, and she complied to oblige her fellow delegates.

On her return to Canada, convinced of the importance of the organization, she advocated a League of Nations section of the Government, to be set up under the Department of External Affairs. Speaking to the League of Nations Society in Ottawa, where Miss Charlotte Whitton was one of the directors, she urged them to continue their work, to move forward. But she was caustic about their membership—it was too highbrow. The

Tours and travels outside parliament

general public, she said, must be brought into this peace movement or there was no hope of its success.

In Parliament she urged a "dollar for dollar" peace campaign, to equal the defence budget. The peace dollars would go to establish a chair of international relations and international scholarships in each Canadian university. The honourable Members took the easy way out of this embarrassing proposal —they "talked out" her resolution, eulogizing peace at such length that the time allowed for private Members' bills expired, sparing them the necessity of voting on the measure.

Agnes had one other suggestion—to the next session of the League of Nations the Canadian government ought to send Tommy Church, an arch-Tory and one who despised all pacifists. "This may seem drastic," she said, "but I found that those who went to scoff, remained to pray."

Fourteen

R. B. B.—and hard times

Even before the stock-market crash of October, 1929, which precipitated the great depression, agriculture had been slipping into serious difficulties, as Agnes had not failed to point out in the Commons. "One dared not go around among the farmers," she remarked, in her budget speech in March, 1929, "and talk about 'prosperity'."

Investment figures were significant : seven dollars invested in agriculture produced one dollar annually, while three dollars invested in the manufacturing industries produced a two-dollar return.

"If farm lands in old Ontario could be sold readily, at least one-half the farms would change hands overnight," she said. And she urged, "The farmers must, not as individuals but as a group, enter the marketing, the financial and the legislative fields."

Following the Wall Street crash, business took on an abrupt slump everywhere, and men were out of work in the thousands. Mackenzie King did not recognize the extent of the damage. He was niggardly with relief assistance when pressed by the provincial governments. He brought down a 1930 budget that completely ignored the pressures of rising unemployment and business strangulation. He faced the electorate in 1930 with bland confidence.

But the Conservatives had chosen a new leader, R. B. Bennett, a talkative, arrogant, nattily dressed Calgary lawyer. He boasted that he would lead Canada back to prosperity by "blasting our way into the markets of the world". Any brave voice was listened to by the voters that year. The Conservatives went in, for the first time since the war, to inherit the sorry task of government in a time of economic crisis that extended across the entire Western world.

But in South-East Grey no Conservative was able to unseat Agnes Macphail, though Bennett himself had come into her riding to speak in support of the Tory candidate, Dr. Campbell, and no expense was spared in his campaign.

Agnes described Bennett's efforts to defeat her.

"He came into my constituency, dramatically waved his hand at a closed factory across the street and said, 'Put me in power and in three weeks that factory will be running full time.' That was not enough; a little child toddled up on the platform and he put his hand on the child's head and said, 'Let us vote right for the children's sake.'"

She led the laughter, in rural schools and country meeting places, at this pompous Tory lawyer who wanted to be Prime Minister.

A Liberal, O. T. Wright of Dundalk, was also nominated, but apparently thought better of it and did not run.

The U.F.O. conducted its campaign with dignity. The *New Trail*, published by the South-East Grey Political Association of the U.F.O., carried on the front page in a box, an item entitled "The Real Issue":

"In South-East Grey, the real issue is: shall we elect a member responsible to the constituency, free to vote on the merits of questions as they arise, responsible only to this constituency, or shall we elect a member who, be he ever so honest and intelligent, is unable to vote on the merits of questions, and who is responsible to his party, not to the electors?"

Throughout, the paper emphasized the weakness of the two-party system and the value of the independent Members. A list of legislation initiated by the independent groups appeared in the lead position on the front page. It included, among other items: rural credit; old-age pensions; bank inspection; greater consideration for returned soldiers; the refusal of clearance papers for vessels carrying liquor to the United States; amendments to the Grain Act beneficial to farmers; closing of Parliament at 11:00 p.m. and the forty-minute limit on speeches; the right of the new groups to move amendments on important questions, and their recognition as separate groups; consent of Parliament to provide productive work for prisoners; amendments to the Election Act, which provides for the non-partisan conduct of elections, coming into effect this election for the first time; the right to pay for halls the night of the meeting; and the privilege of clubs and associations to contribute to the campaign fund of their favourite candidate. An impressive list of accomplishments. (Agnes had said, "About all government legislation springs from private bills that have been buried or talked out. . . . Seventeen out of twenty-two private bills have originated in our group.")

A picture of the candidate, Agnes Macphail, adorned the opposite corner of the front page, showing her looking down, with her hair marcelled, her glasses less prominent, apparently rimless, and a serious but sweet expression around the mouth —a nice change from some of the grim photographs of the past. The accompanying text, "A Message to the Electors", reminded them that they would have the privilege, on July 28, of "approving or disapproving of what I have done. If you approve, remember, 'It is the effort of each blade of grass that keeps the meadow green.'"

The entire back page was occupied by an advertisement for the annual picnic on July 1st: "Complete Program From One to One!" There would be sports, including softball in four categories, football, lacrosse, and horse shoe tournaments. The grounds, it was announced, would be electrically lighted. A Scottish entertainer and a concert party were scheduled to give a high-class concert. There would be addresses by Miss A. C. Macphail and F. R. Oliver, M.L.A.—all to be enlivened by a pipe band, and all evening an orchestra for dancing. Political gatherings were lively and lengthy in those days.

Her loyal people voted once more for "Aggie". There was a great victory celebration in Durham and the surrounding towns, as election returns came in that Monday night. Durham

R. B. B.—and hard times

streets were crowded with farmers' cars and buggies. The town hall and U.F.O. headquarters overflowed with joyful party workers. At ten o'clock Agnes arrived; thunderous cheers greeted her. She told her people she was proud of the clean campaign they had conducted, and that she would rather have been defeated on it than elected by the campaign used against her. She told them :

"I am not in politics for money. I am not making any. But I am giving my whole time and the best of my life and ability in your service."

The new Conservative Prime Minister had an unenviable job before him. The hard times of the 1930's are still too well remembered by most Canadians. The restrictions on daily living, the general penny-pinching and real distress, are part of our family history.

Since the Second World War, ways have been found to steady the economy. In 1945 Canada could face the signs of a new recession with some degree of calm, because economic measures, first advanced by socialists, would check the full impact of the disturbance.

But back in 1930, R. B. Bennett was the man *on the spot,* entrusted as Prime Minister to lead a nation under unprecedented economic stress, and with nothing but a few hunches to guide him. Most of his hunches, at first, were wrong. He tried to cure business depression and unemployment by cutting down government spending, thus decreasing still further the jobs and money in circulation, and by haranguing the nation to bear its trials meekly. His bludgeoning efforts to bend the flow of international trade to suit his liking failed to accomplish anything like the results he looked for.

Agnes liked R. B. B. She loathed his political principles, but she got on very well with him. Agnes could encompass this kind of paradox with the greatest ease. She was attracted by his impulsive generosity in private life, his urbane gallantry. She loved people in vast variety, and colourful, buoyant personalities were especially interesting to her.

And at the same time no one damned the Prime Minister and all his works so forthrightly as Agnes.

"Sir Richard", as Agnes Macphail called him, in the little notes passed over to his desk, was rich, fastidious and egotistic. One unpleasant story relates that he had his rooms changed to the front of the Chateau Laurier, where he occupied a 17-room suite, because he disliked looking down through the north windows at the transient unemployed sleeping under newspapers in Major Hill Park. It was Bennett who sent the Mounted Police to halt the wretched march of the unemployed at Regina. And Bennett's name, to all prairie people, was linked in bitter association to a horse-drawn, stripped-down automobile that could no longer be kept running with gas and repairs—the Bennett Buggy. Bennett lectured the nation to be patient and thrifty and hard-working, while hunger and bankruptcy stalked the land.

He was the man who above all others drove the progressive forces among farmers, city workers and intellectuals to unite in a new political front, the C.C.F.

Fifteen

Formation of the C.C.F.

Mackenzie King, chipping away at the Progressive Party, had shredded it down to a group of staunch independents in Parliament. But from the remaining stump a new organization was getting ready to grow—the philosophical roots of the reform movement were intact.

After the 1925 election, the eleven U.F.A. Members, the three Labour M.P.'s and nine independent Progressives met regularly in a common caucus. Meanwhile, in Alberta the United Farmers and organized Labour had a working understanding for mutual support in elections. And in Ontario, organized labour supported United Farmer candidates when the opportunity arose.

Following the unsatisfactory budget of 1930, nineteen of the Farmer and Labour Members met at Ottawa and drafted a constitution for "Co-operating groups". They agreed to work together formally "in the development of a co-operative system of administration". Each group was to retain its identity.

Agnes Macphail had been most anxious that Mackenzie King, not R. B. Bennett, should attend the Imperial Conference of 1930. That was the reason for her effort to persuade King to defer an election until after the Conference. She knew that Bennett was an ultra-Conservative, with strong theories about protection. She was right. Bennett took a "Canada first" position at the Conference, trying for a scheme of empire preferences. He called a special session of Parliament in September, 1930, for two purposes. One was to pass an Unemployment Bill that provided $20,000,000 for relief, to be spent in conjunction with the provinces. The other was to pass amendments to the Customs Act to give the Cabinet greater discretionary powers in manipulating tariffs, so as to put Bennett's protection theories into effect. His tariff policies were slightly helpful to industry, but put a heavier burden on the primary producers.

When Parliament met again in March, 1931, Agnes spoke in the opening debate on the Throne Speech. She mocked the Tories:

"It has been very amusing to me to note the added touch of arrogance of practically every member of the Government, and especially of their leader."

Criticizing Bennett's protection policy, she said, "A simple remedy, refuse to buy, but sell . . . The thing is so obviously fallacious that it passes my understanding that men of culture, education and brains should really believe it. . . . When the question is one of finding markets in which to sell our surplus goods, the progress has not been so great. . . . Trade has fallen 26 per cent during the fiscal year just ended, under the preceding year."

She quoted Winston Churchill's phrase, "the curse of plenty". Deploring the Government's agricultural policy: "There is mention of 'an increased effort to eliminate parasites'. If that means the cut-throat as well as the cut-worm it is all right. On the other hand, if it simply means there will be fewer bugs, it might be as well to let the bugs have the wheat as not to be able to do anything with it."

She offered a farm programme that would stress co-operative marketing; reduction in cost of processing farm products, through government experimentation; lower tariffs; cheaper farm credit; a vital rural educational system.

Bennett's arrogant attitude in the House was a continual irritation to Agnes. In April she arose to tell him off. His attitude, she said was "unfortunate and ridiculous". He had been "lecturing the House, especially this corner". She said she had been out West during the Easter recess, had herself seen the badly dressed men in crowds walking up and down, aimlessly, on a Winnipeg street; had heard about problems of giving relief in Regina. She advised Bennett to take a look at actual conditions, or at least read the papers.

On the 26th of May, J. S. Woodsworth moved an amendment to the Criminal Code to define more accurately "unlawful assembly". Several left-wing speakers had been denied the use of halls in Toronto. Agnes was one of them. She was very much insulted at finding herself classed as a "dangerous person". Speaking in support of Woodsworth's motion, she said, "The difficulty arose when the Fellowship of Reconciliation attempted to rent a hall in which to have a public meeting to be addressed by me . . . 'a dangerous person'? There are people in the city of Toronto who think that communistic gatherings and propaganda can be stopped by prohibiting the right of assembly and free speech. That is utter nonsense."

The co-operating group in the House recorded that in their opinion, "Changes in our fiscal policy are not of themselves a solution to our modern economic problems, but effective encouragement should be given to the development of co-operative principles, having regard to production, distribution, and the utilization and control of credits." The fact that the farm Members subscribed to this statement meant that they had taken a long step. They had been wedded for many years to the theory that tariffs were the basis of all economic ills. Now they had changed their minds and enlarged their views.

That summer the Western Conference of Labour Parties, meeting at Calgary, invited farmer representatives to attend their meetings. In Saskatchewan a parallel activity was taking place. The United Farmers of Canada (Saskatchewan Section) approved a series of resolutions favouring "social ownership and co-operative production" and agreed that direct political action was necessary to achieve their aims. The convention also declared itself "ready at all times to co-operate with other organizations with similar aims and objectives".

Unemployment in Canada had increased 80 per cent from 1930 to 1931. The total was reported to be 700,000. The 1932 session of Parliament opened on February 4th. The Prime Minister introduced the drastic measure of reducing the salaries of M.P.'s and Civil Servants 10 per cent to save seven and a half to eight million dollars. Gardiner and others protested the measure, not for personal reasons, but because it would further cut purchasing power and depress business. Agnes Macphail voted for it. "The people of my constituency have had to take a cut, not of 10 per cent but of 60 to 70 per cent. They feel very bitter. . . . While I am opposed to this policy [because of the reasons advanced by Gardiner] I will support it, because I believe that a Member should reflect the opinion of his constituency."

She protested strongly against exemptions from the reduction for members of the armed forces, the R.C.M.P., and judges. "There are more highly paid men in the Department of National Defence than in any other department of the service," she said. "We seem to have enough arm-chair generals to swing a good-sized war at any time, and they take no cut in salary."

The Speech from the Throne asserted that in the midst of a serious world-wide economic stress, Canada's position was "fundamentally sound" and "conditions are gradually improving".

J. S. Woodsworth said the Speech revealed "an absolute bankruptcy of ideas in the face of crisis". On March 2nd he introduced a resolution pointing out the obvious failure of the capitalist system and urging a change to a "co-operative commonwealth" based on the teachings of the Fabians of the United Kingdom, with nationalization of large industrial and financial holdings a keystone.

A few days later, Agnes protested an increase in the estimates for the R.C.M.P.:

"A week ago yesterday we had on Parliament Hill a display of force such as this House has never seen before. . . . A thousand unemployed men gathered in Confederation Square, and we had the spectacle of heavily armed men standing at the gates and an armoured car careening all over Parliament Hill. We knew there was a detachment of mounted and armed policemen ready to dash out should trouble occur. Why all this? Because

Formation of the C.C.F.

a thousand unarmed, unemployed, destitute men were gathered to lay their troubles at the foot of the throne. . . .

"I realize that there can be no permanent cure of unemployment without the elimination of the causes of the depression, and that means fundamental changes in our economic system. . . . Just think of the people who have been cared for this year in the dried-out areas of the prairie provinces, and the unemployed throughout Canada. I am asking you, Mr. Speaker, and the Members of the House : how long can this go on as it is now being financed?"

She warned the Liberals that "their only chance of survival is to champion fundamental changes. . . . Canada cannot stand two ultra-conservative parties; the burden is too great."

Outside the House she crusaded on the subjects of the folly of the gold standard, on the desirability of a little inflation to help purchasing power, and on disarmament—sometimes practically in the same breath. For instance, in Hamilton she spoke in the afternoon to the Kiwanis Clubs, in an enlarged meeting including wives and friends. Her subject was "The Changing Trend of Economics." In the evening she addressed the Women School Teachers' Association on "Our Changing British Empire"—an eloquent plea for an aroused public opinion in favour of disarmament.

Outside the House, too, her arch-enemy, Mr. Bennett, was very charming to her, and she responded to his friendliness. He liked to sit beside her and hold her hand at social events, to the dismay of some of his supporters. At one of his parties Agnes remarked to him that it seemed odd that he served liquor lavishly but did not drink or smoke. What, then, was his vice? "Ah," he replied, "I love the ladies!" His followers worried considerably about the possibility of a scandal involving the Prime Minister and the sharp-tongued lady Member. The situation amused Agnes very much, and she certainly played up to it. She genuinely liked Bennett the man, and she genuinely loathed Bennett the Prime Minister. It was a nice change of pace from Mackenzie King and the possibility of a merely political seduction.

On May 26th the House adjourned, with a speech from the Governor-General commending "the fortitude and patience with which the Canadian people have endured the trials and hardships of these troubled times". Some of the people had reached the end of their patience.

That summer, the United Farmers of Alberta returned the invitation of the previous year to the Labour Parties. In Saskatchewan a joint meeting of delegates from the United Farmers of Canada and the Independent Labour Party was held in Saskatoon under the leadership of M. J. Coldwell, and the Saskatchewan Farmer-Labour Party came into being. Delegates were appointed to go to a political convention immediately following the United Farmers' convention in Calgary at the end of July.

Bob Gardiner had become president of the U.F.A. when Henry Wise Wood retired the year before. This meant a change in direction—Gardiner did not believe in the narrow base of "interest groups". The need of the times seemed to be the establishment of a new economic order. At the end of the conference, Gardiner said: "This is a task that we as a farmers' group cannot accomplish alone, even if our industry be organized efficiently not only in Alberta but from coast to coast. We must be prepared to co-operate with other social units who suffer today as a result of the breakdown of the economic system. . . . Co-operation involves continuous consultation and co-ordination of effort. It involves action . . . on a Dominion-wide scale, for it is only on such a scale that the co-operating groups can make a bid for power to bring about the fundamental changes in the economic system upon the necessity of which they are agreed. In order that the whole people of the Dominion may be able to identify the various groups as parts of a great national movement, it is desirable that the nation-wide movement should be known under a single national name."

The political conference that followed this convention was attended by representatives of the United Farmers of Alberta, the United Farmers of Canada (Saskatchewan Section), the Independent Labour Party of Manitoba, the Canadian Labour

Party and the Dominion Labour Party of Alberta, the Socialist Party of Canada from British Columbia, the Independent and Co-operative Labour Parties of Saskatchewan, and the Brotherhood of Railway Employees.

They had all assembled to form a new federal political organization, and there was no necessity for prolonged debate. They got on with the job of forming their Federation—"not a political party, it is a federation of groups which in their own sphere retain their autonomy and identity but in support of a common national programme will make common cause from coast to coast." Woodsworth was made president.

Since the United Farmers of Ontario had not yet been caught up into the new movement, Agnes Macphail did not attend the Calgary meeting. But she busied herself at once promoting the new federation. Her anger and despair at economic conditions, her respect for the opinions of such men as J. S. Woodsworth and his associates in the House, had convinced her that real reform was impossible without a new medium of reform, and that new medium should be the Co-operative Commonwealth Federation. She spoke on the subject at every opportunity. In the fall, she and William Irvine did a tour together. They were reported at North Bay, on the nationalization of finance and credit, social reconstruction, control of key industries, increase in inheritance and income taxes, and contributory insurance. Agnes and Irvine were a great speaking team, both witty and assured. Irvine was very striking in appearance, rather like a nineteenth-century actor, with a great mane of hair, a beautiful deep voice, and the delivery of an evangelist.

Parliament opened again in October. In her speech during the Throne Speech debate, Agnes made fun of the Government's fancy phrases in the Speech : "retrenchment and constructive development", "the enviable financial position of this country", "the integrity of industry", "the resourcefulness of agriculture", "approaching prosperity".

" 'The resourcefulness of agriculture', she scolded. "I understood that very well. The expression really means that the farmer stops taking the daily paper, has had his telephone removed from the house, does without a new winter overcoat, and has his children do without a much-needed tonsil operation. The farmer's wife does not get her new hat or new shoes; they are not able to take the little trip they had planned—oh yes, I understand that.

"I believe it is not inaccurate to say that there is not a farmer in the Province of Ontario who this year can earn his taxes from the proceeds of the land he has cultivated. . . . this great disinherited class . . . The Prime Minister referred to soap-box orators, communists and socialists, who will endeavour to arouse the passions and prejudices of the people. . . . He has done that already, with the kind of speech *he* made. . . . We picture the Prime Minister in his absolute, assured and complete comfort this winter holding out to the unemployed the one hope that if they emerge from the present crisis they will be better people, strengthened by the fires of adversity."

At the end of November that year (1932), the United Farmers of Ontario held two meetings at the King Edward Hotel in Toronto. They were both significant, and Agnes Macphail played a leading role in both. The first was the meeting of the United Farmers Co-operative Company, which was at that time set up as a joint-stock company. W. C. Good proposed that it be reorganized to make it a genuine co-operative. W. C. Whitemore, one of the directors, led the company attack. He criticized the other directors, accusing them of working on a reorganization scheme instead of tending to the business they were elected to do, and compared their very small holdings to their big expense accounts. Agnes was furious. The arguments were hot and personal. She was wildly indignant at such people as W. C. Good being accused of wrongdoing. She pointed out that as it was constituted, the company was interested mainly in efficient management and substantial profits. What they should be interested in was the co-operative principle, with profits incidental. This involved deliberately helping small and struggling co-operatives. She demanded that Gordon Waldron, K.C., the company counsel, be fired. "What business has a lawyer who does not believe in co-ops being the lawyer for co-ops?"

The meeting voted to reorganize into a genuine co-op to be called the United Co-operatives of Ontario. That round was won. Agnes' fighting blood was up, and she waded into the next battle. This was the convention of the United Farmers of Ontario, which followed immediately.

Robert Gardiner and William Irvine both addressed the convention, on the subject of the newly formed Co-operative Commonwealth Federation. But Agnes was the representative of the Ontario farmers, and she spoke with more authority than the best of the outsiders could do. It was generally conceded that her speeches swung the convention. The president, R. J. Scott, tried to fend off the step by proposing a motion to co-operate with a friendly group, without naming the C.C.F. Agnes countered this—"It's putting you in the absurd position of saying you won't co-operate with the farm Members of the House. I'm through running the straw engine Mr. Irvine spoke of last night that goes 'psst' one time for the Grits and 'psst' next time for the Tories."

The Ontario farmers were not too happy about climbing on a wagon that came from the West. Irvine was reassuring on that point. He said Ontario had really led the way—Ontario had been the first to adopt the Farmers Platform years ago. The West had simply followed and taken one more step. Agnes, on her home ground, felt no need to be equally tactful. If they objected to ideas from the West, she asked, "where are your own ideas?" "I like the U.F.O. platform very much," she added. "I am inclined to view the platform as more of a left-wing Liberalism, but I am heartily in favour of every item in it. However, the purpose of the C.C.F. is clearly to change the social order, and that is where my heart is."

She told them that while she thought it would be good for the U.F.O. to join the C.C.F., after listening to them debate for three days she was not at all sure it would be good for the C.C.F. to take them in.

Graham Spry, the new proprietor and editor of the

Farmer's Sun, advocated the U.F.O. joining the C.C.F. He added, rather strangely, "My paper is not going to support it."

Only six hands were raised against the motion to affiliate with the C.C.F. The convention laid down safeguarding conditions:

1. The U.F.O. to retain its identity and all its privileges and powers unimpaired.
2. The principle of constituent autonomy that prevailed within the U.F.O. with respect to direct political action to be retained.
3. With respect to policy, the affiliation of the U.F.O. with the C.C.F. to be limited by the declared policies of the U.F.O.

The *Toronto Star* commented sourly that only three hundred members of a 7,000-member organization were present to take this step.

R. B. Bennett, speaking in Toronto that November, had attacked the newly formed C.C.F. savagely: "We know that throughout Canada this propaganda is being put forward by organizations from foreign lands that seek to destroy our institutions. And we ask every man and woman to put the iron heel of ruthlessness against a thing of this kind."

When Parliament was again in session in February of 1933, Woodsworth said of this speech that it was not only untrue but seditious, in that it advocated the use of force by one class against another. "What would be suggested if I should advocate putting the iron heel of ruthlessness on all capitalists? . . . The Prime Minister went on to say, 'Remember the words of the Man of Nazareth, "The poor we have always with us." Nineteen centuries have passed but it is still so.' It seems to me," said Woodsworth, "positively sickening that a wealthy man should stand up and lecture poor people in that fashion."

He then moved a resolution asking the Government to take measures looking to the setting up of a co-operative commonwealth in which all natural resources and the socially necessary machinery of production would be used in the interests of the people and not for the benefit of the few. Seconding the resolution, Agnes declared herself a member of the C.C.F. She said :

In the last three or four years, as things got worse and worse and the suffering and poverty of the people increased very rapidly, many citizens and Members of the House who do not belong to either of the major parties really expected—I for one at any rate did—that there would be changes of policy on the part either of the Government or of the Liberal Party. I thought there would be on the part of responsible Members a realization that these days we are passing through are not ordinary days and that a change in policy had become necessary. As time went along we saw there was no such realization, and possibly I had better pay tribute where tribute is due, and thank the Prime Minister and his party for the very able assistance they have unwittingly given to the Co-operative Commonwealth Federation. It would not otherwise have been possible to have addressed such vast audiences, nor would such support have come our way had it not been for the policies of the Prime Minister and his pronouncements from time to time. . . .

There was on the part of many people an expectation that the Liberals would turn to the left. But instead we found them talking about personal liberty, religious liberty and constitutional liberty, as though these could be all that they ought to be if they were not accompanied by economic liberty. . . .

I am very glad to say that the Canadian people cannot be reconciled to continued want and privation, suffering, disease and early death in a land of abundance. . . .

May I say that I am an anti-revolutionist. I have never believed in force. . . .

It seems to me that this depression has been so prolonged that there is less and less chance of some accidental happening bringing us out of it. It looks as though we are going to have to think our way out.

It was significant that while Agnes spoke on farm conditions in Ontario and the Western members spoke on both the farm and industry, the industrial workers of the East had no eloquent spokesmen in Parliament. It was a time when the trade-union movement was in a slump, a time when strong trade unions were needed, but unemployment kept them weak and shifting in membership. They were, for the time being, politically impotent. But they were preparing to take action through the C.C.F. And the League for Social Reconstruction was offering a medium for the middle-class intellectual. The League was the nearest thing Canada had to the British Fabian Society, willing to do research and given to earnest study and discussion. The white-collar classes were suffering just as explicitly as the industrial workers and the farmers. Teachers and ministers were on relief, as well as office and store personnel.

The Communists, in their various sects, were busy, like termites watching a new house going up, preparing to move in and either take over or destroy. The Stalinists, the Lovestonites, the Trotskyists, who could not abide each other, were willing to give each other a helping hand to cripple the fledgling democratic socialist party. Their strength, and their nuisance value, lay in some of the labour organizations, and some of the socialist clubs. In those days, the insulting word was not "Red" or "Commy" as it is now, but "Bolshevik"—the shred of memories of the 1917 Russian Revolution.

In July, 1933, the first formal C.C.F. convention was held in Regina, and the delegates of the affiliated groups were confronted by each other and by the Regina Manifesto, the programme of the new Federation. In preparation, Agnes had called a meeting in the spring, a "provisional council". Among the Labour representatives was Humphrey Mitchell, afterwards to become Minister of Labour in a Liberal government. The meeting was held on a Sunday. H. H. Hannam pointed out that the U.F.O. wouldn't like a Sunday meeting. Agnes knew he was right, but it was her meeting and she was stuck with it. The meeting was held—unofficially; discussion went on for hours—unofficially. At midnight, the U.F.O. members arrived, and official decisions could now be arrived at. It took most of the night.

Five carloads of people went out to Regina from Ontario. Many of them were young people, and it was a light-hearted trip if not a comfortable one. It had the air of a prolonged picnic. Nobody had money enough for hotels and restaurants. They napped in the cars, and bought food in paper bags. They took the dust and heat and discomfort as a test of cheerful group sportsmanship.

Two things disconcerted Agnes when they reached Regina. One was the presence of the socialists from British Columbia—"a wild-eyed bunch," she called them, "that were going to reform the world overnight." The other was the Manifesto itself. She considered herself sufficiently sophisticated and politically educated to take these things in her stride, but the thought of the reactions of the Ontario farmers kept her pacing the corridors. In fact, the Manifesto went very little farther than the Farm Platform of many years before. But the word "socialist" seemed to her to be a dangerous one to ask Ontario farmers to accept as a label.

The convention debates were lively indeed, as the delegates strove to make their own ideas a part of national policy. During a heated debate on farm policy, Agnes quite lost her temper. There were doctrinaire socialists present who were sure that the family farm was doomed as an economic dodo. The preservation of the family farm was an absolute "must" in the eyes of Agnes and her group—and indeed, of nearly all farmers. As the discussion got hotter and hotter, Agnes regally declared that if the convention voted against her, she would leave, and take the Ontario delegation with her. She won her point.

A little later, during the debate on Labour matters, Angus MacInnis from B.C. said with a wry smile, "I could threaten to leave if this measure is not accepted, except for the sobering thought that you would probably get on very well without me."

(Agnes was thoroughly affronted by the implied rebuke, and simply ignored Angus for a couple of years. The painful situation was righted when Angus slipped into the temporarily vacant seat beside her in the House one day, and enquired anxiously about the condition of Bob Gardiner, who was very ill. Later Agnes caught up to him in the corridor, and slipped her arm through his. "Angus," she said, "I thought we were not friends, but I always liked you.")

Agnes made her opinion of feminism unmistakably clear at this convention. One of the woman delegates persistently arose and demanded that "a woman" be on each committee being formed—not any specific person, just "a woman". Agnes was invited to speak at a Women's Luncheon. She arrived wearing a cape, a current fashion that suited both her bearing and her sense of the dramatic. She was introduced to the guests. She arose and addressed her rapt audience: "All I have to say is this. I'm sick and tired of all this 'woman' business. In all the time I've been in the House of Commons I've never asked for anything on the ground that I was a woman. If I didn't deserve it on my own merit I didn't want it! That's all I have to say."

She threw her cloak about her and stalked from the room.

The convention adopted the Regina Manifesto as a statement of policy for the C.C.F. In the eyes of the public it remained the official document of the C.C.F., although convention after convention made important policy changes. Finally, in 1956, the C.C.F. found it necessary to issue a new formal statement under the title of "The Winnipeg Declaration."

Sixteen

The C.C.F. in Ontario—the U.F.O. in and out . . .

The Ontario C.C.F. was set up on the same pattern as the national organization—membership was through affiliation of clubs, labour councils, and so on. In the fall of 1932 J. S. Woodsworth addressed a meeting at Hygea Hall on behalf of the C.C.F. Cards were provided for interested people to sign, indicating their desire to join. Over one thousand cards were signed at this meeting. The attendance was largely white-collar, people who had no natural affiliation with either the farm or the labour groups.

After the meeting, Woodsworth appointed a temporary organizing committee. Frank Underhill, from the University of Toronto, was chairman. D. M. LeBourdais was added later. At the first committee meeting, LeBourdais was proposed as secretary. He had a full-time job with the Mental Hygiene Committee and was reluctant to take on such responsibility. Realizing that everyone present had the same sort of reasons for refusing, he accepted the post, and obtained a three months' leave of absence from his job.

The collection from the meeting had been handed over to the organizing committee, and Sam Marks was appointed treasurer. This was an excellent move, as Marks promptly loaned the committee a room at 3 Charles Street, which he equipped with a typewriter, a table, and two chairs. This was considered a very good start.

LeBourdais suggested organizing C.C.F. clubs, which could be affiliated to the Federation. The basis was the federal riding

—a basis which has not been changed. During the next three months one hundred C.C.F. clubs were set up in Ontario.

LeBourdais was summoned to a secret meeting at the King Edward Hotel in Toronto. He arrived late, and found the room full of people. Some he knew, Philpott and Graham Spry, for instance—many he had never seen before. Mitchell Hepburn, the newly elected leader of the Ontario Liberals, was there. As the meeting progressed, it became apparent that it had been called on behalf of Hepburn. The idea was that all the anti-Tory forces in the province should combine behind Hepburn. LeBourdais was called on to state the position of the C.C.F. He arose and stated that while he could not speak for his organization without consulting them, he was sure the C.C.F. could not compromise its position. Hepburn immediately adjourned the meeting.

When the Ontario Provincial Council was set up, LeBourdais was its secretary. The president was Agnes Macphail, the most prominent C.C.F.'er in Ontario, the strongest link with the U.F.O. and certainly a person of great prestige. Wherever she went, whatever her subject, she found crowds of people eager to listen to her. She rode triumphant over pinpricks of criticism.

In January she spoke in Calgary on behalf of Miss Amelia Turner, a Labour C.C.F. candidate in a by-election. Four hundred women turned out to hear her at the Labour Temple. She told them, "Two groups in this country are engaged in an unorganized strike—the farmers and the unemployed. They are refusing to buy—because they have no money to pay for anything."

During the question period she was attacked for a prospectus for an oil company that had failed—her name was on the prospectus. This well was on her uncle's farm near Oyen, Alberta. Agnes had put seven hundred dollars of her own money into the project. She said flatly she was serving as a director without fees, but had not read the prospectus.

Back in Toronto, at an Open Forum, she found herself called on to defend the behaviour of Premier Brownlee of Alberta in his treatment of hunger marchers. It had not occurred to her

The C.C.F. in Ontario—the U.F.O. in and out

that the Farmers' affiliation with the C.C.F. would put the C.C.F. on the defensive for farm governments—in this case, the United Farmers of Alberta. She simply said she would have treated them very differently.

In May there was a slight flurry because she had used her parliamentary franking privilege to send out letters soliciting subscriptions to the *Farmer's Sun*. She was entirely unembarrassed. She had no monetary interest in the *Sun*, and moreover she had supplied the notepaper and envelopes. Another M.P. was in warmish water over the same sort of thing, but he had gone further. He sent out franked letters soliciting jobs for the graduates from his business college, "seeking to ease unemployment", he said.

She was constantly reported in the papers. R. E. Knowles, a prominent columnist with the *Toronto Star*, was given to outbursts of printed slush about her. He seemed, judging by his columns, to make a practice of lying in wait on station platforms to interview her—sometimes he took the train, too. "You are the flowers and the music and the sunlight at Ottawa," he said he told her—she looked "pensively" out the window.

An article about Agnes appeared in *Maclean's Magazine* under the signature R.T.L., which was the pseudonym of the well-known journalist Charlie Vining. Later in the year *Saturday Night* published an article by Robert Caygeon entitled "Agnes Macphail—Romantic Evangelist." This was a clever character analysis, written in the expectation that she would become C.C.F. house leader, if not the prime minister of Canada. It dissected her faults and virtues with wit and good humour, and Agnes treasured it.

In 1933 a redistribution changed the boundaries of her riding and it became Grey-Bruce, constructed from South-East Grey and South Bruce. The new riding was sixty miles across and nearly as long. It contained ten urban and ten rural municipalities, with a population of about 35,000. In June a big meeting at Walkerton introduced Agnes to her new constituents. Elmore Philpott appeared on the platform with her.

She and Philpott were working hard that summer to spread

the theories of the new C.C.F. party. They spoke together at a C.C.F.-Labour picnic in Windsor shortly after the Walkerton meeting. Her theme was largely the necessity for national planning : "There must be instituted at once an extensive system of non-productive public works. There shouldn't be a town or a city in the whole country with a slum section. Every farming community in the Dominion should have its Hydro plant. I say 'non-productive' because such public works ought to be set up, not for profit, but for the welfare of the whole citizenry of Canada."

She spoke several times a week, all over Ontario, and by the end of the summer she was terribly tired and feeling ill. In September she was nominated at a meeting at Hanover as the U.F.O.-Labour candidate for the new Grey-Bruce riding. Her organization was expanded to provide for section executives in the new area.

She announced that she was going to take a rest, but she did nothing of the kind. Her speaking engagements continued all through September and October. In the middle of November the papers announced that Miss Macphail had to have an operation. She went home to Ceylon for a preliminary rest and then in Markdale the operation was performed by her lifelong friend, Dr. R. L. Carefoot. This was a major abdominal operation which had a more serious and long-lasting effect, particularly emotionally, than she cared to admit.

When she accepted the presidency of the Ontario C.C.F. Council, it seemed a natural move, and she had no presentiment of the unhappy experience ahead of her. There were thirty-six members on the Council. The U.F.O. supplied its president, R. J. Scott, and its secretary, H. H. Hannam; Arthur Mould of London and Mrs. Elizabeth Morton were there from the Ontario Labour Council; Elmore Philpott, president of the Ontario C.C.F. clubs, and D. M. LeBourdais, secretary, represented the clubs. Some of the others included F. H. Underhill, H. M. Cassidy, Graham Spry, Bert Robinson, and Miss Isabel Thomas.

Agnes was completely out of her element. She did not enjoy

any part of it. Meetings bored her, particularly meetings which she had to conduct and where she was not the main speaker. She admired brains but not "intellectuals" (an intellectual was a brainy person she did not like very much), and she was uneasy in the presence of too many college professors. She liked and respected the Labour Members in the House of Commons, people like J. S. Woodsworth and Angus MacInnis, but she found the Labour members of the Council a strange breed indeed. They never missed an opportunity to needle the farm representatives, and the farm members sat in stone silence, getting huffier and huffier.

There was constant friction over matters like holding council meetings on Sunday. The Labour people were accustomed to that sort of thing, since the six-day week of the time left them only Sunday free. The white-collar people were indifferent in the main. The farm people were shocked.

Agnes found herself torn between two loyalties, and on the defensive with her farm friends. She did not turn to the women members on the council for friendship. Isabel Thomas was exactly the type she detested, not only an intellectual but a feminist. Many years later she learned to like and appreciate Miss Thomas, but at that time she did not understand her at all.

She was unhappy about the whole organization. Where she had enjoyed sharing the discomforts with her farm friends on the trip to Regina, she hated the shabbiness of the room where the Ontario Council met. Where she had sat through many night sessions in the House of Commons, she resented sitting up for night meetings of the Council. She was profoundly un-interested in the details of running a political party. She was quite incapable of dealing with the tangled situation that arose in Ontario, and she suffered from an entirely new sense of inadequacy.

Years later when she spoke of that period, she managed to make it sound like a matter of climbing creaking stairs into a dim and dusty room filled with conspirators. Most of the Council members were earnest, enthusiastic and serious people, with no resemblance whatever to conspirators. But it was evident that someone was reporting every move of the Council to the newspapers, and suspicion and distrust grew, along with the wrangling sponsored by the various brands of Communists who had wormed their way in.

Elmore Philpott was her confidant and friend in this situation. After meetings they walked away together, happily ripping all the other members to bits. His caustic tongue appealed to her, and his dependence on her liking and advice forged a tie that never loosened, in spite of his subsequent political behaviour—behaviour that she could not forgive in other people.

In the spring of 1934 the storm broke over Ontario. The Trotskyist branch of the Communists had been particularly successful in infiltrating some of the labour organizations and socialist clubs and were determined to use them for their own purposes. Pleading for "labour unity", they insisted that the C.C.F. should join in co-operation with the Communists in defence of the Rev. A. E. Smith, who was charged with sedition. The C.C.F. Provincial Council rejected the proposal. Philpott went to London to address a big Sunday meeting in one of the theatres, and reported that the London C.C.F. Council had decided to take part in protest meetings, in spite of the provincial ruling.

LeBourdais, the secretary, asked the St. Paul's C.C.F. Club to expel their secretary, Wilfred Jones, for Communist activity. The club refused. LeBourdais attended a meeting of the club and found it "packed" against him. He promptly adjourned the meeting and left. Someone immediately telephoned the papers with a lurid story about his being bodily ejected. When Thomas Cruden moved to expel the Communists, he was removed as president of the Socialist Party of Canada. Obviously the Ontario C.C.F. was in deep trouble.

As provincial president, Agnes received a letter protesting the co-operation of some C.C.F.'ers with Communists, and urging action to expel these members. It was signed by J. S. Woodsworth, A. A. Heaps, and Humphrey Mitchell. Hannam and Scott were appointed by the U.F.O. to consider the situation and they were very sceptical of the Council's ability to clean house. Agnes did her best to soothe them, assuring them that pro-Communists would be expelled.

The difficulty lay in the fact that there were no individual memberships; therefore if an affiliated organization refused to expel a person, the only way to get rid of him was to expel his whole organization. On February 23, 1934, Agnes wrote Philpott suggesting a Council meeting on March 3rd, "to read out the organizations that will not conform to the constitution drawn up at Regina. There is no use fooling about the thing any longer."

They had fooled about the thing too long already. A mass meeting on February 18th at Massey Hall had done the final damage. The meeting was on behalf of Rev. A. E. Smith. The principal speaker was to have been W. I. Patterson of New York, but he was not allowed to cross the border, and Rev. Smith took the platform himself. He attacked Justice Minister Guthrie, and Price, the Ontario Minister of Justice, and orated on the dangers of fascism in Canada. He attacked the leaders of the C.C.F., singling out Woodsworth, Philpott and Macphail for special attention. Some of the supporters on the platform were members of the C.C.F., and one of the speakers was Wilfred Jones, the secretary of the St. Paul's club, who joined in the criticism of the C.C.F. leaders.

On the 1st of March a letter from H. H. Hannam arrived, enclosing a letter written to the Ontario C.C.F. secretary, announcing the withdrawal of the U.F.O. from the Co-operative Commonwealth Federation. Agnes wired Hannam, begging him to hold off until after the Council met. She was doing her best to hold the organization together, but she simply could not do it.

LeBourdais piloted a resolution through the executive to expel all the Labour clubs in Ontario. He wrote Woodsworth, asking him to come to Toronto, and saying he had a list of Labour leaders who would co-operate in reorganization. He sent a letter to the C.C.F. clubs, explaining the events that had led to this action. There was a great furore in the clubs, who protested that the action was too drastic to take without consulting them, and that at least the Provincial Council should have been consulted.

In response to the letter to Woodsworth, the National Council ruled that the Provincial Council must meet, and set the date at March 10. But the U.F.O. would not wait. They withdrew from the C.C.F. Woodsworth made a statement :

1. The arrangement with the U.F.O. had not been satisfactory. The farm members were influenced by temporary and local expediency and seemed unaware of and uninterested in the Dominion objectives of the C.C.F.
2. The working agreement with the Labour councils was no good—it had just provided a field for Communist advantage. The Labour councils were obviously unable to maintain discipline.
3. The C.C.F. clubs set up to enable individuals to join the movement were too difficult to integrate. They were a happy hunting ground for cranks and Communists.
4. The Ontario Provincial Council was unable to deal with the situation.

Elsewhere, Woodsworth said, the C.C.F. was in a healthy state. He declared that each local unit must rid itself of Communists. Then reorganization on a different basis would be possible in Ontario. He announced the dissolution of the Provincial Council and said the National Council would take steps to reorganize the province.

This was done, and the new constitution for Ontario resulted in individual memberships.

Meanwhile, however, Agnes was automatically withdrawn when her organization, the U.F.O., left. She lost her place on the National Council as well, as Philpott did when he resigned. They rejoiced together like children relieved of a distasteful task.

Philpott had come originally from the Liberal Party, and he definitely wished to be a Member of Parliament. In a long letter to Agnes he set forth his dilemma, which he thought was hers too. He suggested : "(1) We can go back (or is it stay in?)

the reorganized C.C.F. (2) We can form a new party, either as independents or otherwise. (3) We can proceed for the time being as unattached crusaders."

He decided to stay unattached, but drifted back to the Liberals, eventually being elected in B.C., long after Agnes was out of the House.

Agnes really had no problem. The situation left her as she wished to be, an independent farm Member of Parliament with strong attachments to a congenial group. She had not changed her mind in any respect about the rightness and desirability of the C.C.F., but she was free to vote with the C.C.F. caucus in the House or not, as she chose; she retained her friends; she was no longer the uncomfortable buffer between two hostile forces; and she had no feeling of disloyalty, since it was her organization that withdrew, and the decision had not been hers. She turned back to her own affairs, especially her new riding of Grey-Bruce.

Her riding executive left Agnes very free to involve herself in anything she pleased, so long as she continued to be a sincere and independent spokesman for the farmers and for her constituency. In a measure, this was a denial of the old U.F.O. theory, upon which the power of recall had been based, that a Member of Parliament was responsible to the riding for all his actions in the House. On the other hand, it was a good working arrangement because, like most citizens, the Grey-Bruce constituents were entirely unwilling to follow with close attention current events that were outside their immediate interests.

For instance, her championing of the Nova Scotia coal miners in her first term at Ottawa could hardly have been more alien to her riding. Later, when she became involved in penal reform, her supporters were no more interested; it simply did not concern them. The U.F.O. excursion into the C.C.F. and out of it again left very little residue in local thinking. They had never really become C.C.F. members in that riding; they had only affiliated with the organization and kept the door open for their retreat. Their Member's close association with C.C.F. Members in Ottawa, the fact that she usually voted with them, and that on important occasions she was invited to their caucus, did not bother her executive, so long as she ran exclusively under the farm or independent label in elections.

This freedom carried its penalties, penalties whose severity became apparent only when it was too late. She was never able to change the basic thinking in her riding, she failed to involve her followers in her outside interests. Her main support rested primarily in the hands of farmers whose attention remained focused on farm problems. They admired her, and rightly, for she was their articulate voice in the nation.

But as she became more and more interested in national and international matters, as she became convinced that democratic socialism as practised in the Scandinavian countries was the answer, as she became more sympathetic towards organized labour, the gap between her and her riding widened. And as her health failed, her patience failed with it. She had always been devastatingly outspoken, but as she spent more and more time away from home her criticism fell on native ears less like the warm familiar scoldings of a member of the family and more like the carping of a visiting celebrity.

Local lack of interest was brought home to her by a small incident in the thirties. The ladies of South-East Grey presented her with a patchwork quilt, bearing hundreds of embroidered names of the donors. It was a tribute to her service in Parliament, and she was genuinely appreciative. But she remarked privately that when she had attended the League of Nations and become the first woman ever to sit on the Disarmament Committee, nobody in her riding had seen fit to so much as comment on it.

This was a characteristic exaggeration, since many of the local papers had carried proud accounts on that occasion. Nevertheless it was true that it would never occur to her supporters to commemorate a far-away event like that in any tangible way.

Agnes enjoyed some support from urban voters but the towns were not her best fighting-grounds, and certainly most of the municipal officials were no friends of hers. In 1931 a book was

The C.C.F. in Ontario—the U.F.O. in and out

published in Owen Sound, entitled *A History of the County of Grey*. It was produced in co-operation with the Official Committee, the Sheriff, the County Treasurer, and the several Wardens of the County. It was an interesting book, with many anecdotes of the early settlers—and it virtually ignored the entire Macphail-Campbell connection. It contained a lively chapter on politics, but although Agnes Macphail had been an M.P. for ten years, and Farquhar Oliver an M.L.A. for five, neither of them was so much as mentioned. According to the book, the political history—though not the social—ceased with the Conservatives, Mr. Lucas, M.P., and Dr. Jamieson, M.L.A.

On the whole local papers were reasonably kind to her and often viewed her with great pride. But Agnes' hostility toward city papers and her distrust of their reporters was very deep, rooted in her resentment at their early treatment of her. Many a politician today would be delighted to receive the constant publicity that she took for granted, but she had the conviction —not unreasonably—that reporters were always hoping she would say something they could publish to her discredit.

In the early thirties a pair of young men turned up in the riding representing themselves as reporters and busily spreading stories to the effect that Agnes was being indiscreet, to put it very mildly, with a number of M.P.'s from French Canada. This struck the Grey farmers as so far-fetched that it was hardly funny. They would not have begrudged her a romance with someone plausible, like a farmer Member, even if he were from the West, but to suggest that their Aggie would get tangled up with virtual foreigners was ridiculous. Agnes always maintained that the Conservatives sent the men in to destroy her reputation. Her close supporters blamed the story on an M.P. from a neighbouring riding, and promptly countered with some hair-raising rumours about his own behaviour.

The fact was that Agnes was deeply in love with a Member from the Province of Quebec at that time. But she discovered that he thought that a woman in love would just naturally enjoy darning his socks and performing other little domestic tasks. Agnes was so affronted that the romance died.

Seventeen

The Baynes incident

Among the many plain-bound volumes of reports and commission findings, in the beautiful parliamentary library where
Agnes Macphail was once a familiar figure, there is one that
she was largely responsible for placing there.

To turn its pages today is to be revolted and disturbed at
every passage, for it is the official description of Canada's penitentiaries as they were in the 1930's. It is the Archambault
Report (1938), containing the report and recommendations of
the Archambault Royal Commission. We read :

A man named Price is confined to a penal institution. It is
intended that while there he will acquire a decent respect for
law and justice. These things happen to him :

He is charged with "attempting to incite trouble", tried by
the warden, and sentenced to twenty strokes of a leather strap.
Before administering the punishment the warden reports the
circumstances fully, as required, to the Superintendent at
Ottawa. The Superintendent goes over the evidence, finds it
very insubstantial, but comes to the conclusion, *in his office at
Ottawa,* that the prisoner was guilty of four other offences
against regulations. Therefore, although Price has not been
charged with these offences in warden's court, the Superintendent decides that the twenty strokes, plus twenty-one days on
restricted diet, plus *indefinite* isolation (though the rules say
such confinement should never exceed one month without review) are quite in order, and he so instructs the warden, who
proceeds to carry out this punishment.

Previously, Price has taken advantage of one of the Superintendent's very rare visits to the penitentiary, to complain that he has been very badly manhandled by a guard. This is the only recourse Price has, his only chance to appeal against whatever action the prison officials deal out to him. The Superintendent makes a note, which goes into a file, recording that Price is "a faker", and that he was *"perhaps badly handled by a guard—but not hurt"*. No investigation is made, no action is taken.

There is riot in the penitentiary. Price is in an isolation cell. None of the prisoners in this row can possibly escape; their only contribution to the riot is some additional noise. Yet a gun is fired at Price in his cell, wounding him in the left shoulder. A prisoner in a nearby cell hears Price call out; he attracts the attention of a guard and reports that Price has been shot and may be dying. The guard reports to the deputy warden. No one goes near Price, he receives no food, for twenty-two hours. Two days later he is X-rayed, the bullet is removed, and he is hospitalized for five weeks. This is reported to the Superintendent, who receives reports on everything. The Superintendent describes it as an accidental shooting, makes no attempt to find out who did it or why.

"Brutal and inhuman, a reckless misuse of firearms," the Royal Commission decides. And, citing massive evidence, the Commission draws a simple conclusion : *"There are very few, if any, prisoners who enter our penitentiaries who do not leave them worse members of society than when they entered."*

The Royal Commission is in session in Saskatchewan Penitentiary. They discover, among other inadequacies, that no proper arrangements are made for the treatment of tubercular patients. They are painfully aware of two such patients lying helplessly in the corridor outside their cells, and in the course of the visit one of the patients dies there. . . .

Prisoners complain of disgustingly filthy food. The investigation shows that a storage room is over-run by mice which have chewed holes in salt bags and flour bags, covering food with their droppings. There is a large hole in the lower part of the door jamb where the mice get in, but no one has bothered to repair the hole. . . .

So reads the evidence; it is a grey and sordid story.

Following publication of the Report, the head of the Penitentiaries Branch was immediately dismissed, and the most glaring abuses quickly removed. The report became a bible for those who had long sought to introduce modern methods of penology to Canada, and things were never quite so bad again behind penitentiary walls.

Canada owes this report to Agnes Macphail.

There had been a series of riots and disturbances in the seven federal penitentiaries, during the early 1930's. Officers and prisoners were injured, considerable property was destroyed, fires were started, wholesale floggings were administered, some cases were referred to the criminal courts and sensational evidence was disclosed.

Evidence was given, "eyewitness" accounts were reported; and counter-evidence from official sources contradicted both. What could be said with truth? How bad were the penitentiaries?

Agnes Macphail, in her speeches in the House of Commons and in her press interviews on the subject, showed remarkable restraint. She knew how vulnerable she was, as a woman in public life, to charges of weak "sentimentalism". She tried to move cautiously.

It was a male colleague who made Commons members' flesh creep by brandishing a perforated leather strap, which he denounced as the barbarous instrument of punishment inflicted on the convicts. It was a male colleague who wept for the young lads of fifteen, the first offenders, confined at Kingston with the most hardened criminals. (And this was officially denied.)

It was Agnes Macphail who marshalled authoritative briefs, and pounded home the need for an objective enquiry on the highest level, to get at the truth and recommend reform.

Of course, she was deluged with stories of desperate and outrageous acts. But she avoided using the most sensational reports; she did not want to run the risk of having her statements proved false in detail, to prejudice the main cause.

She was caught only once, at the outset of her campaign. The

The Baynes incident

story of this deliberate attempt to trick her, to subject her to ridicule and shame, is one of the least creditable episodes of recent parliamentary history.

Among the many ex-convicts who asked to see Agnes Macphail and were admitted to her office on the sixth floor of the Parliamentary Buildings, was a fair-complexioned man of apparent good breeding, whose name was Charles Baynes. He first came to Agnes early in 1929. He told her he had just finished serving a five-year term in Kingston penitentiary. She didn't ask him what his crime had been. It was her policy not to ask this question, having learned that she seldom got a straight answer.

But Baynes had resolved to mend his ways, and to make up for whatever he had done by helping veteran pensioners, since he was one himself. He proceeded to work on case after case, assisting veterans who were not getting the full pension they were entitled to. He was astute; his efforts were often successful, and Agnes heard from him at intervals during the next four years.

Charles Baynes is now dead. He is remembered as a plausible person, an excellent bridge player. His manners were exemplary. It did not surprise Agnes to learn that he was the black sheep of a respectable English family, and that his older brother was a highly placed member of the British foreign service, stationed in the British West Indies.

In the late spring of 1933 Baynes came to see Agnes to tell her that a "conspiracy" was afoot against him and his arrest was probably imminent. He had been too zealous, he said, and the Pensions Branch was after him.

However that may be, he was, as he predicted, presently under arrest. Agnes received word from him at Carleton jail in Ottawa, telling her he was to be sent back to Kingston penitentiary for another five years, and he feared for his life. He was receiving a 100 per cent disability pension as a tubercular; he knew there were no proper facilities for the treatment of tubercular patients at Kingston; he begged her to intervene and have him sent to a jail farm where he might have sunshine and fresh air.

A letter came also from the brother in the West Indies, requesting that she do what she could for Charles.

It was late in October, 1933. Agnes sent a telegram privately to Hugh Guthrie, with whom she had crossed swords so often, now Minister of Justice in the Bennett Government.

". . . I am interested that he be sent to Burwash, Guelph or Mimico. I have known this man favourably for four years. He is an ex-service man with a good record. Tuberculosis due to army."

Her telegram was received and duly noted by the Minister.

Agnes visited Kingston penitentiary, the first woman ever to insist on inspecting the whole institution (standing on her right as a Member of Parliament). She observed for herself such things as an insane prisoner making hideous with noise the hospital ward where a man lay after a serious operation, and a bathtub that was used not only for baths but to wash the daily dishes. She made a short speech to the women prisoners, and this was one of the hardest tasks she had ever set herself to do.

The Toronto *Globe* had meanwhile begun a heated campaign for better prison conditions. Prisoners' welfare organizations renewed their long-unrewarded efforts for reform. *Maclean's Magazine* ran a series of sensational articles by ex-convicts.

But no Member of Parliament had tried consistently to force the government's hand. Agnes resolved to do so. As the 1934 session opened, a resolution appeared under her name on the order paper. She urged :

"That a special committee be set up to investigate the causes of crime and to determine whether the penitentiaries of Canada are doing all that could be done towards protecting society by the reforming of the criminal."

The penitentiary system was due for an airing on the floor of the Commons. Agnes prepared her material.

She instructed her secretary, Miss Malvina Bolus, to obtain the file on Charles Baynes from the Department of Justice. Miss Bolus phoned several times, unsuccessfully. She was informed each time that the file wasn't immediately available, it would be delayed, and so on. Despite repeated attempts she was unable to procure it.

M. F. Gallagher, Chief Remissions Officer, later became Agnes Macphail's good friend. And it was then, several years too late, that she learned the file was deliberately kept from her, on the order of the Minister of Justice.

On February 12, 1934, Agnes' resolution was called. But Agnes had just undergone an operation; she was in no condition to present her major speech. And to her grateful surprise, Mr. Guthrie had made a special concession; he had crossed the floor a day or so before to enquire about her health, and to assure her that if she couldn't manage to present her resolution on the 12th he would arrange to have it delayed. Agnes' colleagues thought such an arrangement quite contrary to the rules, but on February 12th when Mr. Speaker called the number of her resolution, the Minister intervened and asked for a postponement, which by unanimous consent of the House was granted.

Two days later Agnes felt well enough to go on.

Harry Anderson, the big, thick-set Toronto *Globe* editor who was waging the penal reform battle tooth and nail, was in Ottawa for the occasion. Through him it is learned that on the eve of this debate a circular passed among newsmen of the Parliamentary Press Gallery, tipping them off to expect something good; Guthrie was going to give Agnes Macphail "a merry ride".

Agnes moved her resolution. She reviewed the many reasons why a full investigation was needed. Midway through her remarks she played straight into Guthrie's hand. She said:

"It is true also that tubercular patients are allowed to mingle with their fellow convicts. I am expecting this statement to be denied, but I may say that it need not be, because I happen to know very well a man who is sentenced to a five-year term in Kingston penitentiary, a man who is a 100 per cent pensioner, very ill from tuberculosis, had haemorrhages as long as three or four years ago and for several months after that was in a military hospital. He is a man with a fine social outlook and very much better than a great many people I know who are not in the penitentiary. I know him well."

When she concluded, another member took the floor, and next the Minister of Justice.

Hugh Guthrie had decided to "get" Agnes, to fix her once and for all. After preliminary comments (he was trying to urge on the House the theory that prison disturbances were Communist-inspired) he lifted from his desk the private telegram that Agnes had sent him three months before. He read it to the House. He stressed that Agnes had "spoken well" of this man. Then he took up the file containing Charles Baynes' record, and read it clearly, deliberately and at length :

"His first conviction was for indecent assault at Winnipeg. His second was for a bestial crime which I will not mention in this Chamber, for which he was sentenced to five years in the British Columbia penitentiary. He was released on ticket of leave to enlist in the Canadian expeditionary force, in which he served, but before he went he was again convicted of indecent assault and sentenced to twelve months. In 1919, after the war, he was convicted in Toronto of forgery. In 1920, again in Toronto, he was again convicted of indecent assault and sentenced to twelve months. On December 22, 1920, at Toronto, he was convicted of theft and sentenced to nine months. On June 17, 1922, at Toronto, he was convicted of theft and sentenced to six months. In August, 1925, at Ottawa, he was convicted on a charge of gross indecency and sentenced to four years in Kingston. In March, 1926, he was transferred to the Manitoba Penitentiary. On October 13, 1933, at Ottawa, he was again sentenced to five years in the penitentiary for indecent assault. That is the case."

To understand precisely what this did to the only woman Member of the House of Commons, it is important to recall the social climate of twenty-five years ago. It was impolite to mention sex at all, let alone its perverted forms. A normal woman of decent circumstances was required to be *ignorant* ; she was not even to suspect that such aberrations existed. This was a dark, immoral abyss into which no one enquired : the Kinsey Reports belong to a different era.

Agnes, in her own words, "suffered anguish". Her old friend, Mrs. Quay, remembers her misery. Her mother, with unusual sympathy, tried to comfort her on a week-end visit home.

The effectiveness of Guthrie's cruelty can be judged by the many people who recall the incident, and in whose hazy recollection Agnes was, at best, very gullible and very rash. "To defend that kind of person!" Few ever heard that she was prevented from finding out what kind of person he was.

Agnes learned that her Conservative opponents in Grey-Bruce planned to distribute a smear leaflet based on the incident. Whether or not this was done, it is certain that the story was used in word-of-mouth campaigning. Agnes, in great distress, dictated a long letter to the newspaper editors in her home riding. She was not yet fully aware of the means the Justice Minister had employed and took some blame upon herself for not persisting in obtaining Baynes' record before she publicly defended him. She said, with rare humility :

"If one is to keep warm-hearted and helpful as life goes on, one is bound to make mistakes. I think it is inevitable, and so, when such a time as this comes, one must be willing to pay the price in suffering."

To Baynes's brother she wrote a letter of reproach, dated March 28th, 1934, because he had not enlightened her as to the nature of Baynes's crime when requesting intervention on his behalf. But she had the grace to add :

"I think our method of dealing with them [sex perverts] is cruel and useless. Had someone of knowledge and broad human sympathies talked to your brother when he was a lad I have no doubt he could have become a very useful member of society."

As for the unfortunate Baynes, tubercular or not, he was shipped to Kingston, where his condition was duly noted and ignored.

There is no doubt that this humiliation hurt Agnes deeply, and yet the following months are not marked by the silence of a subdued lady Member. On the contrary, it was during the next few months that she pressed hardest, in Parliament and on public platforms, for a clean-up of Canada's disgraceful prison system. A sneak attack had the unexpected result of rousing her to real effort.

And so Guthrie tried again.

A convincing array of evidence shows that in April, 1934, the senior Inspector of Penitentiaries, J. D. Dawson, was sent to Kingston Penitentiary for the express purpose of meeting privately with Charles Baynes and extracting from him a statement that this one wretched convict was the source of Agnes Macphail's "information" on penitentiary matters. In particular, Baynes was to "confess" that he had told Agnes about the death of the convict on the stone quarry in Manitoba, though this was not at all the case. This and other details of prison life were to have originated with Baynes, this man whom the public regarded as a particularly low type of criminal.

This was the tactic used, perhaps by direct order and certainly with the concurrence of a Minister of the Crown, to discredit a lone, independent woman Member whose persistent questioning had become an embarrassment.

It may be that Hugh Guthrie believed that conditions in the penitentiaries were much better than they were. A main point of the Royal Commission's report, when it appeared, was the *misinformation* regularly given to the Minister and to the public by Superintendent Ormond. But it is also clear that Guthrie was stiff-necked, unwilling to concede even the possibility of mismanagement, stubbornly opposed to a public investigation, and playing every excuse, such as the presence in Kingston penitentiary of several well-known Communists, for the wave of prisoner unrest and violence.

The first indication Agnes had of the second attempt against her was a letter from the West Indies, from the highly placed brother of Charles Baynes. It was written in obvious alarm. There was an apology for having contributed to her embarrassment, and gratitude for her interest in his brother. And there was a further plea—would Agnes, if she possibly could, visit Baynes? A letter had come from him, so heavily censored that

The Baynes incident

one could scarcely read it, but urging the brother to get in touch with Miss Macphail at once.

Some time elapsed before Agnes complied with this request. The following February she filled a speaking engagement at Queen's University, and the next day made a visit to the penitentiary.

Here she went with Warden Allen to speak to convict Baynes in his cell. She had apparently decided to ignore Baynes' mysterious message, relayed through his brother. But she wished to satisfy herself that the man's tubercular condition was not worse.

Baynes appeared greatly agitated. He asked her if she knew of an attempt to link him with her exposure of prison conditions. When she said she did not, Baynes related that Inspector Dawson had come from Ottawa the previous April, and had attempted to have Baynes sign a statement admitting that he had supplied Agnes with certain information. Baynes had refused. He charged that Dawson used first cajolery and then threats to obtain Baynes's signature, and when he was unsuccessful committed Baynes to a punishment cell. He named a guard as witness.

Agnes was incredulous. She was not going to put any stock in such a story.

A short time later, in Toronto, Agnes was visited at her hotel by an ex-convict who backed up Baynes' words.

This informant was a rogue with a fantastic history, Alfred George Hall. He had got hold of what looked like a good thing. He obviously relished the prospect of causing discomfiture among the authorities who had interfered with his own very profitable undertakings.

So imaginative a career is perhaps worth an aside. Alfred Hall was frequently known as Reverend. He once remarked that religion was, all in all, the best way to collect money, but this was the nearest he ever came to acknowledging that what he did was not exactly legal. Whenever he was arrested he treated the police with great contempt—they were making a particularly stupid mistake. His adventures were various; he arrived in Toronto at one time as an expert on dietetics, and set up a school to train dietitians. Another appearance was as a psychologist, still another as the owner of a magazine agency, and a fourth as a promoter of a chain of beauty salons.

He had an easy method of setting up in business. A large quantity of stationery supplies (including printed letterheads), to the amount of several hundred dollars, was ordered. When it was delivered Hall was absent, and a most superior secretary explained that Dr. Hall was unfortunately tied up in a vital conference and had neglected to leave payment, so perhaps the delivery man had better take it back for the time being? The delivery man, eyeing the enormous package, phoned his company and was instructed to leave the order. No money ever changed hands.

Perhaps his finest effort was in 1930 when, styled as the Reverend Mr. Hall, Psychologist, he created the National Order of Canada with bank assets of $1.31, and hoodwinked the Royal York Hotel into arranging a $1,400 banquet for an estimated 2000 guests, to include the Prime Minister, the Leader of the Opposition, and Senator Sir George Foster. About 180 people turned up, none of their tickets paid for. The Royal York took action in court, and there the defendant appeared in braided black cutaway coat, double-breasted waistcoat, wing collar and grey trousers, playing to the hilt his final scene before he was packed off to Burwash jail.

In Toronto in 1935, Hall told Agnes that he had, regrettably, been confined to Kingston Penitentiary the previous year, and during the April visit of Inspector Dawson had been granted an interview with him to present certain grievances. (For obvious reasons he had been chosen as spokesman by the inmates.)

Dawson came to the interview fresh from his unsatisfactory talk with convict Baynes. He asked Hall if he knew Baynes. He called Baynes "the greatest criminal in Canada and the most unmitigated liar." He said that "this was the kind of criminal who was supplying Agnes Macphail with information." And he added, *"Aggie made a goddamned fool of herself in the House of Commons, but when we are finished with her she will never be able to lift up her head in the House again."*

Hall seized on the words. Spoken by a departmental official against a Member of Parliament, they were surely loaded with trouble. He immediately reported them to the Protestant chaplain and the warden, but while he remained a convict at Kingston nothing came of his accusation.

In telling all this to Agnes, Hall was quite aware that his own very motley record was not going to be of much help in making his story stick. Therefore he insisted on having an affidavit sworn—he made much of the fact that he was now a free man and could be held to account if his word was proven false.

Agnes was now convinced that the incident actually had taken place.

On March 18, in Parliament, she asked for departmental papers dealing with Inspector Dawson's visit to Kingston the previous April. The papers brought down for her were incomplete. They stopped abruptly at April 8th, the day previous to Hall's interview with Dawson. There was no mention of the talk with Baynes. Agnes protested. Guthrie assured her he had supposed the file was complete and would make enquiries.

The following day, when Agnes was absent, Guthrie made a brief statement to the House : "I find that Inspector Dawson went to the penitentiary to make an inspection and report respecting a certain matter which had been referred to him. After he had concluded his inspection on April 8th, an interview was requested by prisoner 3033 (Hall) and it is during the course of that interview I think it is alleged by the honourable member for Grey-Bruce that certain aspersions were made against her character as stated by her yesterday. I can assure her that there is no foundation for the report. The inspector made no report of the interview—however he has assured me most definitely that the name of the honourable member for Grey-Bruce was never mentioned."

Next day Agnes brought the matter up again. She said she refused to accept the assurance of Inspector Dawson. She read

Hall's affidavit. She related what she had been told by Baynes and by Hall, and said she had the name of a prison guard as witness. She said :

"It does not matter that the incident reflected on me, but it does matter whether any member of this House can be put in the position in which I was placed by this sort of thing."

Guthrie tried his old tactic. He told the House in detail about the confidence games of Alfred George Hall. He protested, smiling, that the honourable lady had been imposed upon by "men of this character".

But at her insistence, he at last reluctantly consented to "appoint a county judge or high court judge of Ontario to undertake an investigation . . . into the truth or falsity of these statements."

Agnes replied, "I shall be very glad to have an investigation into this matter. *But what I want is an investigation by a Royal Commission into the whole penal system in Canada, which is a very much greater thing than anything said about me.*"

Guthrie could do no less than institute an enquiry, since, as he admitted, "the honour of a Member of Parliament is to some extent involved." But the restrictions placed on the enquiry were self-defeating from the outset.

Guthrie appointed Judge E. J. Daly as commissioner for the enquiry, and R. H. Greer as commission counsel. Neither was a stranger to Conservative political circles.

Agnes was not consulted in the preparation of the reference to Judge Daly, and was disappointed to find that he had been charged merely to determine the truth or falsity of Hall's statement that Dawson had uttered the words : "Aggie made a god-damned fool of herself in the House of Commons, but when we are finished with her she will never be able to lift up her head in the House again."

Writing to Justice Minister Guthrie, she asked that the enquiry also consider Baynes' charges, that efforts had been made to have his falsely swear to supplying her with information. And she asked that she be provided with counsel.

Guthrie refused both requests.

The Baynes incident

Agnes protested. The refusal to provide her with counsel was particularly hard to take. She wrote to Guthrie:

"The position is this: the case for the Government, and on behalf of the employees of the Government, will be fully presented to the commission by counsel appointed and paid by the Government, while I, a member of the House of Commons whose honour as a member of the House is involved, must present my own case or pay counsel out of my pocket."

She was not to go without expert counsel. No less a person than J. C. McRuer, now Chief Justice of the High Court of Justice for Ontario, agreed to appear on her behalf, supported by Gerard Beaudoin, K.C., who had known Hall in previous adventures. McRuer charged Agnes nothing at all for his services, and Beaudoin kept his expenses to a minimum.

But despite the able and generous efforts of both lawyers, the enquiry was conducted in a spirit completely hostile to the claims put forward by Miss Macphail.

At the outset McRuer was accused by commission counsel Greer of "political ambitions" in taking the case.

Judge Daly permitted himself considerable sarcasm from the bench and rigidly adhered to the narrow limits of the enquiry, refusing evidence that McRuer tried to introduce.

The newspapers were strongly biased. With Hall on the witness stand, they dwelt at length on his bad record, and when he testified that on hearing Inspector Dawson insult the lady's name he had "threatened to smash him on the nose", the ridiculous posturing of the ex-confidence man got full play in the headlines.

Inspector Dawson was called as witness, and flatly denied the charge. His testimony was contradictory and unconvincing. He admitted having no training in penitentiary matters, no association with penitentiary affairs, until his appointment as inspector two years before, yet now he was Chief Inspector and had in fact served as Acting Superintendent on occasion.

He admitted that he had been sent to Kingston primarily to find out if convict Baynes was supplying Agnes with material she used in Parliament.

This testimony was ignored by the press. The newspapers appeared to avoid the implications of the admission. Who had sent Dawson to get such a statement from Baynes? What use was to be made of Baynes' statement if he had agreed to sign it?

Instead, the newspapers cheapened the affair, suggesting it was all a matter of whether or not an official had called Agnes Macphail "a goddamned fool". Said the St. Thomas *Times-Journal*: "She is making a mountain out of a mole hill. She should forget about it."

Agnes met these trials with fortitude and good spirits. Gerard Beaudoin, whose path did not cross hers again after the enquiry, recalls her buoyant humour. He remembers walks with McRuer and Agnes in the mornings—up Ottawa streets, before the day's proceedings opened. He recalls Agnes joining the two lawyers, McRuer a tall and dignified figure, Beaudoin himself a head shorter, and stepping back to look them up and down and laugh, "Well, what's the long and short of it this morning?"

On the witness stand briefly, Agnes emphasized her interest in an enquiry into general penitentiary conditions. She also told of an attempt by Inspector Dawson to meet her privately, and of how Guthrie, hearing of this, ordered him not to communicate with her.

If Hall had been Agnes' only witness her case against Dawson would have been weak indeed, although she and McRuer and Beaudoin were all persuaded that the expert liar was this time telling the truth.

Other witnesses were sought. The Protestant chaplain, Rev. W. E. Kidd, to whom Hall had taken his story immediately after his interview with Dawson, cautiously refused to become involved.

But a stouter man did come forward. He was Colonel W. B. Megloughlin, who had been warden at Kingston Penitentiary during the incident.

Colonel Megloughlin, who died early in 1958 in Ottawa, was a distinguished soldier and a man of integrity. In 1932, when Kingston convicts rioted and the penitentiary was in a state of siege, he was summoned by the federal Cabinet and urged to step into the emergency as warden. He agreed. He went in, unarmed, to a tense meeting with the convicts. He listened to their demands and, agreeing to several (chief of which was the public trial in criminal court of instigators of the riot), brought the situation under control.

He stayed with his warden's duties less than a year—only long enough to acquire a monumental amazement at the conditions that flourished in Canada's prison system at that time. A short time before his death he recalled the incredible stupidity of a court sentence, commonly imposed, which inflicted ten lashes on a prisoner on entering an institution, detained him there for a period of years ostensibly to reform him, and then inflicted a parting ten lashes on him at the end of his sentence, as a sort of Godspeed into the arms of decent society.

Colonel Megloughlin had in his desk when he died a photograph of Agnes Macphail. It was inscribed, "To Colonel Megloughlin who if allowed would make a prison what it ought to be—a defence for society and a hope for broken men."

Megloughlin was called to the witness stand. Under questioning by counsel McRuer he told the commission that Inspector Dawson had come to Kingston to investigate letters which convict Baynes was alleged to have written to Agnes Macphail. When Dawson arrived, Megloughlin advised him to be careful of any statements he might make to Baynes and Dawson's arrogant reply was that "he had interviewed 300 convicts, and there were no bozos in Kingston pen he couldn't handle."

Megloughlin related that on April 9 Dawson had a long interview with Alfred George Hall, lasting several hours. When he arrived back at the warden's office he remarked that he had gone without lunch, and Megloughlin invited him to tea at the warden's house. Dawson was "excited", apparently uneasy about what had happened. He said he guessed he had made a fool of himself in saying certain things in front of Hall, who was obviously clever and might try to make trouble, and he repeated to Warden Megloughlin his now famous remark about Agnes Macphail.

Megloughlin expressed resentment of Dawson's behaviour in conducting the interview with Hall without having a record taken, and in failing to submit a report to him as warden.

Called to the witness stand also was Rev. Father W. T. Kingsley, the Roman Catholic chaplain at Kingston. His manner impressed reporters as "quiet and deliberate". He told the commission of a conversation with Inspector Dawson after the talk with convict Baynes, when Dawson protested that Baynes was "a notorious liar" and various other things, and threatened to make a report that Baynes "was not and never had suffered from TB".

"I told him I admired his tremendous courage but not his lack of prudence," the padre said, adding that all of Baynes' medical records would be against Dawson.

Father Kingsley, who had worked in penitentiaries for twenty-four years, told the commission bluntly that Inspector Dawson was, like his chief, Superintendent Ormond, "full of conceit, self-opinionated, and holding the belief that experience was not necessary in the conduct of the penitentiary."

He said sadly, "I have seen so much inexperience, and the wreck that inexperience could make of the morale of the Kingston Penitentiary. It was very depressing and was becoming an appalling condition of affairs."

There were other interesting bits of evidence. Harry Anderson from the Toronto *Globe* was at hand, and tried to have the commission take note of a conversation he had overheard between two penitentiary guards, one cautioning the other to be careful if he were called to testify, since "the boss wants to land Aggie". But this bit of eavesdropping was not admitted.

The commission of enquiry sat for nearly two weeks in Ottawa, moved to Kingston for a further hearing, and then adjourned.

The report when it appeared some weeks later could satisfy only the most cynical. The testimony of Hall was apparently considered unreliable because of his character, but *the corroborating evidence of Colonel Megloughlin was completely ignored*. Inspector Dawson had not, in Judge Daly's opinion,

The Baynes incident

said to Alfred George Hall, "Aggie made a goddamned fool
. . . etc." The case was closed.

Yet what had happened? A great many tongues had
wagged, a great many columns of newsprint had been filled,
and despite every effort to prevent it, the result had been a
widespread impression that there was a scandalous mismanagement in the penitentiaries system, that a breath of clean air was
needed, that a full-scale enquiry had become essential.

In this Agnes accomplished her main purpose.

Eighteen

The dark prison house

"No man has the *right*," Agnes Macphail said, 'to deprive another of space, and light, and air!'"

She had broken her way through many prison walls in her own forty-odd years. She had refused to be confined and restrained by a rural environment, by her sex, by a political climate that did not favour her reform ideas. She felt an instinctive horror of restraint, and her intense concern over prison problems followed directly from this emotional bias.

Moreover, Agnes Macphail had the ability, which in extreme is almost a disability, to identify herself completely with another person and his hopes and needs. E. B. Jolliffe, with whom she was to work in close association a few years later in the Ontario Legislature, saw through her gruff disguise and said of her that she was always a little afraid of being betrayed by her own soft heart.

She had visited the women's section of Kingston Penitentiary when she addressed the House of Commons in February, 1934, and she said, "As I faced those women I did not feel myself different from them; I simply felt that I had been in much more fortunate circumstances."

Agnes Macphail's greatest work, in a long and busy public career, was in the field of penitentiary reform. When the challenge of this urgent problem confronted her, she was at first extremely reluctant to plunge in. She liked her parliamentary role as the doughty champion of Ontario farmers; she was busy enough with this, and most at home. But the crying need for penal reform touched her conscience, and she could not pass it by.

In January 1938, when the Archambault Royal Commission made its report, Canada's seven federal penitentiaries contained a convict population of 3,250, and the fact that the penal system was failing in its purpose was obvious at first glance, for 72 per cent of these convicts were back in prison for a second, or third, or even a tenth time.

In terms of cost alone, this situation was serious, for each conviction was estimated to involve a cost of $1200, and the cost of maintaining a prisoner in a penitentiary for the average term of eight years and two months was $5,984.83. Recidivism is expensive.

The Archambault Commission concluded as a result of its exhaustive study that the figure of 72 per cent could be dramatically reduced by introducing modern methods of penology. Among its major recommendations were an adult probation system, classification and segregation of prisoners, proper reformative treatment, a *trained* staff, and well-organized schemes of rehabilitation on release. On all these counts, the penitentiaries of Canada were woefully lacking.

The Commission uncovered some very shocking conditions. There was, for example, the matter of the "criminally insane". If a prisoner was discovered to be insane, the penitentiaries sought to have him transferred to a mental institution (and thereby from federal to provincial authority). But provincial governments protested, partly from simple lack of accommodation at their mental hospitals, partly because of an obscure distinction between the "criminally insane" and other mental patients. The result was that in many cases the provinces refused to accept custody of insane prisoners, and the penitentiaries were obliged to keep them, as the Report states : "caged like wild beasts, where there is neither means for proper treatment nor personnel with experience to deal with them".

The entire penal system was characterized by a dreary purposelessness, a lack of constructive policy or practice. Idleness and silence were the absolute frustration to which all prisoners were condemned. Seventeen hours out of every day were spent completely alone, locked in their cells, where every occupation, even so innocent as a crossword puzzle or plaiting a cellophane picture frame, was forbidden, and if a man should be caught in this offence he was subject to punishment. Talk between prisoners and guards except relating to the carrying out of orders was prohibited just as strictly—there was no opportunity, even if a guard were so inclined, to speak any helpful word to a prisoner serving a prison term. In some institutions a corrupt "spy" system using favoured prisoners kept the air vile with suspicion and hostility.

Shop work, equipment and space for teaching a trade, and ordinary schoolroom facilities were wretchedly inadequate or non-existent. In several penitentiaries the younger prisoners who might have benefited most from learning a trade were not allowed in the shops at all because this would bring them into contact with habitual criminals, and this solicitude was the only example of practical segregation discovered by the Commission.

The sixteen riots that exploded behind penitentiary walls between 1932 and 1937 can be traced in large part to the militaristic, "paper" régime set up by Superintendent D. M. Ormond, who shortly after his appointment by the Bennett Government, and without any consultation with his more experienced wardens, issued a volume of 724 regulations to be enforced forthwith.

Though it seems incredible, permission had to be obtained from Superintendent Ormond in Ottawa to replace a five-cent scribbler, or to paint the benches in a mail-bag department, or to buy hinges worth 16 cents for a storm window. One extract from the Report will serve to illustrate :

"In the summer of 1935, a farm at Dorchester penitentiary became overstocked with young pigs. The farm instructor found it necessary, because of the lack of facilities, to keep about 85 in one pen where in a few weeks, many of them became lame, and it appeared that a large number would be lost. However, some wire, which had been purchased for a line fence, was available because it was not yet required for that use. In order to

The dark prison house

save the pigs the farm instructor utilized this wire to divide the pigs into a number of pens and, as a result, saved the entire number. Immediately the emergency had been met he submitted a requisition for more wire.

"When the Superintendent learned that the farm instructor had saved a considerable loss of penitentiary property by utilizing the wire, however, he wrote severely censuring both the warden and the farm instructor because they had not first written to him for permission to use it for another purpose than that for which it had been purchased. If the farm instructor had been as punctilious as the Superintendent in observing strict formalities, $700 worth of pigs would have sickened, and a great majority of them would have died. Correspondence on the subject was maintained for an entire year before the incident was closed."

Small wonder that turn-over in staff during Ormond's regime proceeded at a dizzy rate, and of his three inspectors two soon resigned. One replacement was Inspector Dawson, Ormond's right-hand man, who became publicly involved in an enquiry concerning Agnes Macphail, and who was described in the Archambault Report as *possibly a good accountant* (since that had been his occupation prior to appointment) but without "the capacity or temperament to fulfil the important office of inspector". The Report recommended that he be transferred to other duties.

If the multitudinous rules harassed the officials, they were much harder on the prisoners. In the words of the Report: "The Regulations provide so many trivial offences that may be punished in a drastic manner that it is almost impossible for prisoners to avoid committing some punishable breach of the rules."

Discipline was severe. Trial of prisoners for misconduct while in prison was held in the warden's court, under a procedure which appeared to the commission to be open to abuse. Punishment by shackling was gradually eliminated but had been common, and the prisoner's hands were usually shackled, not at waist height as Justice Minister Lapointe had once informed Miss Macphail, but high above his head. Paddling was inflicted not with a light strap but with a cruel leather instrument three and a half feet long and perforated with a number of holes that drew the skin in such a way that flesh could be, and in some cases was, torn from the prisoner's body. This instrument was applied to a man stripped naked and bent over a table, to which his legs were tied.

A most invidious fact contained in the Archambault Report was the secrecy surrounding the activities of the Penitentiaries Branch, the misinformation given by Superintendent Ormond to the Minister of Justice, Mr. Guthrie, and hence to Parliament and the country.

Thus in 1935 Superintendent Ormond paid a visit to England and on his return, on August 10th, issued a report blandly asserting that a program modelled on Britain's Borstal system was "presently being put into effect". This was in due course proclaimed to the House of Commons by Justice Minister Guthrie, and yet, in fact, *nothing remotely resembling the Borstal system was even proposed for Canadian penitentiaries.*

Again, the Commission discovered so little evidence of any practical training and educational program for prisoners, that one might say there was nothing at all—yet reports were constantly being published to suggest that a well-organized training program was in actual operation. The Report made this point :

"It has not been uncommon to read in the press that judges and magistrates, in sending young prisoners to penitentiary, have declared that they are sending them 'where they will learn a trade'. The gravity of publishing reports that mislead the public in this manner requires no further comment."

The wave of prisoner demonstrations and rioting mounted from the time of General Ormond's appointment.

Agnes Macphail first introduced the need for penal reform into Commons debate in 1925, while she was still a first-term Member of the House. She urged a productive work programme in penitentiaries to keep prisoners usefully occupied and to help offset the costs of the establishment. Her resolution was lost, but

The dark prison house

in 1926 when she introduced it again in a more receptive political atmosphere it won government approval and was passed.

In the sessions of 1927 and 1928 she found occasion to urge the implementation of that resolution, and she drew attention to the generally unsatisfactory efforts of the penal system to *reform*, as well as to punish, our lawbreakers.

In 1929 she brought the case of one convict directly to the attention of the Government, demanding an investigation. This was the death of a prisoner at Stony Mountain, in circumstances which suggested negligence by the authorities.

In 1931 she was back on a new tack, protesting the patronage method of hiring prison officials. Most of them were appointed, she said, "not because they are trained in penology, but because they happen to be the brother, the cousin or the brother-in-law of some person in authority."

She spoke again during the 1933 session on the imperative need for a more constructive approach to the whole prison problem.

And in 1934, having received an overwhelming abundance of proof that conditions were bad throughout the prison system, she brought in a resolution urging the Government to make a special investigation. The treatment she received at the hands of the Minister of Justice when she presented this request, has already been described.

In this major address in the House of Commons, on February 14, 1934, Agnes reviewed the work of previous commissions of investigation in 1914 and 1920, and pointed out that little or no attention had been paid to their recommendations.

She urged several specific reform measures. Prisoners ought to be classified as soon as admitted, according to their capabilities and previous training. The warden must be assisted in this work by a trained psychiatrist. (No psychiatrists were at that time attached to the staffs of any of the penitentiaries.) There must follow the attempt to use the prisoner's term of incarceration "to educate him to a better condition".

Work must be provided. "Every effort must be made to induce him to like some kind of work." And some slight payment for his labour, some tangible return, should go toward the support of his dependents in the world outside. "There is no doubt at all," Agnes said, "that the man who is in prison and is no longer in any way responsible for his family is apt, if he is a good type, to feel disgraced and, if he is not a good type, to feel relieved. In either case it is very much better for him if the responsibility for his family remains his own, and if he knows that by his own work he can discharge it."

Health measures and sanitation at the penitentiaries were intolerable. Sterilization of instruments used in the barber shops was completely unknown, to quote one small item from a shocking list.

The too severe and too frequent punishments for infraction of rules must be modified. And a new system of parole, and of supervised readjustment to civilian life, was urgently required.

Concluding her address that afternoon (just before Justice Minister Guthrie launched his poison shaft), Agnes said, "While society must be protected and the offender punished, unless these men come out with a social consciousness, society is really punishing itself rather than the criminal. This is the changed viewpoint which up until now has not expressed itself in legislation, regulations or administration."

The House was side-tracked, then, by Guthrie's recital of the criminal record of a tubercular prisoner whom Agnes had "spoken well of". Her motion for a complete investigation of the penitentiaries did not come to a vote, but the Minister had made it obvious that he did not endorse the move. He also quoted a refusal given by his leader, Prime Minister R. B. Bennett, when "on two occasions Red-tinged groups asked him to appoint royal commissions."

To urge an investigation, then, was to run the risk of being called Communist.

While Parliament was still in session, during the winter and spring of 1934, several more prison disturbances occurred, especially at Kingston. Deliberately, Guthrie avoided bringing down the estimates for his department (which would give members an opportunity for debate) until June 25th, in the final week of the session. By this time several sensational incidents had been featured in the press, and Agnes Macphail was ready, as soon as the opportunity came, to carry the attack in the Commons.

Speaking on June 25th, she questioned the minister closely about the death of a Kingston convict, Sam Behan, alone and unattended, in an isolation cell, one month before. He had been paddled for creating a disturbance in his cell, he had been confined to isolation and there had died, of coronary thrombosis according to report.

She questioned the Government about the "wholesale punishment" meted out in April, after convicts had staged a protest demonstration to coincide with a visit from the Governor-General. Twenty-two men were reported to have been paddled on that night, without proper trial procedure.

And lastly she protested against the absurd practice of compulsory attendance at Sunday chapel, where the chaplain was protected by an armed guard while delivering his sermon.

"Unless we intend to make our penitentiaries simply whipping institutions and places of vengeance, we should try to get these things in harmony," Agnes concluded. "It is not possible to bring people to an understanding of the gospel, of the philosophy of love, at the point of a gun."

The House rose before the Justice Department estimates were passed; they were left over again until the last possible moment, on June 30th. Then Agnes was on her feet again. She protested the lateness of the debate, the obvious intention of the Government to prevent discussion of prison matters. She pressed for more information—about the case of one John O'Brien, held in solitary confinement for two years without any charge being formally laid against him; about the firing of shots deliberately and directly into the cell of Tim Buck, Communist leader, during an earlier riot.

"I feel that the Government of Canada should no longer refuse to have an impartial investigation. If they do, the responsibility must be entirely on the shoulders of the Administration."

To this the Minister made the astonishing reply that he really couldn't give her an answer, because the Governor-General was on his way to Parliament Hill to dissolve the House.

There was a flurry of indignation among Members at this choking off of debate. J. S. Woodsworth protested strongly. Guthrie curtly agreed to postpone progrogation, and the session was extended another day.

Guthrie was thus obliged to make reply, and his defence was not convincing. He attempted to throw some blame on Warden Megloughlin, who had now resigned but who had during his brief régime introduced baseball games during exercise periods at Kingston and allowed inmates to talk to each other during recreation hours. The ball games had been discontinued and Superintendent Ormond recommended that talking be once more prohibited. Guthrie cited Megloughlin's short-lived reforms with disapproval. The remainder of his speech was a denial of the "lurid charges" of various published reports.

Agnes spoke again, before the final bell. She admitted a few minor improvements in the prison routine as a result of a great deal of public protest. The heads of inmates were no longer shaved, for example. But she had still a formidable list of basic reforms, and these she put on record again.

She summed up, "It is in the public interest to have an impartial investigation, which in all probability will result in far-reaching recommendations, that will change the spirit of our penitentiaries."

This time she got scattered support from members of other parties in the House, and several briefly added their request for a Royal Commission. But the House prorogued with no further reply from the Government.

Speaking engagements at far-flung points, and the activities of the new C.C.F. party, kept Agnes extremely busy during the remainder of 1934. But prison reform was not forgotten as she addressed women's clubs, university students, farmers, and various other audiences throughout Canada and the United States. She also found time to *learn*, to read all that she could of penitentiary reports and treatises.

The 1935 session was the final round in Bennett's inadequate

The dark prison house

attempt to browbeat the Depression out of existence. There were exciting political development in many fields, but Agnes did not let the cause of penal reform fade from the public mind. Her first encounter with the Government, in March 1935, was the personal issue of the offence against her by Inspector Dawson, and the enquiry into this incident received considerable play in the press, though not much of it was favourable.

The Baynes and Dawson affair was quite incidental, in Agnes' view, to the main cause. Whenever she was on her feet, battling with Guthrie for a fair settlement of this account, she seized the opportunity to repeat her demand for a Royal Commission.

"But what about a penal system," she demanded, "marked by demonstrations and riots and fires from one end of the Dominion to the other? . . . Yet the department headed by the Minister will not have an investigation into the penal system of Canada!"

On June 15 she called attention to a new fire outbreak, with $35,000 damage, at Kingston Penitentiary.

On this occasion Guthrie commented brusquely, "Regarding the question of a commission . . . I am proud to say that Canadian penitentiaries today stand higher than or as high as those of any other country in the world."

He defended Superintendent Ormond. He also announced that the long-desired practice of *paying* inmates for their labour had now been introduced! Prisoners would henceforth earn five cents a day or thirty cents a week. Of course, it was now necessary to charge them for their tobacco, at the rate of thirteen and a half cents a week. And a prisoner might now accumulate up to thirty or forty dollars against the day of his discharge—but if he accumulated anything, of course, he no longer received the ten dollars which had formerly been handed to him free!

It was during the debate that day, June 15, 1935, that another Conservative, a certain Mr. Bell from Hamilton, served as spokesman for some of the opposition and criticism which Agnes Macphail had to face in this difficult struggle.

He began with exaggerated "sweet talk"—"the honourable member's great womanly sympathy", "her trusting nature", "her sweet femininity".

Agnes growled, loud enough for Hansard reporters to hear and duly record, "Cut out the cant."

Bell then regaled the House with a story to the effect that when Agnes had toured the penitentiary she came upon a group of inmates who piously began to sing, "Abide with me."

This was the level of counter-attack.

Agnes had now inspected both Kingston and St. Vincent de Paul penitentiaries. She detailed for the House the impressions of her visit. She invited members to consider the sage opinions of Thomas Nott Osborne, outstanding penologist. She quoted Honourable W. P. Nickle, a former Attorney-General of Ontario, who had joined her in advocating a Royal Commission. She went over again the list of most urgently needed reforms, including segregation, useful work, trained guards, attendant psychiatrists, a parole system, and so on. She pounded home the continuing urgent need.

Again she was joined in her demands by several other members, including one very significant name. Ernest Lapointe, former Minister of Justice and now in the Opposition benches, asked the Government to consider Miss Macphail's request. In a very few months Lapointe would be back on the Government side again, in a position to grant what Guthrie had withheld.

And so it turned out. A fall election in 1935 removed Bennett from the Prime Minister's office and Hugh Guthrie from the job of Minister of Justice. And Mackenzie King's new Administration gauged the weight of public demand and decided that reform action could be taken with majority approval—a nice point that Mr. King was most adept at defining.

Ernest Lapointe, in February, 1936, announced the appointment of a Royal Commission to Investigate the Penal System of Canada.

The learned chairman of the commission was Justice Joseph Archambault, and appointed to serve with him were R. W. Craig and Harry Anderson. Agnes was especially delighted that the hard-fighting *Globe* editor was made a commissioner. And Anderson wrote to her (March 2, 1936): "Accept my hearty congratulations on the vindication of your courageous course in placing the need for prison reform before Parliament and the public and in bringing about the proposed investigation."

But bad luck dogged the commission as it got under way. Mr. Justice Archambault met with two successive severe accidents that kept him in hospital. And on April 28, Harry Anderson died suddenly in Toronto.

There was delay in choosing a successor to Anderson. After some deliberation the name of J. C. McRuer was proposed, and Agnes, remembering his generous efforts on her behalf during the Dawson enquiry, was delighted with the choice and wired McRuer urging him to accept. But to another acquaintance she sent a wry note:

"We have certainly had a run of bad luck. Archambault, the chairman, having two legs broke both of them—I am sure if he had more they would have gone also. Harry Anderson, in whom we settled our hopes, died, and after that the editor of the *London Free Press,* who also recently departed this life, was to have been appointed to the commission. I believe now McRuer, the lawyer who gratuitously acted as counsel for me in the minor investigation a year ago, is to be offered the third place. Much as I want him to accept it, one fears for him if he does."

The commission surmounted these difficulties and began hearings in October, 1936. Its recommendations, after a year and a half of study, were far-reaching and bore out to a remarkable extent the reforms that Agnes Macphail had urged for so many years.

"Complete reorganization" was proposed, including the placing of authority in a prison commission instead of in the superintendent. (Ormond was to be dismissed; this was put into effect immediately.) A training school for penitentiary officers was to be established, and their pay was to be "brought up to a reasonable standard".

Classification and segregation of prisoners were recommended, and prisons were no longer to be required to house, indiscriminately, the insane, the mentally deficient, and the recidivist drug addict.

Discipline was to be greatly modified, and corporal punishment abolished except for major specific acts of violence within the prison. The new discipline was to emphasize "a firm dignity" with "no place in it for weak sentimentality or for cruel severity".

The educational system, the medical service, the prison industries, were all to be "completely reorganized" along constructive lines. A probation system was recommended, new rehabilitation measures were proposed, and numerous other detailed recommendations would serve as a guide to future government action.

The report was tabled in Parliament in April, 1938. It remains an outstandingly civilized document, a most valuable contribution to progress in Canada's penal system. It must, however, be assessed as a blueprint for reforms which have only begun to be realized, even today. Penal reform is not a closed book. The great significance of the Archambault Report was the light it shed into dark corners.

The copy that arrived at Agnes' desk had this inscription: "To Miss Agnes Macphail, M.P., courageous pioneer and untiring worker on behalf of prison reform in Canada. Joseph Archambault."

This major achievement is on public record, and all who look at the history of Canada's penal institutions will recognize the contribution made by Agnes Macphail. But what can never be known, because no record was kept, are the many personal acts of charity and sympathy that this woman extended to the individual men and women whose lives were marred by a prison term.

Her secretary from 1935 on, Miss Lilla Bell, has recalled one of the many. On this occasion it was a young man, recently released from a penitentiary in Western Canada, who had come to Ontario in a vain search for work, and on the way, riding the freights, had met with an accident. One foot had been injured and had received no medical attention, so that it remained swollen and deformed and was wrapped in a clumsy bandage. He came to Agnes' office to ask her to help him find a job. She knew before she answered the door that he was another ex-con, for now she recognized the knock, the peculiarly diffident and defiant approach of a man who has small hope left in him. She invited him in and heard his story. She picked up the phone and made several calls, hoping to find an opening for him as a chauffeur. She then phoned an Ottawa shoemaker asking him to fit the man with a special last so that he could once more wear a shoe on his injured foot. When the bill came Agnes herself would pay it. This ex-convict left, with some money from Agnes' purse to tide him over. Then Agnes turned back to her desk and suddenly gave way to tears. Even now, after hearing it so often, the hardship of the people who sought her help was not "an old story".

Miss Bell found a news item a short time later in an Ottawa paper, which she took care not to show to her employer. The young ex-convict had been arrested for stealing a car, and was on his way back to jail.

Sometimes assistance brought a genuine change for the better in a troubled life; sometimes it seemed to accomplish little. Agnes was always upset by the ungrateful and unreformed, but never to the point where she could turn away the next suppliant.

However, there was one notorious criminal of that period with whom her name was quite unjustly linked, for there was a widespread impression that she was partly responsible for his parole.

The man was "Red" Ryan, a psychopath who managed to convince prison authorities completely of his reformed character, and who was released on parole, amid considerable fanfare, in July 1935. It is said that Prime Minister R. B. Bennett was personally responsible for parole being granted, so convinced was he of a metamorphosis in this criminal. But a few months later Ryan was killed in the act of holding up a bank. In the gun battle he had killed a young Sarnia policeman.

Agnes' chief concern was that this ill-judged case would prejudice the system of parole, as in fact it did. Public reaction was violent, and Agnes came in for quite unjustified abuse. Letters addressed to "You wretched woman" accused her of "coddling crooks and criminals", blamed her for the death of the policeman and the grief of the policeman's family, and denounced her as an "hysterical sob-sister". Agnes requested and received an official letter from the Remissions Branch asserting that she had never made a request for Ryan's parole, but this sober truth was noticed by few. As an outspoken advocate of prison reform, she must bear the blame when acts of mercy miscarried.

Writing to a sister of Harry Anderson, Agnes said, "The kindest thing we can think is that he [Ryan] was not wholly responsible. It is most unfortunate that he was ever paroled because his rash act has set back penal reform by many years."

Privately, and in the Parliament of Canada as long as she remained a Member, Agnes continued to strive for better treatment of prisoners. Her work extended into her later years, to her terms in the Ontario Legislature and almost to the time of her death.

The final word of tribute can be left with those most truly concerned with all she sought to do. In February 1958 a special issue of the Kingston Penitentiary *Telescope*, a publication written by the inmates, published these words:

"As inmates, most of us are prone to take for granted the privileges we have today, without remembering that it was not always so in this penitentiary. However, those of us who suffered from day to day and lifted our eyes to 'Aggie', as she fought for humane treatment of inmates, know that it was not always so and quietly revere and bless her memory, which the passing years have not dimmed.

"Aggie is dead but lives on in the hearts of countless prison inmates who knew her and loved her. When the bell tolled for Aggie on February 13, 1954, it tolled for the inmates of every Canadian penitentiary."

The dark prison house

Nineteen

The cause of labour too

In 1935, at the eleventh hour of his term as Prime Minister, R. B. Bennett had a sudden change of heart. As election time loomed near, he astonished the nation with a series of radio broadcasts setting out eight sweeping reforms to safeguard the rights of labour and bolster the purchasing power of the people. Many dismissed the whole grandiose scheme as mere window-dressing, inspired by panic—especially after much of the legislation was subsequently disallowed by the courts on constitutional grounds. Agnes told a Newmarket audience that the Prime Minister "is five years too late with his speeches. Those speeches show how powerful the C.C.F. has become."

But M. J. Coldwell was sure that Bennett had been persuaded by the arguments of his brother-in-law, W. D. Herridge, at that time a minister to Washington and apparently under the influence of Roosevelt's "New Deal". There was a private meeting to which A. A. Heaps, the C.C.F. member for Winnipeg North, was summoned, to his immense surprise. The Prime Minister questioned him bluntly, almost naïvely. Minimum wages, the forty-eight-hour week, unemployment insurance— were these really the answer to the depression? Heaps' answer was sincerely given : these things were indeed the answer, the only possible solution. And Bennett's decision was very typical of the man : "If the system needs changing, *I* will change it."

When the eight pieces of legislation were rammed through Parliament, in the early spring of 1935, Agnes expressed considerable doubt and apprehension. Her farm bias, her cautious rural approach to any change that might adversely affect her

215

own kind, prompted her to speak sharply against the eight-hour-day bill that her C.C.F. colleagues were supporting.

"I cannot sit and listen without entering a very vigorous protest," she said.

"What are the farmers getting out of this much-talked-of reform program? They are getting the chance of a loan from the $90,000,000 [Farm Loan] fund, at a rate of interest that will probably be at least 5% and may be $5\frac{1}{2}$%.

"At the bottom you have a group like the fishermen and the farmers, who are hardly organized at all, and they have to pay all this increased cost—because there is no use blinking the fact that such legislation as that for a minimum wage, an eight-hour day and unemployment insurance puts additional weight on the backs of the already burdened unorganized primary producers. . . . We have many groups in this country, and our program should be a balanced program. The farmers were here first, they were the pioneers who cleared the land and opened up the West; let us not now serve them last."

J. S. Woodsworth had just delivered a vigorous speech urging the Government to carry through the eight-hour-day legislation. He had made mention of the farmers, but with a touch of impatience had advised them to "use their heads" and "organize". Taking a rather remote and visionary view, he argued, "It is quite possible on the farm to have two shifts or if necessary three, just as they have in industry."

Practical Agnes could not swallow that bit of high-flown idealism.

"The Honourable Member for Winnipeg North Centre, much as I respect him, talks about two or three shifts on a farm, when the farmer, with himself and his family working themselves nearly to death, cannot break even—and after all, it is today we are living in, and this bill is being passed today to regulate hours of work which are going on from this day forward. The farmers could no more think of putting on double or treble shifts than flying to the moon! . . .

"They know just a little bit more about hard work and about saving than any other large group of people; they are an admir-

The cause of labour too

able class in the national life of Canada, and I think it is not going too far to say that they are the bedrock of our whole national life. Therefore, although I hope for an eight-hour day and I would welcome a four-hour day instead of fourteen, as we have it in this House—I feel that we have now altogether too much disequilibrium between the country and the city."

Thus spoke the farmer's daughter, out of a deeply ingrained loyalty to her own people and out of the hard memory of farm days, of the daily round of chores from sun-up to sun-down, and the steaming drudgery of a farm wife's kitchen.

The press, of course, seized on the exchange with relish. Agnes was fulsomely praised by editors for her "horse sense" in joining their attack on the outrageous eight-hour day. Mackenzie King commented with considerable pleasure that the House had now heard the "two opposing views of the Co-operative Commonwealth Federation on social legislation".

She probably did not go so far as to regret that impulsive speech, for Agnes seldom bothered to repent what might prove to be politically unwise. But it is quite wrong to conclude that she was anti-labour, for many of her statements, obviously quite as sincere as those on the farmers' behalf, prove otherwise.

In fact, as early as January, 1926, during a parliamentary debate on Glace Bay mining conditions, Agnes Macphail went on record :

" I think the labour men, the miners, should be given every opportunity to organize, and that the almost contemptuous propaganda that has been circulated against class organization in this country should cease. The miners have just as much right to organize and to work aggressively for better living conditions as have the manufacturers or bankers or farmers or any other class group."

These were no doubt her "official" views, her reasoned approach to labour problems, strongly influenced by her C.C.F. associates J. S. Woodsworth, Angus MacInnis and A. A. Heaps. Later it was to be more fully confirmed.

There was great political ferment in 1935 ; many people were discontented with the conduct of both major parties but unwilling to get into anything so radical as the C.C.F. The Reconstruction Party under H. H. Stevens took a brief canter in Canadian politics at this time, and there was a move towards a "League for National Government". The papers wanted to know what Agnes Macphail thought of these things. She said she had not been approached by the League for National Government, but that she was not only not interested in a Liberal-Conservative coalition, which was what she considered this, but was very wary about a party with George Drew and George McCullagh in it at the top.

Her riding executive flirted with the idea of supporting the Reconstruction Party. To many people it looked like a genuine reform movement; to others it was just a group of disgruntled Conservatives putting on pressure. Agnes was wary about this, too, and the executive decided that she was in a position to help Mr. Stevens whenever she agreed with him, but should not get involved with the organization.

On September 16 a story appeared in the Toronto morning paper announcing that Agnes had endorsed the program of the Reconstruction Party in its entirety at a meeting in Ceylon. This was apparently based on the fact that the Grey-Bruce executive had decided to write a letter to the new party thanking them for not running a candidate in opposition to Agnes. The *Toronto Star* promptly checked with Agnes by telephone. She was indignant. "It is quite the other way," she said. "They have endorsed me by not opposing me."

The election campaign of 1935 turned out to be a tougher proposition than any of the previous ones. This time she faced two opponents. Her former riding had been altered to include a part of Bruce riding—as it happened, the most *Liberal* part of Bruce riding. Dr. Walter Hall of Walkerton, who had been the Liberal M.P. for Bruce in the previous House, was nominated to run against her. The Conservative candidate, Dr. Lewis Campbell, she had beaten before and expected to beat again. But her fighting blood was up as she matched campaigns with Dr. Hall.

On nomination day a joint meeting was arranged, accord-

The cause of labour too

ing to custom, in the centre of Durham. Agnes marched to the platform bearing a very large stack of Hansards, the official record of parliamentary debates. Pink slips protruded from the pages to mark the times she had spoken on the floor of the House; one lone marker showed Dr. Hall's contribution to the work of Parliament. She "threw back in his teeth" a statement attributed to Hall a few days earlier—that Agnes secretly received Liberal campaign funds. And as for his insinuations that she was against the Catholics and against separate schools —she absolutely denied both charges, and it was a provincial matter anyway. Candidate Hall did not appear on that platform on nomination day; he had his own reasons, doubtless, for remaining absent.

Now Agnes had two foes to battle, and her position as an independent to defend. She discussed the "terrible economic conditions" revealed by Stevens' Price Spreads Report—"yet Mr. Bennett sat pat and talked much, while as for Mr. King he sat pat and said nothing—which he does superbly."

Bennett would be swept out of power, she predicted confidently. But she had this sober reflection to make about "Sir Richard" : "He is a very clever man. If he had had to work harder when he was a young man, probably on the farm forking hay or something like that, he would be a very great man. . . . But Bennett and King live remote lives, so that they cannot be in sympathy with the average person."

Conservative candidate Campbell, striving feebly to stem the tide, persuaded the ladies to organize a meeting on his behalf in Chesley. The ladies were not very effective. Their main speaker said sweetly, "It would be a dreadful thing for Canada if we were to turn out Mr. Bennett. Miss Macphail is a very fine person but she is not exactly the best person to represent this riding. She is absolutely alone in the House. There is nothing she can do. I would urge your support for Dr. Campbell."

To this Agnes roared back, to a packed hall at Paisley, to a large crowd which came through pouring rain to hear her :

"Some of the finest bridge players in Canada are old-party members of the House of Commons, who retire to the lobby and play bridge really seriously—while the independents struggle to help the people."

And when the votes were in, Agnes had beaten both her opponents very handily. To her 7,210 votes, Dr. Hall had polled 5,727 and Dr. Campbell 5,100.

Bennett's last-minute social welfare legislation did not impress the voters, who threw out his government with a vengeance. Conservative strength in the House was cut to 39, and King led his Liberals back into office with a comfortable 171. The Conservatives were so soundly beaten that they would not rally again until long past the days of Agnes Macphail.

In this election the new C.C.F. party fared badly also, electing only seven members, while such stalwart United Farmers of Alberta members as Robert Gardiner and H. E. Spencer went down to defeat.

The old labels, United Farmers and Progressive, all but disappeared from the political scene. Agnes Macphail, the "freak" woman member who had arrived in Ottawa on the crest of the Progressive tide, was the only survivor of that spent political force.

On October 17 the Walkerton *Herald Times* commented in picturesque fashion on the election results:

"There was a prediction made by skeptics in 1921 that the U.F.O. would soon peter out, until its Ontario representation would be able to ride to Ottawa on a bicycle. In fourteen years that prediction has come true, and Agnes Macphail rides the bicycle. . . . Her victory at the polls is a personal triumph."

She had successfully contested five elections. She went back to Ottawa for a new term of office, during which she was to demonstrate her full powers as a parliamentarian.

Agnes was to discover from this time forward that no politician living in Ontario can hold aloof from labour's problems. As she became more personally involved, she was quick to take the side of the workers. Shortly she was heard exclaiming in the House that "a really mediaeval attitude toward organized labour" existed in a furniture plant in her riding, where she had

The cause of labour too

learned of "men with wives and families losing their jobs because they wanted to organize".

By 1937 the anti-labour policies of Mitchell Hepburn forced most politicians to take sides, and Agnes plumped for labour. In June that year she declared, "Large-scale organization of labour is inevitable. . . . While I regret the loss of life in connection with the steel strike in the United States, it is nothing compared to the sacrifice of human life before mass organization of labour started. Workers paid a terrible toll in premature deaths, injuries, and killing fear of losing their jobs, before unionization began."

It was a sad blow when her protégé, Farquhar Oliver, fell that summer under Hepburn's spell. The dynamic young Liberal Premier had come into power on a sweeping wave of reform and new ideas. For a few years his star shone brightly, and then fizzled out. Agnes was caustic about him. She coupled him with Duplessis of Quebec, and indeed they were much alike in their passion for provincial autonomy, their running battles with the Federal Government (some Liberals claim the party in Ontario was destroyed by this split), their contempt for labour, and their high-handed methods. When they tried to tell the House of Commons how to vote on a matter involving hydro-electric power, Agnes commented on their presumption : "Imagine! The very idea of that precious pair telling us what to do ! They make the decisions for these two provinces, they have their photographs taken with their smiling faces and their double chins. These two silly little Mussolinis and Hitlers." (She called Hepburn a "tinpot Mussolini" several times.)

There was a rumour that Farquhar Oliver might be offered a cabinet post in the Hepburn government. The U.F.O. as a political force was very dead, and Oliver was far more alone in the Ontario Legislature than Agnes Macphail was at Ottawa. Agnes had separated herself only technically from the C.C.F., and she had the comfortable feeling of companionship. But she could not excuse Oliver. To her, his side-slipping into support of Hepburn was one more—and the most heart-breaking—

instance of the independent farm member being seduced by the Liberals.

During the provincial election campaign of 1937, the defection was only a rumour supported by Oliver's friendliness towards the Liberals, in and out of the legislature. Agnes made it very clear that she was supporting Oliver but not Hepburn. She blasted the latter thoroughly for his labour policy; she called his behaviour in sending tanks in to a strike situation in Oshawa "fascism".

Oliver was holding joint meetings with the "Liberal-Progressive" candidate in North Grey. Agnes called this, ironically, "international border relations between two ridings", and promptly set up her own border relations by turning up at a C.C.F. meeting in Owen Sound, where King Gordon was the speaker. She was invited to the platform, and accepted the invitation. She said, "I came, not with the intention of being on the platform, but to listen to at least one intelligent speech in the provincial campaign."

It was not until after Agnes' defeat in 1940 that Oliver made the formal move to the Liberals, becoming a cabinet minister and, later, leader of the party provincially. Agnes never saw him alone after that time. She seldom talked about him, but when she did she was bitter, in a way she was never bitter about Elmore Philpott. The cruelest thing she ever said was, "Farquhar was always afraid of being too far out in front—he need not have worried!"

Twenty

On the crest

Agnes Macphail's best all-round work in the House of Commons was undoubtedly done during her fifth term, from 1935 to 1940.

She had hit her stride. Her skill in debate, her clear and provocative presentation, now commanded respect on every side. When her tall straight figure rose in the Chamber and her deep voice called, "Mr. Speaker. . . ." members stayed in their seats to listen, and not from chivalry.

These were her last four years in Parliament.

Now, after all the early mockery had died away and the trials arising from her inexperience had been lived down, she established the truth that being a woman need not hold back a good Member of Parliament.

Her voice was heard on every occasion, arguing social reform. She urged health insurance : "Certainly it is the human and civilized way of going about the matter and the sooner we do it the better."

Subsidized low-rental housing : "Good housing for all the people is the greatest investment we can make."

Scholarships, which, she observed, were already common practice in other countries such as Great Britain, Japan, the United States, Australia and New Zealand : "Unless we follow suit we are going to be placed in a very unfavourable light and naturally hinder our development."

Improved Old Age Pensions, and pensions for the blind : "I have never felt very comfortable about the fact that we as a country have not been able to do anything toward taking care of our blind fellow citizens. We as a Parliament ought to be ashamed to say that we cannot afford to take care of the blind when they need care."

When a pension for the blind was passed she turned to another group : "I am thinking particularly of people who are so crippled that they are unable to sit, and must lie prone; of others who can sit but cannot walk; and yet others who can walk only a few steps"—the crippled victims of rheumatism and arthritis.

And to pay for all these pensions, in the hard times of the thirties? Agnes Macphail delighted in supplying this answer too :

"There are some birds of passage, rather wealthy birds who fly to the Bahamas. . . . One of them is Mr. Harry Oakes, and he is justifying his flight on the ground that he might avoid taxes." Other such birds were Sir Frederick Williams-Taylor and Sir Herbert Holt. "If they care to go there it is all right with me; but at least I would see, if I were in the seats of the mighty, that they did not take with them all the great gifts which this country has so richly bestowed on them. . . . I suggest that allowing those people to avoid taxation is an affront to all hard-working and destitute Canadians."

The tragedy of wasted youth during this period became of special concern.

She argued for a programme of rural community recreation: "Even if we do not solve our economic problems as rapidly as we should like to do, we could help to brighten rural life all over Canada by helping the young people to develop a satisfactory social and recreational life."

A widowed mother's letter on behalf of her four children impelled Agnes to place before the House an urgent plea for aid to youth. All four of this woman's children were working, none were idle or shiftless. Yet the eldest, a trained teacher, unable to find a school, earned $3 a week at day labour; the daughter, a trained stenographer, earned $1 an afternoon in an office three times a week; the next son learning to be an operator in a theatre earned $1 a week, and the youngest boy, with a paper route, also earned $1 a week. On these pittances the family must live!

Agnes defended youth's bitter protests. Of course they wanted jobs, and fun and fellowship as well. "Why should they not want these things, and how much less would we think of them if they did not!"

"In my generation," Agnes reflected, "youth did not worry about a job. We worried about learning to do the kind of work we were preparing ourselves for; we worried about examinations, about a diploma, about apprenticeship, but not about finding a job. I recall, when I applied for my first job, just in order to be safe I applied for five and was accepted for all five . . . It is more likely that when a young person applies for one job today there will be a hundred other applicants."

For farm youth she made a repeated plea to the Government to provide loans at low interest rates, repayable over a long term, to enable true farmers to remain on the land.

The only people worth keeping on the land, from a production point of view, cannot now get loans to enable them to buy farms. Anyone who has money today is afraid to lend it to a farmer.

So many of these men are forced off the land into the cities, where they may be employed but are certainly displacing someone else. Somewhere in the line someone is displaced from a job and goes on relief. Then in a city like Toronto or Winnipeg, or maybe in Ottawa, some person thinks up a scheme of putting that fellow who knows nothing about farming and never will, "back on the land".

And he never gets a chance, for he is not taken and put on land in Ontario and Quebec in a neighbourhood where there are schools and churches and neighbours, but up in a part of the country where a goat could not live. . . . What we ought to be doing is to provide loans at reasonable rates of interest, amortized over a long period, to young skilled farmers.

The times were badly out of joint. There were crackpots and cure-alls aplenty. But the voice of Agnes Macphail was a plain, common-sense voice, sharp sometimes with exasperation at the Government that would not or could not act to meet the desperate plight of a sick nation.

It was during this term, following the 1935 election, that Agnes lost all confidence in Mackenzie King. The Liberal leader, having routed Bennett at the polls, had proceeded to test the eight social-reform laws in the courts, and almost all were declared invalid, infringing on provincial jurisdiction. But instead of devising new means to achieve these reforms within the framework of the constitution, King withdrew into his fussy Edwardian retreat at Laurier House, where he perfected the political art of temporizing and delay.

"Canada now has two Conservative parties," Agnes announced.

She was a reformer always. Experience in Parliament merely proved to her the grain of truth in some of the most daring early proposals of the U.F.O. She still stoutly believed that party politics was a poor basis for government. The Owen Sound *Sun Times* quoted her thus, midway through her last parliamentary term :

"I believe the day will come when the Cabinet will be a body elected by the Members of the House. They will share equally in blame and praise and the situation will not be as it is now, namely, when the Government does something really fine the Opposition is in despair."

Those who praised her prowess as a politician did so without overtones of cynicism, as a kindly editorial in the Toronto *Star Weekly* (of February 28, 1936) indicates :

"She has sat in the Commons for fifteen years and some of the male members would like to know how she does it. She does it, we think, by treating her constituents like friends and talking to them like neighbours.

"She sends articles every week or so to all the papers in her constituency—well-written, interesting, 'homey'. The other day the papers carried two : one from Ottawa and one about

Agnes' trip to the southern States. In the Ottawa one she pointed out that the mourning required at the House Opening made it impossible for some of her guests to attend because they could not afford the necessary new black dress—something that would be discussed in many homes. But her genius was revealed in her account of the U.S. trip. Well down in her article she began to tell about Southern cooking and how she found it just as good as people had told her it would be. And then—no man would have done it—she planked down a recipe with the remark that some of her readers would like to try it. Of course they will try it. And at every table where it is served it will be called 'Miss Macphail's recipe' for years to come. How can anyone hope to defeat a woman like that?

"It should be said, however, that it is not just political guile that Miss Macphail practices. If that had been the case she would have been found out long ago. The fact is that she has a natural friendliness and an interest in human beings and a capacity to write entertainingly and chattily. She cultivates her political garden, but it's because she really likes gardening."

In the summer of 1936 she joined a party of seven Canadians on a tour of the Scandinavian countries and Russia. The group was headed by Dr. Leonard Marsh of McGill (later the author of Canada's most extensive social-welfare scheme) and included Miss Malvina Bolus, Agnes' former secretary in the House. Through Sweden, Finland and Denmark they travelled, visiting co-ops and folk schools, enormously impressed by the "middle way" of life enjoyed by the Scandinavian people and their emphasis on social welfare.

She told a Women's Canadian Club on her return: "The middle course taken by the Socialist governments of Sweden and Denmark in their effort to evade Communism is unbelievably sensible—so sensible that we will never get it here. It is much too sensible for us, to have our government own 90 per cent of the stocks in liquor and tobacco, the dividends of which are used for social-service work; to have the government break monopolies by operating factories, the products of which are sold at a minimum of profit; or to have our government and business enterprises build enormously in times of depression and very little in times of prosperity."

The trip to the Scandinavian countries had a profound influence on Agnes' thinking. There she saw democratic socialism at work, and successfully at work. She was enormously impressed with the way the co-operatives and socialists worked together, and most of her impatient criticism of the C.C.F. was based on the failure of the Canadian democratic socialists to set up anything resembling this. She was convinced that the farmer's enthusiasm for co-ops could be directed into the political field by people who knew and understood farmers. She felt it essential that the farmers be organized among themselves first, in a more militant group than the non-political Federation of Agriculture, and then drawn into political action through their unions.

The stay in Russia, however, was the high-light of the tour. Here again Agnes toured relentlessly, exhausting the other members of the party. "The Russian cities are beautiful; the Russian people dull and dreary. You don't hear any whistling or singing. I'm 150 per cent glad to be a Canadian.

"The women wear blouses not intended to go with any skirt, and least of all with the skirt it does go with. Coming breathless with admiration and surprise from an inspection of the magnificent underground railway called the Metro, you come suddenly upon the street cleaners of Moscow, women with silly little brooms made of twigs, busily sweeping the over-wide streets."

It was in Finland that Agnes briefly encountered Sir Oswald Mosley, who by chance saved her the ordeal of a Finnish bath. On their way through the streets of Helsinki to try the baths, Agnes and Malvina met Sir Oswald, who had attached himself that morning to their party. Mosley was obviously exhausted. When he informed them that he had just emerged from the baths, Agnes and her companion lost heart and retraced their steps to the hotel for coffee and cognac.

The taste of Europe, the introduction to older cultures and a more cosmopolitan way of life, had two diverse effects. Agnes' insatiable love of life responded promptly to these wider influences. But this broadened outlook, which made her undoubtedly a more effective public figure, began inevitably to drive a wedge between Agnes Macphail and the Grey-Bruce people with whom she had once identified herself completely. The difference began to show in testiness, in irritation and quarrelling with many of her political workers back home. The end was in sight.

But ironically it was during this period that her most constructive contribution was made to Canadian agriculture. She met and warmly admired John Bracken, Premier of Manitoba. When Bracken presented an able brief to an agricultural conference in Montreal, Agnes supported his views in the Commons.

"The farmers now have their own economists," she exulted. "They know what they want, even to the point of drafting the right legislation."

During these years she pressed for stronger marketing legislation, outside provincial scope, to meet the larger problems of interprovincial and export trade. She argued, sagely, against the move to introduce mixed farming in the West. Let the West stick to wheat, she insisted, and the East to mixed farms. It was a good, natural division of interests. And to maintain this arrangement, let the Eastern farmers not object to the subsidization of Western wheat when the prices fell.

"It might be well for me, if I were playing politics," she said, "to take the position taken by some Eastern farmers, that the West is getting much more than it deserves. I do not believe that. I think the West has suffered to an extent that is affecting not only the West but the whole Canadian economy."

Agnes held out firmly against government agricultural policy, which was aimed, with a false, assumed optimism, solely at methods of *increased production*—in a period of deflated prices and large surpluses. In the middle thirties an "Ag Rep" sported a motto on his office wall that read, "Wasn't the depression terrible?" Such an attitude was worse than foolhardy, Agnes insisted.

"What is the use," she cried in a widely quoted speech, "of

making two blades of grass grow where one grew before, if you can't sell either one?"

Emphasis ought to be on better marketing, on a subsidized price structure, on the encouragement of co-operative handling of farm products to cut down delivery costs.

She spoke boldly, in advance of her times, in support of a "two price" policy for agriculture.

"A comprehensive study must bring us to the conclusion that we cannot allow domestic prices to be set by very small surpluses, and in this regard I think we shall have to take a leaf out of the manufacturer's book. He has always sold his surpluses abroad at lower prices than he got in the home market. Even though the transportation charges might be very high, his surplus was sold in foreign countries for very much less than at home. I think we are coming close to the time of a two-price agriculture."

In September, 1939, Parliament assembled briefly for the one purpose of declaring war on Nazi Germany. Agnes spoke but once during that session. In that black week when she, like so many others, felt all her warm faith in humanity betrayed, she made a single speech. Faced with the unknown pressures of a new social upheaval, she spoke on behalf of the farm people who had sent her five times to the House of Commons.

"Agriculture in this country must not be sacrificed on the altar of mistakes in foreign policy.

"The farmers have been paying for the last war ever since it ended. . . . One does not need to make an argument about it; the shabby countryside which one sees everywhere . . . shows all too clearly that the farmer went on producing at a loss.

"We cannot allow our Government or any other to fix for agricultural products prices which would mean a continuation of the semi-starvation which the farmers of this Dominion have endured.

"I entreat the Government to listen to me on this occasion."

They were her last words, her final speech in Parliament.

Twenty-one

Colleagues and other people

One March morning in 1936 Agnes Macphail received at her office in the Parliament Buildings a large bouquet of crimson roses, with a card that identified the donors as "The Old Guard —J. S. Woodsworth, Angus MacInnis and A. A. Heaps." It was her birthday. Agnes was forty-six.

That birthday, occurring at the height of Agnes Macphail's career, was a happy occasion. In the afternoon she attended a tea given by the wives of the Cabinet Ministers, and at night a dinner in the parliamentary restaurant with a group of close friends. She was loved and honoured.

With her own associates in the C.C.F. party Agnes had come to share the special affection that belongs exclusively to comrades in a minority political group. She looked to J. S. Woodsworth not quite as a leader, for her independence was something she guarded jealously, but certainly with a degree of respect and loyalty she accorded no one else.

Angus MacInnis, for many years Woodsworth's right-hand man and perhaps his closest friend, ruffled Agnes' feathers frequently, with a tongue as sharp as her own. But between the spats they enjoyed each other's company. Basically, they were in politics for the same reasons, and this was the bond that held throughout the years.

The coming leader of the C.C.F. had been elected to Parliament in 1935. At first Agnes was not impressed by M. J. Coldwell : he seemed to her a shade too respectable, while Coldwell, for his part, looked slightly askance at Agnes' extravagant ways.

But mutual respect and regard developed, as they sat in caucus and shared the round of Commons duties.

In caucus Agnes was, according to some witnesses, not the obdurate or egotistic presence that might be expected in one who insisted on her "independence". If the C.C.F. group included prima donnas, Agnes was not one. She had a canny sense of good tactics in most political situations. Her political antennae were sensitive, and her common sense was a cohesive force in this group of her peers.

She was less at home, less sure of her ground, when the caucus met with the party "intellectuals". David Lewis and Frank R. Scott were slightly suspect, because of their academic background. She got on better with the common or garden variety of politician. Her political philosophy was not a studied thing ; it was in fact a hodge-podge of various truths picked up at odd times and places, and glued with a tremendous love of life.

Just as she was not quite at ease with the intellectuals, so she felt a certain diffidence, with a streak of snobbishness added, in the company of those from a different social background. She was always conscious of her plain rural upbringing. A fascinating contrast in personalities emerged in the meeting of Agnes Macphail and another outstanding woman of the C.C.F. movement, Mme. Thérèse Casgrain of Montreal. Thérèse, the daughter of a Cabinet Minister, moved in a circle of prominent Quebec families from which she turned, audaciously and with consummate grace, to become a tireless exponent of women's rights and the democratic socialist cause. Before that time she came to Ottawa as the wife of the Speaker of the House of Commons. She held dinner parties to which Agnes Macphail came ; she handled skilfully the delicate matter of inviting a suitable man to take Agnes in. Agnes was less aware of, and cared less for, the niceties. On one occasion when Mr. Speaker and Mme. Casgrain invited her to a luncheon, and politely suggested an hour "or thereabouts", she took them at their word and didn't trouble to be punctual, arriving in fact very late to

Colleagues and other people

the embarrassment of other guests and the extreme annoyance of M. Casgrain.

When Thérèse developed an interest in left-wing politics, Agnes was overjoyed, and ready to encourage her. A picture of Thérèse was hung in a place of honour in Agnes' office. Years later there was a touching, and awkward, occasion in Cobalt, Ontario, when Thérèse Casgrain, National Vice-President of the C.C.F., was guest speaker at a women's conference, and Agnes, having been asked to introduce her, insisted on coming to perform this office, despite her illness. She was scarcely able to complete her introduction, for her voice thickened with tears. To her, naïvely, it was a wonderful thing that a woman of rank and social privilege should join the people's cause.

By the time her parliamentary career drew near its close, Agnes had won for herself not only acceptance among the men of the House of Commons, but almost universal goodwill and affectionate regard. The insults flung at her in her first term were long past. There were compliments on every occasion now, and she responded warmly. When the Commons congratulated Ernest Lapointe on the 34th anniversary of his election to Parliament, she could rise and say with real conviction: "The Minister of Justice has always conducted himself in such a way as to restore my faith in my fellow-man and in the Members of this House of Commons."

Her standing among her colleagues was so secure that she could rib them publicly, as she did in the famous Beauty Contest that enlivened the proceedings of 1936. The session was unusually dull, from the newsmen's point of view, and it was a news reporter who egged Agnes on to name "the ten best lookers in the House of Commons".

Agnes obliged in a hilarious half-hour. Denton Massey, Conservative member for Toronto-Greenwood, was her first choice; Hugh Plaxton, Liberal member for Toronto-Trinity, stood second. She liked tall, dark men best, she said. T. A. Crerar, Ian Mackenzie, Grant MacNeil and Earl Rowe were on the list, while R. B. Bennett got marks as the "most distinguished".

A Liberal from Saskatchewan, George McPhee, rose to protest that the dignity of the House was in jeopardy, but they laughed him down. When "distinguished" R. B. B. later rose to speak there was facetious applause. The newspapers loved it and printed full-spread pictures of the "10 Best". The Members loved it too, and a dozen or so notes were hurried to her desk by page-boy—the select ten expressing their gratitude at the honour, some who had been overlooked professing chagrin, because "we had on our best suits, too".

There is no doubt that Agnes dearly loved the role of queen bee, although in fact she was not the only woman member during this last term in Parliament.

Twenty women candidates had entered their names in the 1935 federal election. One other besides Agnes had been elected —Martha Louise Black of the Yukon. The circumstances were peculiar—the Yukon seat belonged as though by divine right to her husband, George Black, a veritable legend in that region. George finding himself ill and unable to carry on when the 1935 election came along, his wife was conscripted by their friends to "hold" the seat until her husband was himself again. Under these conditions Martha Louise Black, a lady of considerable spunk and talent but with no knowledge of public affairs, came to Ottawa.

Agnes did not, being Agnes, disguise her caustic reaction to this casual approach to politics. She was fiercely anxious that woman members should acquit themselves well, for she wanted women to be accepted in this field, and she felt that only by proving themselves as good as the best of the men could they achieve acceptance.

A letter from Martha Black, expressing interest in the compilation of Agnes Macphail's biography, was written in 1957.

"I remember Miss Agnes Macphail very clearly. She was considerably younger than I was and at times showed her lack of personal feeling for me. It also seemed to me, perhaps mistakenly, that she felt that I was not serious enough for the questions at hand. She evidently did not realize that at my age I had known little or nothing concerning women in politics. It

Colleagues and other people

was all new to me. Many friends voted for me simply for the reason that I had lived in the Yukon so long and everyone in the country knew my husband and me.

"Although often she made me impatient when matters did not quite suit her, I grew to like her and appreciate what the change in public feeling towards women in politics meant to her."

The impatience was mutual.

"It is time, if women really care about the franchise, that they got into the work," Agnes told the National Council of Women in Toronto's Royal York hotel in 1935. A formal banquet was honouring such founders as suffragists Dr. Augusta Stowe-Gullen and Dr. Margaret Patterson; the guest speaker for the occasion was Agnes Macphail.

Agnes declared sternly, "You can get into the House of Commons when you're a friend of the people of any constituency, if you want to. . . . Women are long past the resoluting stage."

Mrs. Rex Eaton of Vancouver had introduced her as a woman admired by all present for her honest convictions. The Toronto *Mail and Empire* said, "A few years ago it was definitely noted that she would not have been welcomed by the National Council. Last night she was applauded to the echo."

Had Agnes Macphail *arrived* among the genteel females of her native land?

If so, it had not curbed her tongue. She was outspoken about the need for prison reform and had something to say, too, on the problem of the mentally deficient. "They must be stopped reproducing their kind. There is no modesty about shutting our eyes to this situation. And nothing will be done until we start a row about it."

Once her patriotism had been held in question over minor matters, but now she was able to say bluntly of her fellow Canadians, "We fill the back seats always—a poor, conservative people afraid almost of our own shadow, showing great lack of confidence and always afraid of being misunderstood. We carry the tang of rural life—we are kind and hospitable—

a heritage from our pioneers. We love speeches and argument and like to be stirred emotionally by speakers. It gives us the urge to do to a pleasurable degree, with not enough to put us doing it."

A rare example of bluntness, even for Agnes, was her speech to the Peace Committee of the Royal Empire Society in Montreal High School in March, 1936. Miss Idola Saint Jean, a persistent fighter for woman suffrage in her province, had invited Agnes to speak. Agnes began her remarks by saying she hadn't realized what organization Miss Saint Jean had in mind when the invitation was extended.

"The Royal Empire Society has not been my long suit—I cannot fool myself that any Empire that goes around conquering people for that people's good, is right. I am not strong for imperialism—but I am very keen about and extremely interested in King Edward VIII." (Applause!)

How did she get away with it? An American woman friend had her views in the matter :

"I am so delighted that your tour is going well. You go down because people feel that you are saying what you think; and you must remember that so many people are talking on public platforms today and have all the superficial elements that are required for public speaking, that it is a relief and a tonic to get someone who is as real and vital as you. You are . . . very magnetic and it is extremely unfair and annoying to others to have to work for what you gain before you need to begin to work at all. It often quite annoys me that you can say a few words in your lovely bass voice which seems to convey the impression of inevitability, whereas if your voice had been three tones higher, your height five inches less, your hair scurfy and thin and your legs fat, they would not be considered indisputable at all. These things are of the fundamental inequities of nature."

A handful of press notices of this period bear out the disgruntled friend's impressions :

Said the Walkerton, N.Y. *Daily Times,* in March, 1935; "Miss Macphail's address (to the American Association of University Women, at St. Lawrence University, Canton) which she sub-titled 'A Challenge to Women', sparkled throughout. Her buoyant personality revealed itself in the wit which enlivened her entire talk. With the skill bred from her long experience in politics, Miss Macphail kept in constant and intimate touch with her audience, making her points clear by vivid illustrations coupled with the force of her own personality."

Said the *Christian Science Monitor,* in February, 1936; "The possession of a beautiful voice, combined with a clear, concise exposition of facts and grasp of essentials, makes Miss Macphail a most acceptable speaker beyond Canadian borders. This winter she will make her fourth annual visit as one of the favourite speakers of the Dallas Open Forum."

And in *The New York Times,* in November, 1937, an interviewer extracted from Dr. Russell Potter, Director of Columbia University Institute of Arts and Sciences, the opinion that women lecturers were not in great demand, since they had many unattractive features, but a few notable exceptions included: Eleanor Roosevelt, Dorothy Thompson, Ruth Bryan Owen and Agnes Macphail.

Her appearances in American lecture halls had expanded into annual tours that occupied several months of every year. In December, 1935, an enterprising lecturers' agent from New York, Harold R. Peate, arrived in Toronto and booked Agnes Macphail for a lecture tour in January. Interviewed, he said, "She's a natural. She is good copy and talks well."

Under Peate auspices, Agnes again visited Dallas, Fort Worth and Austin, drawing large crowds and getting press reports loaded with admiration, with topics such as, "Should the American Continent Keep out of European Wars?" and "Money, the Key to the Situation".

She was so well received that Peate signed her again for a fall tour, and in 1937 and 1938 she went back to renew acquaintance with audiences in Texas and other Southern states, and with an increasing number of American friends.

The Peate agency was no small enterprise. Its lists of lecturers were star-studded, with names like Otis Skinner, Grant Wood, Thornton Wilder, William Rose Benet, Thomas Mann, Stefan

Zweig, Irvin S. Cobb, and the Right Honourable Winston Churchill.

To Agnes the additional income was welcome. She received $400 a week plus $10 a day for expenses. With an eye to the future and possible political mishaps, she purchased an annuity that would assure her a small fixed sum each month. Current expenses were heavier also, for her mother took a new house in Ceylon and Agnes helped establish her in it.

The Ceylon house was home to Agnes. It was brick, in the familiar Ontario country style, and stood on a sharp rise of land, giving Mrs. Macphail an opportunity to create and maintain a large and very beautiful garden. Her passion for flowers came to full expression here. Agnes loved flowers too, although her admiration took the form of impulsive buying of quantities of boxes of seedlings in the spring, and presenting them to friends and relatives, who then had the problem of planting and caring for them.

Agnes was firm about the pattern of her life. She would not be domesticated, even at home. She liked to do her serious reading and studying in the morning, and usually wore a dressing-gown until noon. She was also said to have introduced cotton "beach pyjamas" for leisure wear, which brought a mixed reaction among Ceylon neighbours. A nap in the early afternoon refreshed her for whatever came along—visits or visitors, and meetings in the evening.

This pleasant haven was disrupted when Mrs. Macphail became seriously ill in 1937. Agnes was on tour in the United States when she received a wire telling of her mother's condition. She cancelled the rest of her tour and flew home to be with her during her remaining days. Agnes' early resentment toward her mother had faded away as she matured and learned to understand her. A gentleness, mixed with warm humour, was evident between them at the last, and there was consolation for Agnes, too, in knowing she had "made her mother comfortable", in the local phrase. Mrs. Macphail died in September.

It is a long step from the out-of-the-way village of Ceylon, Ontario, to the banquet salons where Agnes Macphail spoke to literate groups of North Americans. Sometimes it taxed her strength to the utmost, and she paid for exacting social demands with periods of complete fatigue.

Mrs. Tinker, the lady who had helped her through her first term in Parliament, was hostess to her on several lecture trips to Detroit. On one occasion Agnes was guest speaker at a formal dinner given by the Women Lawyers of Michigan, with an audience made up of judges and other dignitaries. She acquitted herself well, making an outstanding speech, and afterwards joined in the dancing. But next day, at Mrs. Tinker's home, she spent the entire day in bed. Mrs. Tinker offered to bring in a tray, but this was a service Agnes didn't care for. "I have to eat with my feet under a table," she said. So she emerged from her bedroom long enough to eat breakfast and again for lunch, and went back to bed until evening.

A good friend at this time was Nellie McClung, one of the best-known Canadian writers of the period and a reformer too at heart. Mrs. McClung was Agnes' senior by some years; Agnes had read the McClung novels to her school-children. Now that both were frequently in Ottawa they saw much of each other, gossiping together of farm matters and problems of social reform. When Agnes was off on lecture tours she would receive brief, busy letters from Mrs. McClung, pointing out the urgency of abolishing capital punishment or doing something for political refugees in Europe, in the hope that Agnes would make these matters plain to her audiences.

Agnes got on well with the people of the United States whom she met on her travels. She had a large circle of friends in Texas and Louisiana, where she returned many times to speak. Returning from one visit to Louisiana State University she wrote a casual account for the benefit of home papers, remarking among other things that her American hostess was hopeless when it came to making tea. Inevitably, the article came to the attention of Dr. Harriet Daggett of the Law School faculty, Louisiana State University—who had been the hostess in question. Dr. Daggett thereupon informed Agnes that while she was very welcome to come again she must bring her own tea with her and look after the brewing of it. On her next trip Agnes did so.

American audiences, then as now, were agog over the affairs of the British royal family. Agnes took up the cause of King Edward VIII, Duke of Windsor, and spoke at length on the subject of his abdication to an enthralled public. Quite carried away by all the romantic implications, she urged, "The heart should rule, for any frustration of such an ardent love would leave the lives of both less rich."

Good judgment also took a holiday when she expressed a firm conviction that Louisiana's demagogue governor, Huey Long, was not so bad after all. She arrived at this conclusion chiefly on the evidence of Long's big contributions to the State university, which enabled it to achieve a much higher standard in the space of a few years. There were some American intellectuals who assured her that in "a state like Louisiana" democratic methods wouldn't work anyway, and Long, the champion of the people, was going about reform in the only possible way. Strangely enough, Agnes accepted this view, and chose to disbelieve or ignore Long's strong-arm political tactics. She had met him and she said, "He was the most vitally alive human being I ever came across in my life."

Colourful, history-making personalities had become flesh and blood to her. She liked Ottawa because so many interesting foreigners passed through, and she frequently met them and added new close friends to an almost endless list. Madame Anna Helen Askanasy, a Viennese lady married to a Hungarian, who fled Europe with her family in the late '30's, was an intimate friend. Mme. Askanasy, who wrote books under the name of Helen Mahler, held various strong convictions, including a belief in matriarchy as the only successful form of government. She ran a ranch in British Columbia after an unsuccessful campaign in Ottawa to effect the transfer of the entire Viennese Philharmonic Orchestra to Canada. The orchestra members happened to be Jewish, and only one is known to have survived the Nazi régime.

Agnes finally found the Peate tours too taxing, and in 1938

wrote to tell Harold Peate that she would undertake no more in January, since they left her too exhausted to do her best work in the House.

"It is not fair to my constituency and I will not do it again," she wrote. "Democracy needs the best we can give it, if we are going to save the thing." Shades of Huey Long!

Even Agnes' abundant energy could hardly cope with all she sought to achieve and to experience in these full years. Her private life was as varied and crowded as the engagement books that recorded her public appointments. Men by the score were in love with her. The "magnetic, buoyant personality" that shone from the lecture platform had its more subtle charms as well. In Dallas, Texas, a good friend waited impatiently for her return each year, taking great pains to ensure that her headquarters for the tour would be in his vicinity. In Montreal a man friend argued the many good reasons why a Montreal speaking engagement ought to be undertaken. It was far too difficult, he complained, to see her even once in a while. "That is the devil of falling for a woman with a career."

And another ardent suitor back home in Grey viewed excursions to Montreal with dark distrust, writing jealously, "I hope you are having a lovely time and that you are dining in a very luxurious place. . . . I can almost see you all dressed up and most likely being very nice to some damn' man."

"*You and your loveliness mean the world to me. . . .*"

"*When I measure the time in connection with my yearning for you. . . .*"

Men sometimes resisted a hostess' invitation to meet Canada's female M.P.; then they met her and were added to the score of others who found Agnes Macphail a completely captivating woman.

Robert Gardiner had once asked her to marry him, and she had refused. Having failed to gain re-election he was cut off from Ottawa, and he now isolated himself even from his friends and associates. He lived alone on a remote homestead. Zella Spencer, Agnes' friend, wrote in 1936 to tell of her honest regret that Gardiner had been re-elected as U.F.A. president : "I feel it was a great mistake, when the U.F.A. needs an active person. . . .You know as well as I do that Bob has—well, I always felt as though death had set in when I went in to that smoke-laden, frigid room. I am sure that physically and mentally a sort of numbness has begun."

For Gardiner this state of lonely "numbness" increased until his health broke down completely. He was ill when Agnes travelled West in 1940. She broke her journey to stop over at Macleod, and was deeply hurt when he refused to let her visit him. When he died in 1945 he left the bulk of his estate, several thousand dollars, to her.

Asked to recollect Agnes Macphail as a Member of Parliament, Judith Robinson, political journalist, remembered first her magnificent deep voice, and second her characteristic firm stride. Agnes did not move briskly and elegantly, as a city-bred woman might, but with something of the countrywoman's strong, lithe, unstudied ease of movement. She was tall, and with her pince-nez and her cape, a rather haughty figure. Well-tailored black, often with heavy silver accessories, was a favourite costume. She indulged herself extravagantly in buying shoes, for she was vain about her well-shaped hands and feet. Her thick, softly curling hair was now always well groomed, and sometimes her secretary, Lilla Bell, would brush it for her when Agnes was tired. She sent Miss Bell, too, to bring her dresses for approval from the "French Room" of Ottawa's biggest department store. And Miss Bell, far from resenting such chores, was so deeply attached to Agnes that to be assigned to another M.P. later "just didn't seem right".

Women responded quite as readily as men to her special radiance. Wherever she visited, letters followed her home full of deep affection, tinged with surprise at having been so stirred. One woman wrote from Kalamazoo, Michigan : "The thought of your visit here still warms the cockles of my heart."

Another, Miss Lena Phillips, New York president of the International Federation of Business and Professional Women, wrote : "It was a keenest joy to meet you. . . . I did not know in advance that you and I would come to know each other so easily and so happily. You see, I am taking you at your word; and I know, as doubtless you do, that under the skin you and I are off the same piece. . . . Thank you . . . for just being."

And Nora Frances Henderson, one-time controller of the city of Hamilton, wrote after a week-end spent together: "I always hear echoes of our laughter for days after—it is one of the happiest experiences I have known."

She had achieved a rare degree of personal fulfilment. She had never planned life quite this way, but had taken the opportunities and the challenge as they came, always finding within herself the vital strength to meet the immediate task. In the act of trying so hard and so ardently she had shed many successive narrower selves. She had won a personal greatness, to which sensitive people everywhere made an immediate response.

Ottawa was her home now. In March, 1939, she took a new apartment and bestirred herself to furnish it, writing to a Ceylon neighbour, Mrs. Mel Hogarth:

> Now, I need some things. Send me three complete changes of bed linen; six sheets, six pillow-cases, the best ones. Go through them all. The spread Mother gave me, the one that is now in the front room. The woollen blanket with the green end; I think it is on the back bed. . . .
>
> Send me, besides, three knives with white handles and forks to match them out of the pantry. . . . If it fits into any of the bags, you could send me one good picture; I think the one in the back room on the wall next the bathroom. You could send, too, some huckaback towels from a drawer in the white bureau upstairs and a good many glass towels—at least half a dozen, I think more—from the hall seat.
>
> Go through the tablecloths and send me one or two very small good-looking ones, especially the one with a lot of green in it, and some serviettes, any kind of good serviettes. . . . Affectionately . . .

She was presented to the King and Queen during the royal visit to Ottawa in May, 1939. When T.C.A. launched its inaugural flight that spring, she was an honoured guest in the picked company of foremost Canadians who took the first T.C.A. plane to Vancouver. (John Bracken, Manitoba's Premier, was her seat-mate, and entertained her with agricultural chit-chat on the way. They were immediately attracted to each other ; Agnes was outraged when he later consented to lead the national Conservative Party.) At the high moment of the play one does not anticipate the end. But the year was 1939.

The fireworks that marked the gala royal visit on Parliament Hill sputtered out. As summer advanced an oppressive dread fell across the whole country, a shuddering sense of a catastrophe that couldn't happen to Canada, yet was going to happen.

Of what use were all the reforms so ardently put forward, when the people one knew and loved and tried to serve were being sucked into another world war?

Twenty-two

1940: defeat

In 1935 Hitler came to power in Germany, and during the next four years the exponents of peace in the Western world were caught in a bitter dilemma.

Canada had "renounced war" in solemn international undertaking, in Paris in 1928. Agnes Macphail had said that obviously, war being renounced, we must disband our military forces, and "not be cynical, but believe that all the people of the world are fine people, and if we treat them as though they were, they will treat us in the same spirit."

All the debunkers of "jingoism", all those who had proved triumphantly that war benefited no one, whether victor or vanquished, these bold prophets of peace were forced by the march of events to accept the necessity of waging war again. Yet only twenty years had elapsed since the war that had seemed too terrible to repeat.

The disillusionment that shook the Western world in 1939 seemed to deal a death blow to the innocent idealism that flourished between the wars. Peace talk has never been revived with any great conviction. The firm belief in man's essential goodness and peaceableness has not so far been restored.

Between 1935 and 1940 Agnes trod the grim path from outright pacifism to support of Canada's participation in the Second World War. Her public speeches of those years reveal her effort to maintain an honest conviction, in the midst of shifting world events.

In May, 1935, she told a peace rally of 2000 people in Toronto's Massey Hall : "Canada should decide now what she

245

will do in case of a European war. What I want is for Canada to say, 'We are keeping out of war; we won't go into any European war.' We should say it now, to strengthen the hands of those desiring peace in the old land."

A year later she was deeply disturbed by the obvious inadequacies of the League of Nations. An abortive disarmament conference underlined her fears.

"Canada has never taken the work of the League of Nations seriously. The main block of our delegates should come from Parliament, and they should come back and report to the Parliament of Canada," she said. "We should raise the status of our representation at Geneva."

"This House," Agnes said in March, 1936, "has run along timidly with a short step in the direction of peace and a long step on the military road. We are a long way from Europe, and there does not seem to me to be any reason why we should forever be thrown into the settling of European disputes. I have lost patience with a continent that cannot manage its own trade and language and racial problems. . . . It may be that neutrality is not possible, but . . . the first thing that I should like to see tried is to remove the causes of war through collective action; but may I say quite frankly that the second thing is the maintenance of neutrality at whatever cost."

But she spoke in growing alarm to a Montreal public meeting: "I thought after the last war that never again would we be lashed into a fury of love and hate, stirred by propaganda. I don't think that any longer. The tide is moving strongly and very rapidly."

In September, 1936, Prime Minister Mackenzie King had made a speech at Geneva that was widely interpreted as isolationist, and the anti-war exponents took new heart. But when Parliament met in January, 1937, with the civil war raging in Spain, the Germans establishing new military bases in the Rhineland, and the Japanese renewing their tactics of intervention in China, King's speech to the House of Commons was no longer very definitely on the side of the neutralists.

Agnes condemned his vacillation between "the collectivist

school, the imperialist school, and the North American school. . . . In my opinion the Government deliberately refrained from being too specific."

Agnes herself had veered to a "North American" line of defence. She disavowed any great love for Great Britain, and thought the British Government should be informed that the temper of the Canadian people was not as obediently loyal as it had been in 1914. "No entanglement in European wars" was still her policy.

In 1938 came the turning-point, the painful moment when it was no longer possible to be sure of the pacifist position. Hitler had seized Austria, and the Sudeten territory.

In the Canadian House of Commons the national-defence estimates were increased, though not nearly enough to satisfy those who took war seriously. At the same moment domestic finances were desperately low ; it had just been announced that thirty-five country schools in Saskatchewan had to close their doors because the school districts had no money left to support them. And Agnes drew a deeply troubled contrast.

> If we must fight another war to save democracy, we can be pretty sure that it will be the end of democracy. It seems uncivilized that we are able to find $36,000,000 for defence while in Saskatchewan we have thirty-five rural schools closed because money cannot be found with which to keep them open . . . and almost, if not quite, a million people in Canada are still on relief.
>
> I am speaking more from instinct than anything else— I feel more and more North American in my point of view, because less and less I trust the great powers in their diplomacy and in their secret undertakings. I fear Canada being drawn into a world conflict which is none of our doing. . . .
>
> I do not know that one can say more. I do not know whether one ought to strive to have the estimate cut down. . . .
>
> Frankly, I say to the Minister I would rather open the

schools in Saskatchewan. If we are going to do a lot towards killing everybody off, then let us do the best we can for them up to the last minute.

Then 1939 came; Hitler's armies were spreading farther over the face of Europe. First-hand accounts of Nazi ruthlessness had come home to Canadians. Madame Askanasy had escaped from Austria with her children; her husband had been captured and killed.

Suddenly Agnes' loyalty jumped the Atlantic; she was no longer a "North American". In one of the most moving speeches of her career she revealed the doubts that had overwhelmed her. Her reaction was to shrink from them, to turn to what local good was still possible of accomplishment in her own land.

In these days of confusion and tragedy abroad one's mind turns to things at home, to things that one can understand. All over the world we are seeing liberty, freedom and personal security being swept away for thousands, yes even millions of people. We see democracy backing away before the onslaught of fascism. What surprises me more than anything else is the fact that the conscience of the world has been seared to such an extent that we can endure the tragedy of China, the betrayal of Czechoslovakia and the unparalleled agony of Spain without doing something about it. . . . Quite apart from what was in our innermost hearts, we listened to the Prime Minister of Great Britain being lauded the world over in the name of peace, or this new word "appeasement", for having delivered democracy into the hands of the fascists in response to a gigantic bluff on the part of the greatest dictator of them all.

She urged her parliamentary colleagues to realize that "the simpler days", when "political scrapping" was still possible, were gone. "When I heard the speeches of the first day or two at the opening of the session I thought, 'Can it be that we must all session hear this drivel again?' " She urged an awareness of

1940: defeat

the severe economic problems that still beset Canada, she asked her fellow-members to become "partisans in favour of democracy, both political and economic".

And she proceeded to lay before the House once more, in terse, hard-hitting prose, a program of reform for agriculture, for a youth-training program, for unemployment relief.

During the summer of 1939, Agnes went about her affairs in a mood of grim depression that seldom lifted. In September the crisis came. Hitler invaded Poland; two days later Great Britain and France declared war on Germany.

The policy of "no European entanglements" vanished like a puff of smoke. Canada was completely committed at the outset, and Canadians knew it very well—hence the national sense of shock.

The C.C.F. party executive called an emergency session of its National Council and caucus. Agnes was there. Leaving aside minor matters, the decision facing this meeting was the C.C.F. position in the certain event of war.

Agnes was usually a vociferous member of such meetings. During this two-day discussion she said not a word. She sat in heavy silence. When both alternatives are wrong, what is there left to say?

She gave only one indication of the way her vote would go. When a highly emotional lady sitting next her delivered an overwrought plea for peace at any price, Agnes hitched her chair away, in an obviously disgusted gesture. That was all.

J. S. Woodsworth, the C.C.F. national leader, broke with the party he had helped bring into being, and held to his pacifist faith. The others devised at first a compromise policy of participation by arms overseas, while Canadian men (as yet untrained) would be asked only to defend Canada's shores, and wealth was to be conscripted to prevent war profiteering. It was the thin edge of the wedge, and as the war progressed—after the first "phony" phase of the war under Daladier in France and Chamberlain in England—the C.C.F. altered its stand to full participation.

The tragic break with the national leader was a soul-searing affair for all his close associates, and for none more than Agnes. During these later years she had shared a front-row seat with Woodsworth in the House of Commons. He had become quite frail in health, and he had suffered a slight haemorrhage behind his eyes that left his vision badly impaired. Agnes had become used to reading to him and lending him assistance in the House, but when it occurred to her that he might like Angus MacInnis to fill this role, she offered to change seats.

"You wouldn't leave me, would you, Agnes?" Woodsworth asked.

By dint of writing notes in a very large hand, and relying heavily on his well-stocked memory, Woodsworth was able to continue his work despite poor vision. Agnes once said:

"Some day when political controversy is forgotten and J. S. Woodsworth is gone, he will be recognized as a great man. He has no interests other than improving the conditions of the people. Neither praise nor blame touches him at all. I have seen him standing speaking in the Commons, and in the galleries he sounded strong and aggressive when his knees were shaking so they would hardly hold him. His body is just an instrument for his will. If it hurts it to do what he wants, that's just too bad for his body. He brought an integrity to the Commons. . . ."

Many times in the Commons she had testified to her high regard for him and for his beliefs, as when she said on February 24, 1936:

"I have never doubted that what he seeks is to serve the people in the best possible way. He hopes that to them will come happier days, and ultimately a time when all the people will have access to the learning and the amenities that are now the privilege of the few."

J. S. Woodsworth had seconded her annual attack on cadet training, her personal campaign against war. He had stood behind her strongly in her battle for penal reform. It can hardly be told how much it cost her to desert him now. There was always the haunting fear that he was right about it, after all. If enough people could be found to take an immovable stand of passive resistance. . . . But where did you find such people in this old, bad world?

When the House of Commons assembled for a one-week special session, on September 7, 1939, the Government produced its declaration of war by way of the Speech from the Throne.

The almost plaintive résumé of events by the Prime Minister was an accurate reflection of attitudes across the country. Canadians felt they had done nothing to deserve this calamity. King said:

"I never dreamed that the day would come when . . . it should fall to my lot to be the one to lead this Dominion of Canada into a great war."

In an unexpected and generous gesture, King then paid public tribute to J. S. Woodsworth. It was as though this man was the conscience that twinged in each politician's breast, as he stood confronted with the enormous responsibility of declaring war. King said:

"There are few men in this Parliament for whom, in some particulars, I have greater respect than the leader of the Co-operative Commonwealth Federation. I admire him in my heart because time and again he has had the courage to say what lay on his conscience, regardless of what the world might think of him. A man of that calibre is an ornament to any parliament. I do not know what my honourable friend's views will be. I know he feels deeply that anything in the nature of war should not be countenanced at all. . . .

"But when it comes to a fight between good and evil," King protested, "if we do not destroy what is evil, it is going to destroy all that there is of good."

When Woodsworth rose, the House paid him the respect of silence. He spoke for himself, he said; the position of the C.C.F. would be stated by someone else.

I suggest that the common people of the country gain nothing by slaughtering the common people of any other country . . . I have every respect for the man who, with a sincere conviction, goes out to give his life if necessary in a cause which he believes to be right, but I have just as much respect for the man who refuses to enlist to kill his fellow-men and, under modern conditions, to kill women and children as well, as must be done on every front. . . .

Last century made the world a neighbourhood; this century must make it a brotherhood. . . . The choice is that or the deluge.

He declared it was always easier to fight than to rely on faith in God. "To have peace requires both courage and sacrifice." He said, "I believe that the only way to preserve liberty is by an appeal to the moral forces which are still resident among our people, and not by another resort to brute force."

In the matter of faith in God and in the ultimate goodness of mankind, "I take my place with the children," he said.

A note in Agnes' jagged handwriting was before him as he sat down.

"You are a saint."

And being less than a saint, she voted with the rest of the House of Commons to accept the Speech from the Throne and the declaration of war on Germany.

King had promised Bob Manion, leader of the Opposition, that another session of Parliament would be called before an election took place, for an election was now due. The House was called into session on January 25, 1940—and adjourned the same day with an election announcement.

Parliament had seldom been treated in so cavalier a manner. Agnes, and most other members, were furious. A major consideration was the loss of a sessional indemnity that year. Members of slight resources were confronted with an election campaign, several thousand dollars poorer than they had expected to be.

King, moving adjournment, said that since an election must take place they might as well have it as soon as possible.

Agnes interrupted: "In the winter?"

To which King replied, "What about the men who are fighting overseas? They have to face the winter."

"I'd like to see them drive over our roads," Agnes growled.

King reassured her: "Before the end of March, the roads will not have been broken up."

"They will be piled up, fence-high," Agnes said.

By which she earned the claim to prophecy.

It was a disgruntled and deeply disturbed Agnes who faced the voters of Grey-Bruce in March, 1940. She wasted considerable campaign time in berating King for going to the country: no astute politician thus admits herself unready to face an election contest.

The Liberals nominated a strong candidate, Walter Harris. This was a personal blow, for Grace Harris, his wife, was the daughter of J. J. Morrison, and had played the piano at many a U.F.O. rally. Such family connections swing many votes in the older rural ridings. While Agnes protested scornfully that no lawyer could truly represent the farmers, the Morrison connection could not be dismissed.

And Agnes herself was less truly a farmers' representative in 1940. A gradual and inevitable change had drawn her away from Grey-Bruce, though it was difficult for her to admit this. Thus she was capable of making the political blunder, at a big open-air rally in 1939, of referring in derogatory fashion to "horse-and-buggy days", while back in the shade of the trees stood the farm horses and buggies that had brought some of her most loyal supporters to that gathering.

She had quarrelled with members of her executive. Her organization was no longer the invincible force it had been.

And the war brought other factors into play, none of them to her advantage. Agnes dealt very briefly with the war in campaign speeches. She said that war had come, and her great hope was that it could be quickly ended. This impressed no one very much. The Liberals and Conservatives made full use of her many past anti-war statements.

Worst of all, her position as an Independent shrank in value with the advent of war. There was a feeling in Grey-Bruce that the Conservatives must be kept out of office, and the Liberals given a strong majority for the *cautious* prosecution of the war —the Liberals were promising that there would be no conscription, and this counted heavily with the farmers.

To top the many factors contributing to her defeat, the worst snow and storm conditions of many years prevailed through most of March, and election day arrived with the entire countryside blocked with snow. The farm vote dropped sharply. There were twelve- and fourteen-foot drifts across the back roads.

"It was terrible getting to the poll," one loyal voter told her. "I sat on the sleigh with my eyes closed so I could not see the horses plunging."

Another devoted farm woman wrote:

"We only had to go about a quarter of a mile to the polling booth, but the horses crowded and broke harness and we were over the hour going and coming. When we came out after marking our ballot someone said to Joy (age five) 'How did you vote, Joy?' She said, 'For Aggie Macphail.' They all had a good laugh but it was the only consolation I had because the snow was so deep and the votes coming in so slowly, we were all sick at heart. . . . If the cars had been running, 'our lady', as my dad says, would be going back to Ottawa."

Whether they called her "Aggie", "our lady", or both, the band of fiercely loyal supporters had dwindled and divided. The election results, which gave the Liberals a sweeping majority across the country, revealed that Agnes had run third in Grey-Bruce, losing out to Harris, who topped the poll, and the Conservative as well.

The taste of defeat was so bitter that she could not bring herself to put a good face on it.

When an Ottawa reporter called her late that night, she told him she blamed her defeat on "a reactionary wave across the country", and "the drifts".

"What are your plans now?"

"Who wants to know?" was the answer he got. "I haven't

any idea what I'll do. How could anyone expect me to make up my mind so quickly?"

She went up to Ottawa almost immediately to clear her desk, and again was churlish with news reporters. The election had not been "fair". She said, "Party politics are the curse of this country. I went down there to serve my country irrespective of any party. And what has it brought me? Nothing!" she announced grimly that she was "looking for a job".

When an Ottawa friend, Magdalena Eggleston, met her in the parliamentary library and offered a warm word of sympathy, Agnes turned her face away, unable even to speak of her defeat.

Then the public and private tributes began to arrive. There was an air of obituary about them. One paper even titled its editorial "The Passing of Agnes Macphail."

Judith Robinson, in the Toronto *Globe and Mail*, wrote obliquely of the tragic loss to Parliament of the "United Farmer-Labour Party" (this was Agnes' political label): "No other party in the House equalled it in usefulness, interest, courage and public spirit. None could touch it for deflating pomposities. At least three parties and four party leaders could have been better spared."

Letters and telegrams arrived in great batches.

"My heart nearly broke," wrote Nora Henderson.

"Very sorry that you failed to make the grade," wrote Lucy Woodsworth for her husband.

"I was awfully sorry to hear of your defeat in the elections," wrote F. A. Hardy, Parliamentary Librarian.

Thoughtfully, many began to assess what Agnes Macphail had been in Canadian politics over the past nineteen years.

A prominent Toronto barrister remarked on her success as an independent: "You have thoroughly demonstrated, as General Sherman did in Georgia, that neither bases of supply nor lines of communication were necessary in public life."

Another, this time a woman lawyer, Margaret Hyndman, stated her appreciation:

"I think every Canadian woman owes you a debt of gratitude

which can never be repaid, because you have so conducted yourself as to make it easier for woman members of Parliament who
come after you. Never once have you asked, or left any room for
anyone to say that you have asked, any quarter because you are
a woman. That in itself is something of inestimable value to all
of us."

From Denton Massey came this message : "You have made
a contribution to the debates of the House of Commons that is
more valuable, I am quite sure, than you yourself realize."

All expressed a curious finality. There were a few suggestions
that she would be back in Ottawa next time.

And for Agnes herself, the defeat was so stunning and decisive that she was unable to contemplate the prospect of rebuild-
ing her organization and trying again. She felt that "her
people" had let her down, and suffered accordingly.

She took her papers and files and pictures away from the
office on the sixth floor. She began, in belligerent, almost arrogant fashion, to seek a job to make up her loss of income.

The heart had gone out of her. She no longer belonged to
Canada's Parliament, and she could only stand enraged, like
a great lady of the theatre caught on the wrong side of the
curtain in the final act.

Twenty-three

No safe harbour

The task of adjusting to the fact that she was no longer a Member of Parliament was too difficult and complicated to be accomplished quickly. Agnes Macphail, M.P. was her rightful name; she had lost part of it, and with it her confidence of being beloved and trusted. It was not a part of the political game to her, not the right of voters to change their minds, but a betrayal. And that betrayal coloured her attitude to everyone for a period. She expected, she almost sought, rejection.

Added to the emotional upheaval was the fear of economic insecurity, a fear that was to haunt her for the rest of her life. Solvency was the foundation of self-respect in her home surroundings. She had always been extravagant, but in addition to her natural bent, she had learned to appreciate expensive things. She liked good hotels and first-class travel, pleasant restaurants and clothes of excellent quality; and she liked to be able to give presents and make loans. She had been able to provide for all these things by her own efforts. But now her source of income was cut off, and she did not know where to turn. She owned the house in Ceylon, and she had some money, even some security for the future. She had put part of her earnings as a speaker into an annuity. She was very proud of this evidence of thrift, but it was the first thing she had cut down when her tour was shortened by her mother's illness. It is necessary to realize how obsessed she became with financial security to understand some of her later actions.

She was indignant that she could have spent so many years in public service and find herself at the end of them without tangible recognition and without resources. She was convinced that if she had been as outstanding in the country's affairs as a member of one of the old political parties, some provision would have been made for her, some job would have been found.

This theory was well founded. Away back in 1926, a federal judge from Quebec died. Mackenzie King, the Prime Minister, having a soft spot in his heart for the widows of federal judges, went to Mr. Woodsworth to talk to him about this particular sad case. Mr. King explained that he thought something should be done to help the poor widow. He proposed to put her on the Pensions List of the Dominion of Canada, and he asked Mr. Woodsworth not to oppose the move.

Mr. Woodsworth said he certainly would oppose it. He'd oppose it loudly and continuously until the old people of Canada had pensions, until there was legislation to provide them for people who were not widows of distinguished judges or distinguished anything else—just old people who needed help. So Mr. King dropped the subject.

But in the early fifties, Mr. Coldwell, national leader of the C.C.F., was on the board of the Parliamentary Library and had occasion to look over the list of employees. He noticed a familiar name—a name very well known in Quebec politics.

"Who is this?" he asked. "That's the widow of Judge So-and-So," was the answer. "And what does she do here?" Mr. Coldwell inquired. "Well," he was told, "she used to come down and get her cheque once a month, but she's over eighty now and we have to send it to her."

There was nothing like that for Agnes.

There is a difference between conceit and a well-founded good opinion of oneself. Agnes had an excellent opinion of herself and she felt that she deserved consideration. She could not afford to retire to unpaid good works, and she busied herself at once to get paid employment.

She applied at headquarters for a paid job with the Ontario Co-operative Company. There was no opening for her there and she was regretfully refused. This infuriated her, and she said some very cutting things about the years of service she had given and the disappointment of being denied help when she needed it so badly. Her attitude could have destroyed a very precious relationship, but people like H. H. Hannam and R. J. Scott, and her very good friend and brother-in-law, Hugh Bailey, understood her feeling of frustration and simply bowed before the storm, knowing her fury would subside and her genuine attachment to the co-operative movement would return.

Suddenly a door seemed to stand ajar for Agnes to return to Ottawa. The death of W. G. Brown, M.P. for Saskatoon, opened a seat in Parliament, and the by-election was called for August. Mr. Brown was a minister who had worked among the unemployed and was a very popular figure. Agnes had introduced him in the House of Commons and had great respect for him. They thought alike in most matters. They disagreed in the matter of Communists—Mr. Brown thought it was possible to work with them in a good cause; Agnes knew it was not.

Brown represented the United Reform Party, a local organization. The party had elected another member, Mrs. Dorise Neilson, of Battleford, who had inherited not only Agnes' office in Ottawa, but her secretary, Lilla B. Bell—a piece of tact on the part of the Government towards Mrs. Neilson that Agnes considered misplaced indeed, although she had friendly feelings towards the new Member.

The Unity Party, as it was generally known, telephoned Agnes from Saskatoon asking if she would stand as their candidate. Any doubts were swept aside by the possibility of returning to Ottawa. She accepted and left for the West.

She was very favourably impressed with the executive of the Unity party when she met them in Saskatoon, but dismayed to find their funds extremely low. They had spent a lot of money re-electing Mr. Brown, and a by-election so soon was too much to handle. Agnes hunted up a cheap hotel to stay in. Parliament was in short session, so Mrs. Neilson was in Ottawa and Agnes was disconcerted to find that the executive did not wish to start the campaign until Mrs. Neilson returned. The three people who were most insistent on this were those whom Agnes suspected of being Communists, and she became more and more uneasy.

Mrs. Neilson returned and the campaign got under way. But there was a preliminary tour of Mrs. Neilson's riding, and that of Mackenzie King, a tour that roused in Agnes a passion to get back into Parliament and raise her voice on behalf of the Western farmers. Agnes had seen plenty of the depression, but this country was worse than anything she had imagined, and she was torn with pity and anger. Here, in a wheat-growing province, people were considered lucky if they possessed a little flour. Drought and depression had combined to lower honest farmers into grubby destitution. Mrs. Neilson's own house Agnes described as "no better than a henhouse".

Agnes was nominated on July 30th. Her candidature was approved by the C.C.F. caucus in Saskatchewan, and some of the C.C.F.'ers took an active part in her campaign—unfortunately these were members who were later expelled from the party for Communist sympathies. The only genuine C.C.F. member who helped her was R. R. Knight, later M.P. for Saskatoon. He drove her around the country, but did not speak for her. But her association with the C.C.F. did her more harm than good, in that area at that time. The fact that she was a woman—even the woman she was—told against her, and the fact that she was an Easterner was worse. Moreover, she was astonished to find that her speeches, which were radical indeed in the East, were "pretty tame" in the West.

Lilla B. Bell arrived, having driven Mrs. Neilson's children out from Ottawa. Agnes sorely needed sympathetic company by this time. On the Friday before the election she faced the fact that some of her executive were, not merely suspect, but definitely Communists. She liked Mrs. Neilson personally, but it was pretty obvious that she was Communist too—indeed, later on Mrs. Neilson openly declared herself as one.

Agnes was caught in a nasty dilemma. She could not fight her executive at this point in a campaign—could she handle them if she were elected? She knew the riding needed her, she knew she could do a good job as their member of Parliament. She

No safe harbour

refused to try to deal with the situation. She left it to fate, and fate took her off the hook.

The Unity Party supporters were mainly farmers, poor farmers with no means of transportation to the scattered polls. The party was too short of funds to supply transportation. The seat was won, by a shaky majority of 741 votes, by Alfred H. Bence, a young Conservative lawyer, tennis champion of Saskatchewan, a home-town boy. Agnes' reaction was a sincere "Thank God!"

Lilla Bell suggested, "Lets ramble"—and ramble they did. They boarded a bus and went out to the west coast. Miss Bell stayed with friends of her own, and Agnes visited the Philpotts and her old friend Madame Askanasy. Here she found sympathy and appreciation, and some of her wounds were healed. Her preoccupation with her own affairs was submerged in anxiety for the progress of the war. London was being severely bombed.

Agnes came home from her adventures so low in funds that Miss Bell paid her return fare. She busied herself to get a job. She applied in all directions, including the *Globe and Mail* in Toronto, and the Government at Ottawa. In March, 1941, she had a telegram from Ernest Lapointe, telling her Mr. King was trying to reach the Civil Service Commissioner on her behalf. Soon a second wire asked her to come to Ottawa to meet Gardiner—"matter was discussed in Council today." A third telegram informed her, "Both Norman McLarty and McNamara would be pleased to see you Saturday if you come to Ottawa."

Agnes had an offer from the *Globe and Mail* tucked away in her sleeve by that time; but she went to Ottawa to see what the boys had to offer, as the thought of working for George McCullagh's paper was not very attractive. The Ottawa interview went badly. Agnes was kept waiting, and impatiently and insultingly used the office telephone to call a friend and say quite clearly that she was "being given the old run-around as usual". A psychologist might suspect that she really could not face the prospect of taking a favour from the Liberals, and made it difficult for them. She said afterward that she was offered a job writing publicity for the Liberal party—which could be translated into a publicity job in one of the departments. The Ministers concerned, who had gone to some trouble for her, were quite ready to wash their hands of her. She announced that she had accepted a job with the *Globe and Mail* and went back to Ceylon.

On April 7, 1941, Agnes' first column in the *Globe and Mail* appeared. It was headed "Farm Betterment", and was published three times a week until March 12, 1942—"a long time", Agnes commented, "for George McCullagh to stand me". Her first column dealt with the plight of the Ontario farmer, the dearth of cash return for his work, his insecurity, the difficulty of making enough money so the farmer could retire and let his son carry on : "Today they cannot afford to retire from the farm. They retire on it, and if without a son they, in too many cases, have to revert to old-age pensions, with the farm reverting to the Crown to the extent of the pension after the death of the owner. If the farmer has a son he often is dissuaded from marriage by the prospect of bringing his bride to live with the parents . . . a situation which is hard for everyone."

Her columns were authoritative, and ranged from specific situations in hog marketing to the benefits of credit unions, with excursions into reminiscences of her family homestead. She found it extremely hard work. In Ottawa her reports to the riding had been done with the help of her secretary who gathered and sorted material, typed for her, and helped with the editing. Agnes was inclined to write as she talked, with parentheses and excursions. She found the discipline of limited space very trying, and she had no illusions about her style. However, the work paid fifty dollars a week, kept her busy, and maintained her connection with farm problems.

War-time rationing of gasoline and tires made it difficult for her to live in Ceylon and work in Toronto. She decided she must move to the city. She found a house for rent—a very large house on St. Clair Avenue, in a pleasant district. She promptly rented it, and gathered up paying guests to finance it.

She hired an excellent cook and a maid, Japanese Canadians who had been expelled from British Columbia in the hysteria of war. She was thus freed from the grim necessity of doing housework, her expenses were paid, and she had good company. Her clientele was mostly teachers, but she had a few business men as well. She also had three young girl cousins, daughters of an uncle, who lived with her and went to school. It made for a busy life.

A small episode in this period illustrated Agnes' combination of generosity and impatience. She was appealed to by a woman whose ancient aunt had been evicted from her home and had no resources and no place to go. Agnes took her in. She was not the type to mingle very well with the guests, so Agnes had her meals served to her in her bedroom. She had clothes made for her. Everything should have gone very smoothly, but it did not. The old woman was discontented, lonesome, and disagreeable, and did not suffer in silence. Agnes moved her to another boarding-house, where she paid for her but did not have to listen to her. At least, that was her intention. But the complaints went on and were relayed to her; the new landlady found her too difficult to handle. Finally Agnes became utterly exasperated, called the niece and told her to remove her ancient aunt. "Put her anywhere, put her in an institution—as long as I don't have to see her again."

Towards the end of her employment by the *Globe and Mail* she was invited to a luncheon given by George McCullagh. It was a large and swanky luncheon, intended to launch a campaign for the more militant conduct of the war. "Committee of Something", Agnes described it, with George McCullagh and George Drew very much involved. The host came over to her table and said he hoped she would support him.

"I cannot," Agnes replied flatly, "now that I have seen the people here." She felt, quite logically, that her days on his paper were numbered.

She was quite right. A new editor was hired, Mr. Farquharson, a friend and admirer of Agnes'. One of his first duties was to discharge her. She felt so sorry for him that it took the edge off her regret at losing the job.

Her last column appeared on March 12, 1942. There was no farewell in it, but Agnes took the opportunity to express her feelings on rural life and on education. She replied to various correspondents. One woman had written accusing her of condemning academic training. Agnes wrote :

"Nothing could be farther from my thought. . . . It seems that education in our secondary schools stresses the advancement of the individual to the neglect of development of social consciousness. The acquisition of an education is too often thought of as a way to make more money with less effort, rather than the acquisition of knowledge the better to serve mankind and the small section of it called the community."

Another letter, this one from an agricultural teacher in a good vocational school, complained that parents would not register their children in the vocational course, but put them into the matriculation course instead. Agnes replied :

The parents are doing mistakenly what they think best for their children. Education has been so associated in their minds with "white collar jobs" that they do not think knowledge of engines and what makes them work, and chemistry as it is used in farming, is education at all. That is understandable in view of the difference in the standard of living of professional families as compared with industrial workers' and farmers' families. . . . Rural people, instead of encouraging the continuity of rural life through their children, too often have as their sole ambition what they mistakenly call "educating them for something better" . . . . The first job is to convince the parents that the rural life is a good life, satisfying and profitable enough to maintain a standard of living in keeping with modern life. When that is done the farm children will want to continue to live in the country. . . .

Education could be so closely related to the rural life

No safe harbour

around it that the boy who was planning to farm would get all he could of it, that he might be a better farmer and a better citizen in his community. . . .

Sir Josiah Stamp said : "Education has a threefold purpose ; it should fit us to get a living, to live a life, and to mould a world." That is the sort of education I want for rural people and for all people.

Twenty-four

A change of pace

The Ontario C.C.F. wanted Agnes Macphail back as an active member. During 1941, E. B. Jolliffe, soon to be elected provincial leader, and Andrew Brewin, chairman of finance in the provincial executive, approached her. The three of them had luncheon together on several occasions. The result of these meetings was that she returned to membership in March, 1942. She was formally welcomed by the Ontario president, Professor George Grube. She replied:

"After an absence of eight years I return to membership in the C.C.F. You will recall that the U.F.O. left the C.C.F. in a body, largely because there was no understanding of agricultural problems. From the farmers' point of view it was an impossible situation at the time. My first loyalty was to agriculture. And so I went with them. And now return alone as an individual."

She commented on the excellence of the C.C.F. farm policy for Ontario, "though not yet known to the farmers. In many years I have been making speeches and taking almost the identical attitude of the C.C.F. It seems senseless to stay outside."

Late in May, Brewin reported to the provincial executive that Miss Agnes Macphail was willing to undertake organizational work for an experimental period of three months at a salary of $100, and travelling expenses of $100 a month. She was hired.

As time passed, there was some doubt in the executive about the wisdom of this appointment. Agnes had never done organizing of this kind before, and it did not occur to her that she should make reports of her progress, or even of her itinerary. She was not proclaiming herself a C.C.F. organizer, feeling she would make no progress if she did. Instead she was travelling through farm areas, attending farm meetings of all kinds— co-ops, federation, local conferences, and so on—getting in her C.C.F. work during lunch hours and leisure time.

Her experimental appointment terminated at the end of August, and the provincial secretary, Bert Leavens, opposed her reappointment, both because no tangible results had been achieved and because "her understanding of C.C.F. principles was insufficient." The latter point was well taken, for Agnes was not even concerned with C.C.F. principles except as they coincided with her own—anything she disagreed with she cheerfully repudiated. Her picture of democratic socialism had been formed in her visit to the Scandinavian countries years before, and she was not concerned with anything that did not fit into that picture.

Jolliffe pointed out that winning the Ontario farmer back to the C.C.F. was not a matter of a few weeks, and persuaded the executive that Agnes was really doing a good job for them. Shortly afterward she sent in a long and detailed report, describing the meetings she had been able to arrange with farmers, and announcing that she had arranged a farm conference to take place in October at the King Edward Hotel in Toronto to form the Agricultural Committee of the C.C.F. All the people were coming at their own expense, so she had not asked anyone from Northern Ontario.

A special fund had been raised for the purpose of using Agnes Macphail as an organizer. This fund was now depleted and the question of finance was a serious one. Agnes had become fascinated by the work, and recognized, like Jolliffe, that it was a long-term undertaking. She proposed to continue for expenses only—$25 a week until the end of the year. "Then I will get a job and be as active a member of the C.C.F. as is possible under the circumstances." This offer was accepted with gratitude.

Her report to the executive in November, after a very successful farm conference, was enthusiastic. At the end of the year she recommended that her expenses be discontinued. The executive agreed, with the proviso that they could call on her for special organizing, and that her expenses would be paid under those circumstances.

The fortunes of the C.C.F. in Ontario were on the rise at this time. Agnes was nominated as C.C.F. candidate in the riding of East York on June 11, 1943. At that time, East York was a suburb of Toronto, beginning to expand, and far more heavily populated than her old federal riding in Grey. She had not the feeling of neighbourliness towards this riding that she had enjoyed so much in the other; she was not as interested in provincial politics as in the federal field. Nevertheless, she felt needed, and threw herself into the campaign, not only on her own behalf, but for others. She made an extremely effective tour of Northern Ontario. She had lost none of her oratorical ability, none of her gift for charming audiences. She had become the famous "Aggie" long since, and people were delighted to have her in the Ontario field.

Speaking in Kenora in July, she attacked the Liberals, who were on their way out in Ontario. Writing after Agnes' death, Judith Robinson in the Toronto *Telegram* described the incident:

Mitch Hepburn was done, his machine was broken and more than one cautious Liberal politician had grasped time by the forelock and retired to the bench. Miss Macphail made reference to the fact in her speech and went on.

"Judges," she said, "are all political heelers or they would not be judges."

Next day in Ottawa a question was asked about the reports from Kenora of Miss Macphail's speech. It was answered by Right Hon. Louis St. Laurent, Minister of Justice and custodian of all the power englobed in the Defense of Canada Regulations, including the wartime power of censorship designed to prevent publication of

A change of pace

information useful to the King's enemies. Mr. St. Laurent's words were these :

"I will draw the attention of the censors to this dispatch and see if arrangements cannot be made that publicity will not in future be available for matters of this kind."

When startled parliamentarians rallied enough to ask what the new Minister of Justice meant, Mr. St. Laurent defended his proposal as quite proper. He regarded Miss Macphail's remark as neither respectful nor polite and he felt that it was a legitimate use of the powers of censorship under the Defense of Canada Regulations to censor impolite remarks about the judiciary.

Agnes retorted via her speeches that her opinion of judges was not very censorable, and of course nothing ever came of the extraordinary threat.

Her old enemy, the *Telegram* editorial page, took out after her as usual. The editors dug into the files and produced speeches of hers that were both isolationist and pacifist, ignoring her agonized change of heart. They also disinterred her old involvement with her uncle's oil well in the West. An editorial announced that the socialist candidate in York East had been an oil promoter in 1932.

York East voters were not impressed. They elected Agnes Macphail as their member of the Ontario Legislature. The C.C.F., with thirty-four members, formed the official opposition, under the leadership of E. B. Jolliffe. The Progressive Conservatives, under Premier George Drew, formed the government. It was a lively and bad-tempered legislature.

Agnes was rather like a world-famous actress who had slipped back into playing summer stock. Everything seemed very small and rather dingy. After the House of Commons with its 265 members, the Chamber at Toronto, with ninety, was like an ante-room. There was no comparison in prestige, either. As Agnes put it, "In Ottawa you meet all the queer people from all over the world. In Toronto, the city is so big and the Legislature so small that it just doesn't matter."

269

She had very much of the *grande dame* manner in the House, and she was, in fact, very much deferred to. But she nursed a sincere and vehement dislike of Premier Drew, and he had no reason to be fond of her. There was none of the between-sittings friendliness that she had enjoyed in Ottawa. They were enemies in Parliament and out.

She had the discomfort of sitting in the same House with Farquhar Oliver, who had been returned from her old riding and was a constant reminder, not only of her own failure, but of her personal disappointment in him. He had been questioned by the press, and had made it very clear that his alignment with the Liberals was permanent—or at least that he had no intention of going with the C.C.F.

The only bright spot at first was Ted Jolliffe. He had taken the place of Oliver in her political affections and had become very dear to her personally. She was equally fond of his wife, Ruth, and as their children were born she was as delighted and concerned as if she were indeed a member of the family. Jolliffe's purchase of a farm, and his intense interest in it, was the final satisfaction—at last, for Agnes, the Ontario C.C.F. had a genuine farmer as leader.

She had dropped her old animosity toward the party caucus as a waste of time, and now considered it a necessity. She was altogether impatient with Mrs. Rae Luckock, the only other woman member, who was inclined to stay home and do the family washing on Monday morning instead of attending caucus meetings. On the whole, she got along very well with the other C.C.F. members, although she and C. H. Millard of York West were inclined to form a partnership of their own on some questions, such as liquor, and make statements in the House quite different from the general feeling of their party. Agnes' habit of getting interested in some side issue during her speeches sometimes resulted in remarks that had nothing to do with C.C.F. policy. She complained that the caucus often failed to treat her with proper respect and consideration, but in fact they were very indulgent with her, and Jolliffe reported that

A change of pace

she was the one member whose shortcomings were never called to his attention by the others.

The Legislature opened on February 22, 1944. Agnes attended in a wine-coloured dress, duly reported by the papers along with Mrs. Luckock's blue gown. The Speaker was W. J. Stewart, and he was in for a rough session. Antagonisms were very high, interruptions were frequent, members from all parts of the House were willing to instruct him in his duties, and Agnes' audible comments on other members' speeches were not the least of his trials.

When she arose for her maiden speech on the second of March, Agnes was warmly applauded in welcome. She was a little patronizing, explaining that much of the agricultural problem lay under federal jurisdiction, but still many things could be done in Ontario. She paid a tribute to J. J. Morrison, the agricultural leader who had influenced her so profoundly. She also said kind words about Tom Kennedy, Minister of Agriculture, a popular man and a farmer, and Agnes found nothing wrong with him except his politics.

She could not resist talking about tariffs, a federal matter, and about lend-lease: "We have learned we can give food away . . . They call it lend-lease or mutual aid or something. It would be shocking to call it a gift . . . so they think of some other way of saying it."

When she descended to provincial affairs, it was to comment on the government proposal to take over the stockyards. "I'm glad they've been converted to socialism," she said, but remarked it would be more sensible to socialize the packing-plants instead. "If they had just waited a little longer the stockyards would have fallen into their hands, for every year a greater and greater percentage of stock is being short-cutted past the stock-yards direct to the packing plants. The government must be killing two birds with one stone, letting the shareholders out of a hole and seeming to please the farmer in the good old traditional manner."

She added, "The farmers are very interested in all the talk about a price floor for farm prices, but what they most want to know is at what level the floor will be put. A floor at the bottom of the basement would not help very much."

She demanded a municipal health scheme, more farm marketing boards, and the removal of the Ontario College of Agriculture from politics. Thus she labelled herself once more a representative of the farmers. Her loyalty to them did not waver, though she found herself drawn away to other interests as she had been in her public life at Ottawa. She was unable to bring them back into the C.C.F., as she tried so valiantly to do. The farm conference was held in the office of the opposition, and she was successful with them as long as they were treated as a separate group. But the Ontario C.C.F. had long since become an organization of individual members, with policy-making a matter for the annual convention. The farmers were uneasy, in a way that labour people were not, in an atmosphere that took it for granted that their problems were only part of a general struggle for betterment. They could not operate as part of a whole. They had thought of themselves as "the farming community" for too long, and had been wooed by politicians as a separate class for too long. Agnes scolded her party for failure to understand them.

She was made chairman of the C.C.F. caucus committee on reform institutions, and made a start by visiting Mercer Reformatory for women in downtown Toronto. It was all she detested most—badly located, crowded, old-fashioned, and under full prison discipline. Agnes took along Lloyd Fell, the provincial member for Parkdale, a handsome young man whom she instructed to distract the matron, Miss Milne, so Agnes could talk to the inmates without supervision. The little plot failed because the girls would tell her nothing. She felt they were completely cowed by the discipline. No doubt they were, but as this was their first encounter with Agnes, they were probably cowed by her, too.

She began again, in this new and smaller provincial field, the long, slow job of reform. But it was some time before she made a definite move.

Meanwhile the skirmishing in the Legislature continued.

A change of pace

Family allowances had been introduced by the Federal Government. Premier Drew had made violent speeches against them. Now he realized that he had made a mistake; family allowances were being accepted by the public as a step forward in welfare legislation.

By prearrangement with the Speaker, a member could address the House before the regular business began with the Orders of the Day. This privilege was often used by members who considered themselves insulted or misquoted in newspaper stories, injured by extra-parliamentary speeches by other members, or desirous of explaining some of their own statements outside the House. But the Premier was in the habit of using this period regularly, not for brief statements like the others, but for haranguing the House. It was not a popular habit, and the member from East York resented it audibly.

In his efforts to persuade the Legislature that he had not changed his mind—that, in fact, he had never really opposed family allowances—Mr. Drew made a speech in which he leaned heavily on British custom, British loyalties and privileges.

Agnes was thoroughly exasperated. She arose and complained that the Premier was incapable of saying plainly that he had been wrong and had realized it, a simple matter, it seemed to her. Instead he wrapped himself in the Union Jack.

"Don't you like the Union Jack?" a voice queried.

"Yes, but not with the Premier in it."

"You'll never have me, in it or out of it," retorted Mr. Drew.

Agnes said that was all right with her. The exchange caused something of an uproar, and to Agnes' astonishment, Mrs. Luckock accused her of bad taste. To Agnes, this was not only *lèse-majesté*, it was nonsense. Her view was confirmed when she received a note from Tom Kennedy, Conservative Minister of Agriculture, saying, "I enjoyed it. George gets a little too patriotic."

Outside the House she continued to be popular as a speaker, in addition to her work with the co-operatives, and her frequent contributions to the C.C.F. paper. She may have become somewhat queenly in the city, but there was no aloofness about her in the country.

On one occasion she made a speech in a rural area near Toronto, which was attended by a group from the Workers' Educational Association as well as the local farmers. The W.E.A. people made a picnic of the occasion and were allowed to use a church kitchen to prepare the tea. The women found, to their annoyance, that the last users had left the place in a mess—unwashed dishes had mould on them, "the remains of cake and sandwiches on the plates looked like miniature forests", as one of the women reported. There was no soap to be found and the women set to work to try to get the utensils clean enough to use. In the middle of their work, Agnes Macphail stalked in, impatiently wanting to know what they were doing—she was ready for a cup of tea.

She assessed the situation at once, and disappeared, returning in a few minutes with a pot full of pebbles, to use in loosening the sediment in the pots. Then she primed the pump and carried in four pails of water. The women were tremendously impressed, particularly when she made them promise they would not mention the incident to anyone, because "the women of the parish might be embarrassed".

A change of pace

Twenty-five

Defeat and recovery

Nineteen forty-five was a bad year for Agnes Macphail in all directions. Her pleasant living arrangements were broken up, her political career ground to a temporary halt, and her health gave way, never to be restored.

The big house on St. Clair Avenue in Toronto was sold, and Agnes was notified to move out at once. She fought the order and won a two months' extension. Her tenants had to find somewhere else to live; her Japanese-Canadian helpers had to be dismissed; and Agnes retreated to the Ceylon house.

The 1945 provincial election campaign was stormy, and Agnes found it extremely wearing. As usual, she was expected to assist in the campaigns of other candidates, and she did so. She spoke in Kingston, and spent most of the night following her speech on the train, returning to Toronto. The next night she spent consoling a dear friend whose son had been killed in action. It was too much. She had an attack of cerebral thrombosis. She carried on as well as she could, but was defeated at the polls.

It was in this campaign that E. B. Jolliffe sprang his charges that the Drew Government maintained a force of state police, separate from the Provincial Police force, used for labour spying among other things. He used the word "Gestapo" in this connection, and Ontario was affronted at the idea of such an accusation. Alvin (Jack) Rowe, of the Ontario Provincial Police, had come to Agnes about the situation, and through her to Jolliffe, although Rowe was not the only source of information. He was a star witness in the case when it came before a Royal

Commission, which found against Jolliffe's accusations. Agnes had a very high opinion of Rowe and, too, was deeply concerned over Jolliffe's position. To her, it was another Dawson inquiry and another heart-break.

Rowe lost his position in the Provincial Police, the C.C.F. was reduced from thirty-four to eight members in the Legislature, and the office of the Provincial Police separate from headquarters was closed.

Agnes was ordered by her doctors to avoid strain and excitement for the rest of her life. She was quite ready for a long rest. She packed up and went to Mexico, with her old friend Mrs. Tinker, who had been her first landlady and social adviser in Ottawa. She vegetated in the Mexican sun for three months, recovering her health and her energy at least enough to make her restless and anxious to get back into some kind of action. The kindness and hospitality of the Canadian Ambassador, Hugh Keenleyside, and his wife had made her stay a very pleasant one.

After the Mexican interlude, Agnes went back to the house in Ceylon and relaxed as far as she was able to. She had had a genuine fright, and had no desire to shorten her life by activity against the doctor's orders. On the other hand, was life worth prolonging in a complete backwater? Ceylon had been for years a beloved retreat, where she went for physical rest and mental quiet. But as a permanent home, it was impossible for a restless woman concerned with what was going on in the world.

She had joined the board of directors of the Ontario Co-op in 1936, and always took her responsibilities seriously. She was active and helpful in the local co-ops. She made occasional speeches. She was a vice-president of the Ontario C.C.F. But she still felt out of things.

In 1948, with a provincial election looming in sight, the League for Women in Government (predecessor of the Inter-Club Council) in Toronto, conducted a series of meetings to allow the various political parties to put their views before the membership. The C.C.F. sent Grace MacInnis, daughter of J. S. Woodsworth and wife of Agnes' old friend and sparring partner, Angus MacInnis; Gladys Strum, M.P. for Qu'Appelle, Saskatchewan; and Agnes Macphail. Later, someone remarked to Agnes that the C.C.F. meeting had been much the best in the series. "Of course it was," Agnes replied. "Where would anyone else get three such speakers?"

While she was in Toronto for this meeting, a delegation from the East York C.C.F. approached her and asked her to stand as their provincial candidate. Agnes accepted the invitation and threw herself into the campaign, in her own and other ridings. She was not quite as generous with her time and energy as she had been in the past—she wanted to live to take her seat again. She was elected in June, 1948, along with twenty other C.C.F. candidates. Once more she was a member of the official opposition, with her dear Ted Jolliffe as leader.

She moved into Toronto and made her home with Mrs. Rowe, widow of the provincial policeman, who had died tragically in a plane accident. Agnes' health was uncertain, she had begun to put on weight, but her magnetism was unimpaired. She had become a legend, and her eccentricities and mannerisms —even her lapses into bad manners—were not only tolerated, they were cherished and made the subject of anecdote. She had become thoroughly tired of listening to other people's speeches during the years, and sometimes when she was on a platform with other speakers, she appeared to go to sleep. At other times she carried on a running commentary. The napping did not disturb her fellow speakers, since they were unaware of it. But the comments, in Agnes' deep and carrying voice, were very disconcerting. On one occasion when she was making a political tour with Grace MacInnis, she indulged in the habit once too often. The next time they were together, Grace began her speech by saying, "Now, I don't mind heckling from the audience; I'm used to it and I can handle it. But I do object to attacks from the rear!"

"I'll be good!" said Agnes, very distinctly. And she was, with Grace, for whom she had both affection and respect. Other people did not fare so well. She was very restless, and at a women's conference in London, she distracted the attention of the entire group from a speech on problems of the aged being given by a social worker, by prowling around the back of the hall, gazing out the window, and so on.

"Don't mind me," she said, when she became aware that the speaker had stopped. "I just can't sit still." She was quite unpredictable with the press on her travels. Sometimes she gave them long and sparkling interviews, and sometimes she refused to have them present when she spoke. Nevertheless, reporters were always eager to listen to her, she was good copy.

During the summer she spoke at many rural picnics and meetings, and was as effective as ever, and as cutting. In one Ontario farm area, she was asked her opinion of a millionaire who had originated there, and still came back for holidays. He was an impressive figure with a beautiful white beard, and with strong church affiliation, but his connection with a hard-boiled packing industry made him unpopular with the farmers. "Well," Agnes replied, "when he dies, St. Peter will have to keep his wits about him—he looks so saintly that he might easily get into heaven by mistake!"

The Legislature opened in February, 1949, a very changed Legislature. Mr. Drew had moved on to the federal field, where he was now leader of the Progressive Conservative party, leader of the federal Official Opposition. The ambitious provincial members of the Progressive Conservative government in Ontario were jockeying for position to replace him. Meanwhile, Tom Kennedy, the former Minister of Agriculture, was Premier. He was a very popular man, elderly and amiable, and with no intention of trying to keep his high seat.

In comparison with the former sessions, the Legislature was good-tempered and polite—most of the time. In fact, one of the Labour Progressive members went so far as to say, comparing Kennedy with his predecessor, that it was "Arsenic and Old Lace".

Agnes Macphail's attitude had changed. She had come back happily this time. She felt at home; she was pleased with the calibre of her party companions, and willing to co-operate with anyone who brought in legislation that suited her. Her opening

Defeat and recovery

speech, in the debate on the Speech from the Throne, was almost benign, though she indicated politely that there was trouble ahead.

One of the government proposals was to lower the age of release of girls from training school from twenty-one to eighteen years. At the time, girls picked up on parole were sent to Mercer Reformatory with the older women. Agnes approved of the change, and said there was "something wrong with Mercer".

Mr. Dunbar, the Minister of Reform Institutions, was polite but nervous in his reply. He thanked Agnes for her advice but asked for "no reflection on Miss Milne", the superintendent, who had sent in her resignation because of age and health. He said he would welcome suggestions for her replacement. This was shadow-boxing on both sides.

Penal reform was still one of Agnes' deepest concerns. Old-age pensions was another. The old age pension was $30 a month, with a means test, paid by the federal Government. The Ontario government had stated it was willing to pay 25 per cent of an increased federal old-age pension. Agnes said she was glad to hear it. "But when? These people were seventy years of age before they started on pension. They are old. Generally the age of seventy is not so old, but when you are worrying all the time about how you will live, that lessens your strength."

She compared the pensioners with Canadian senators, who are appointed for life. "Did you ever notice to what age a senator lives? He does not worry. . . . I have seen them wheeled into the Senate when they were ninety years old. They could not get in by themselves, and they were given a handicap of ten to fifteen minutes, when they rang the bells, so that the old fellows who could walk could push in the ones who could not, in time for the three o'clock sitting."

A member interjected, "They get $40 a day."

"Well," Agnes replied, "I want $40 a month for every old-age pensioner in Ontario and I want it this year, this session. . . . Only the federal Government can lower the age limit and eliminate the means test. But Ontario can supplement by $10 a month their share of the total pension. It would cost $700,000 a month. All right, it costs $700,000 a month and I can sleep better at night and enjoy my meals more, and so will you. Any honourable members who can say 'It does not make any difference to me,' let them stand up and be counted."

She told the House about a Christmas dinner prepared by a church women's association and sponsored by the East York Kiwanis club : "A fine turkey dinner for pensioners in the area —a fine Christian thing to do . . . but everyone was disappointed. . . . The old people could eat only a little—their stomachs could not stretch to contain a reasonably good meal. We have no welfare, no visiting people, no counsellors for old-age pensioners. . . . We have done nothing at all to make them feel that the end of their life is good."

The debate on the Speech from the Throne is an occasion when members can discuss an extensive range of subjects in which they are concerned, and Agnes roamed far and wide. She appealed for better pensions for teachers; her special plea was for those who had retired some years before, who had "paid in good money for their pension fund" and now found the cost of living so high that they were receiving depreciated dollars.

She complained bitterly about the accommodation for members of the Legislature who were in opposition. Their offices were inadequate, she said, the chairs were decrepit, there was no place to do the necessary study and dictation, filing space was cramped. She remarked that the Labour Progressives had quite a decent room, with a carpet, but their filing space was one drawer in a cabinet.

Salsberg, of the Labour Progressives, interjected, "But we have no window !"

Agnes : "They were afraid to let the light in. It might dissolve the party."

She had taken quite a fancy to the new member for Durham, John Foote, V.C. He was a war veteran still under treatment at Sunnybrook, the military hospital. He seemed to her to show evidence that he was thinking and studying and genuinely interested in public questions. But she warned him that he might get into trouble if his conclusions did not "suit the Tories"—

Defeat and recovery

members of his party with ideas of their own were apt to fail to get renominated, she said. In passing, she spoke kindly about Tom Kennedy and added that the only thing wrong with him was his politics. She could not forget her old enemy George Drew, and took a swipe at him :

"I am a democratic socialist and I am not ashamed of it. . . . I would not want to be a defender of capitalism in this day and age. There was a time when we were all in favour of capitalism because we did not know anything else. . . . Anybody who is a student of public affairs knows it is slipping. . . . I am reminded of a statement made by one who used to be the Honourable Premier of this House. That we, the C.C.F., were National Socialists. A man who does not sit in this House said it was like saying that a certain man had yellow fever and that was based on the fact that he was Chinese and had a yellow skin and that he had a temperature; therefore he had yellow fever."

She finished her speech with a characteristic mixture of the urgent and the trivial: "I want old-age pensions to be raised from $30 to $40 a month; and if they cannot manage to do that and supply a few chairs, I am willing to make do with these squeaky chairs for another year. I want teachers who have taught thirty-five, forty-five and fifty-five years to get a supplement to their pension which will be liveable, and I do want to see a battery of filing cabinets put in Opposition caucus room and Liberal caucus room, and finally I want the Labour Progressives to have more than one drawer each."

Two weeks later the House voted against a $10-a-month increase for old-age pensioners. It was another example of the kind of party discipline Agnes had criticized all her life—voting the party line, not the considered opinion.

The next day she had a chance to keep the issue open. The House discontinued a subsidy to hog producers, and practically in the same breath raised the stipend of the Ministers of the Crown by $2000. (The increase had been voted some time before but it was not proposed to put it into effect.) Agnes resented the withdrawal of assistance from her farmer friends; and at the same time pointed out that while she did not consider members of the Legislature, or even Ministers, well paid, there was a great contrast between the Ministers' "stipend" and the old-age pension.

She was battling also for an improvement in institutions for the aged, and used her usual technique of specific instances, and personal experience in visiting people in these places.

March 24 was her birthday and Jolliffe, in inviting the House to wish her well, reminded them that she had been elected by the largest vote for a provincial candidate in the history of Ontario. Leslie Frost, Provincial Treasurer, spoke on behalf of Premier Kennedy, who was ill, and asked Agnes to present Bill No. 12 on behalf of the whole House. Bill No. 12 was a welcome to Newfoundland on the occasion of its joining the Confederation and becoming Canada's tenth province. It was all very amiable.

In April a new struggle began when she seconded a motion by Eamon Park, member for Davenport and on the staff of the Steelworkers Union, that demanded equal pay for equal work for women. The measure was close to Agnes' heart and she had plenty to say about it.

"I think this is a straight case of justice. If a person does the work, who they support is their own business; whether they support many or a few, I do not think that enters into the thing at all. . . . I will think that argument has some meaning when bachelors are not paid as much as married men for doing similar work, when a man with five children gets higher wages for certain work than a man with one. . . . I think it's a disgrace to men that they are not willing that women should get the same pay for doing the same work. . . . Is it because women, in their homes, do a lot of work—well, I would not like to say without pay, but certainly not for a stated sum? It has become a habit of mind, that may be it; some explanation must be found to let the boys down, Mr. Speaker, so I will advance that one—that it's simply that they are used to women doing a lot of work for nothing, so they do not see why in factories and other places of employment they should not do the same. . . . If it took Dr. Pan just thirty years to get through the Act giving married women

Defeat and recovery

the right to own property, probably we will not get it this afternoon, but some time this will come. Then we'll wonder why in the world it did not come sooner."

Agnes was a vice-president of the Ontario C.C.F., but she gave up none of her own opinions in the interests of expressing party policy, either in caucus or out. She was impatient with the people she considered slow-witted, and would not stop to explain to them, if they were members of her own party. Those who knew her realized that some of her abruptness was due to her state of health. Those who had not known her at her best considered her crotchety. But her position as a distinct asset was assured.

The C.C.F. considered rent control to be essential in the post-war confusion, with its increase in population and its overcrowding of cities and towns. Agnes considered rent control a monstrosity and said so. She owned a duplex in East York now; one of her tenants paid $40 a month and the other $120. This struck her as ridiculous.

In moments of discontent her mind was apt to turn nostalgically to the old days of the U.F.O., and when that happened she made speeches indicating that she really thought that only a separate farm party could be of any use to the farmers. Most of the time she thought nothing of the kind, and did her best to get the farmers into the C.C.F., but she was quite unpredictable on the subject, so that organizations inviting her to make speeches in farm areas did so with trepidation.

Living in Toronto, she was able to keep in closer touch with her sister Mrs. Hugh Bailey. Her other sister, Mrs. Reany, did not live there. Agnes' talent for separating her public life almost entirely from her private life was most apparent in this relationship with her family, as it was with her non-political friends and those whose politics differed sharply from hers. She was simply a different person with them, with different interests. She loved being a devoted aunt to her three nieces—two of them Baileys and one Reany. When they were small, she had enjoyed buying presents for them, particularly dresses. As always, she liked to do things her own way, so the three dresses must be exactly alike, a source of great boredom to the seamstress who made them.

With the Baileys she had the strong tie, besides her family affection, of their mutual involvement in the Ontario Co-op, where Hugh Bailey was secretary and Agnes a member of the Board of Directors. They travelled together to conventions and enjoyed each other's company.

Mrs. Bailey remembers vividly a trip to a Co-op convention in Chicago. A large group went from Canada, and when they arrived they found that something had gone wrong with the arrangements for their accommodation. The rooms they expected to occupy in a good hotel were simply not available. They were sent instead to a thoroughly run-down hostel. Agnes disappeared into her room, saying she was very tired. The Baileys went into their room, and found it unfit to occupy. It was genuinely dirty. A conference with others in the party resulted in one of the younger men being despatched to find rooms elsewhere. He was successful, and they got ready to move. The young man was sent to notify Agnes. He paced the corridor outside her door for awhile, nervous about knocking, remembering the legend of her fussiness about accommodation, her quick temper, and her propensity to let fly at the first person she encountered.

Finally he knocked, gently; and then more firmly. A delay ensued, and then Agnes came to the door, looking sleepy but calm. He explained that they had decided to move.

"That's nice," Agnes replied cheerfully. "I've had a nap. I took off the dirty pillowslip and found the pillow was quite clean, and I took off the dirty sheets and lay on the blanket."

Agnes was unpredictable.

She took possession of the upper floor of her duplex on Dunvegan Road, and her cousin Ruby Campbell moved in with her. Ruby had lived with Agnes for a while in the big house on St. Clair, along with her sisters. She was now a teacher.

The Legislature opened in February, 1950, and again the atmosphere was different. Leslie Frost had become Premier. When he was Provincial Treasurer Agnes had remarked in the

House, "He looks so nice, and as if he would not say a nasty or mean thing, and it always disappoints and surprises me that at the core of him he is a Tory." Her technique with Mr. Frost followed a pattern—she generally began with a pat and followed with an uppercut. Speaking on March 1, she said : "May I say I have very warm personal feelings for the Prime Minister. I used to think when I heard him speak other places, that he had a delightful 'folksy' way of speaking, but now I think it is a little oily."

The opposition offices had been greatly improved and Agnes congratulated the appropriate officers warmly. She went on to remark that the government should have appointed Foote to the Ministry of Education instead of Dana Porter, who was also Attorney-General.

She spoke wryly : "It is a long time now since I first became interested in government of one sort or another, and in all that time, it was not the game or the fame, which is very short-lived at best. I had a letter returned from Ottawa, I think it was yesterday, which said, 'Not known here'."

Unemployment was abroad in Canada and Agnes was concerned. She did not propose to sit silent and see the country slip back to the terrible conditions of the thirties. "Are we going to go through the soup-bowl, flop-house régime again? It is to be done all over again? Have we learned nothing since the thirties?" The Minister of Labour had assured them this was just a seasonal unemployment. "Well, Mr. Speaker, that does not make the boards any easier to lie on ; that does not make them any warmer without a blanket. The difficulty is that we do not think about them as if they were ourselves. There are a lot of fine-looking men in this House, none of them finer-looking nor more debonair than the Hon. Prime Minister (Mr. Frost); but he would not remain that way if he had to lie on a floor and cover himself with an overcoat—if he had one. . . . I do not know of any words of mine that will move a government which is not moved by such conditions as are appearing in the papers day after day . . . the federal Government talks a lot about the 'shelf of public works' which it has. Well, it must be a high shelf, because they do not seem able to get any of them down."

She asked for industrial training, particularly for the children of women on mothers' allowance. The allowance ceased when the child reached sixteen years of age. Agnes wanted it continued to eighteen, along with training, so "they would have some ability to earn a living when they go out and try . . . It would not cost so much to carry them on and train them as it does to take care of them in reformatories and jails and penitentiaries."

She asked for help for the totally disabled, for a hospital insurance scheme to cover everybody, for a more sensible and humane system of dealing with old people, and for genuine welfare work among them : "The case load of the investigators is too heavy, and the spirit of the people who have gone around has been to find out if it is all legal, and if they are not getting a little of the Government's money they should not have, and so on."

Charles Millard introduced a private bill to amend the Liquor Control Act, which Agnes seconded ; and he in turn seconded her motion to amend the Mothers' Allowance Act. Mr. Scott, Minister of Lands and Forests, had arranged for a tour of Northern Ontario the previous fall, which had greatly impressed the members who had gone, among them Agnes. She immediately demanded more roads to open up the North.

A Bill to amend the Marriage Act was introduced by the government. Somehow the impression got abroad that Agnes opposed the section on civil marriages, a controversial subject that brought out many impassioned speeches in the Legislature about marriage being a religious rite. She supported the Bill in its entirety, "including," she declared, "Section 25. I do not think that many will want civil marriage. If they do want civil marriages I do not see why they cannot have them. . . . People who are married in churches make vows and then break them." The Bill passed unanimously.

On March 23, the day before her birthday, Agnes introduced a resolution "that in the opinion of this House, the Government of Canada should be requested to eliminate the means test as a condition of old-age pension and to assume responsibility for the full amount of any expenditures involved."

Mr. Frost was going to a conference in Ottawa, and Agnes urged that the Ontario members should help him by agreeing to her resolution. "After all, the federal Government has the most money and they waste a lot of it in 'Patronage Harbour' and the like, so there is no reason they could not do some good things."

The air was more hospitable to the idea when it was proposed that the money should not come out of the Ontario budget. The Legislature agreed on principle, but Mr. Frost moved to adjourn the debate, to allow the question to be considered by a non-partisan committee in Ottawa. He promised to confer with Mr. Jolliffe to decide whether or not it should be brought up again. This was definite progress.

The truth was that in this smaller provincial arena, Agnes had far more opportunity to speak than she had enjoyed at Ottawa; and while some of the exchanges could not be called urbane, she was perfectly at home in a verbal rough and tumble.

She had lost none of her conviction that it was important to keep in touch with her constituents, and at one time wrote so many letters that she was told the franking privilege might be withdrawn from the whole House if she did not use more moderation. Her East York riding was very different from her home county of Grey. The constituency was politically partisan to a much greater degree, and this was reflected in her exclusion from community gatherings, school ceremonies and other things of that kind, where the old party officials, the M.P. and munici-pal personnel, were invited rather than the provincial member. The riding was much more urban than Agnes was used to, and she found herself losing touch with the farmers, except through the Co-operative movement.

She was always gentle with Tom Kennedy, who was once more Minister of Agriculture. In discussing a government grant to Women's Institutes, the organization so important to farm women, Agnes begged the Minister to make the grants to farm institutions genuinely free of political strings. She objected to the exclusion of political discussion from the Institutes and the

Federation of Agriculture, which she felt was based on the fear of losing the grants if they offended the government.

"It is soon to be," she said, "that nobody in the Chamber knows anything about politics because nobody will find out anything about it. . . . We have the Federated Farm women, they do not talk politics, and the Institute of Women is for 'home and country'. Home and country today without an understanding of politics is just nonsense. We cannot understand either the home or the country unless we understand political implications. . . . I feel any grant which comes from the government comes from the people of Ontario. . . . I hope therefore that the Hon. Minister will liberate these grants so everybody who receives them will feel they are still a free individual."

She seized every opportunity to further the cause of better education, pleading for improvement in teacher training, particularly in the normal schools, which produced public-school teachers; but her hostility to the "academic" slipped out almost unconsciously: "It has always amazed me that lecturers in universities do not need any training, apparently, on how to teach. I think a lot of them do not know much about it anyway, and I suppose by that time the pupils are so smart the teacher does not have to be so good."

In July of 1949, W. E. Hamilton had replaced Mr. Dunbar as Minister of Reform Institutions. Agnes' opinion of him was that he was a good man personally, with no understanding whatever of frail humanity. She had made a tour of the reform institutions, getting information and ideas, and when he made his report in the House in April of 1950, she was lying in wait for him. They had a sharp encounter, Agnes asking specific questions about the intentions of his department for providing probation officers, moving the Girls' School at Coburg to a more suitable place, provision for the mentally defective, and allied projects. She received vague and discouraging answers, and at one point remarked, "I am afraid the Hon. Minister does not realize what I am talking about." Agnes would have to wait for another Minister of Reform Institutions to get action of any kind.

Defeat and recovery

Twenty-six

The last battle

In the summer of 1950 there began a serious move to have Agnes Macphail made a member of the Canadian Senate. To those who believed that an appointed Upper Chamber had some value, it seemed that her presence would be of advantage to the country, her alertness and critical gifts a stimulus. To those who considered the Senate useless except as a reward for party stalwarts at the expense of the taxpayer, it seemed that Agnes Macphail deserved a rest, and a well-paid, secure Senate seat, without the strain of an election campaign, was just the thing.

Agnes was of two or three minds about the proposition. She said that if she had asked for a Senate seat from Mackenzie King when she was first defeated in 1940, she would have obtained it. But this remark ignored the fact that in 1940 she not only despised the Senate, she despised Mackenzie King as well, and she would never have given him the opportunity to make a generous and non-partisan gesture that would have increased his own prestige as well as hers.

Now she was tired out, though she was still expending her energy at a reckless rate, considering the hazards of her physical condition. But she was being careful about accepting extra speaking engagements, and resting as much as she could.

She still disapproved of a government body that was not elected; but she was beginning to waver. She vacillated on the subject, sometimes declaring she would never accept, at other times complaining that she was not likely to have the opportunity of rejecting it. This, of course, was perfectly true, as Mr.

St. Laurent, the Prime Minister, certainly would not make the offer unless he was positive of her acceptance. He was unable to bring himself to offer it at all. Senate seats were rewards for party activity and Agnes Macphail's activity had been undeviatingly in the service of the wrong parties. She had remarked once that she would like to be in the Senate just long enough to make a motion for its abolition.

When the Legislature opened in February 1951, Agnes thanked John Foote for publicly nominating her to the Senate, a friendly gesture on his part which meant nothing practical. She said: "I would not want the Hon. Member for Peel (Tom Kennedy) whom I have publicly acclaimed, and about whom I have said very kind things, to think that I am transferring my affections; but at least I am dividing them."

She remarked that she thought people like herself and Mr. Nixon and Mr. Kennedy "deserve something when for thirty or thirty-two years we have listened to speeches". She was not sure, she said, that it should be a senatorship, but she did think that there should be a retiring allowance for members, some sort of superannuation after a certain period.

John Foote had become Liquor Commissioner, and Agnes was very disappointed and said so. "The Hon. Member for Durham and I see almost identically in the need of reforming offenders against the law. . . . He believes as I believe, that most offenders against the law caught young enough can be reformed, and no matter how long they have been an offender . . . there is still some chance if they are treated as human beings. . . . We agree on treatment for alcoholics . . . but there my agreement ends. . . . that we should make it so easy for people to sop up liquor to such an extent that they are a bother to everybody around. We should not go on creating heavy drinkers if any way can be devised to stop people making fools of themselves."

She was bitter about the federal Government's delay in removing the means test for old-age pensions, pointing out that the Ontario House had agreed on the subject, and requesting the Ontario Liberal leader—her one-time protégé, Farquhar Oliver—to use his influence with the Liberal Government at

The last battle

Ottawa. "I am wondering," she said, "how many more elections the Federal Government—the Liberal party—is going to win on the pension-without-means-test, without keeping their pledges. . . . My personal opinion is, to win elections at the expense of suffering aged people is a diabolical performance."

Speaking on the teaching profession : "One more reference to Mr. Drew—and this will be the last one, for today at least. When he was part-time Minister of Education—and we have been cursed with part-time ministers of education . . . apparently the Government which was elected in 1943 does not think much of education to put half a man in charge . . . all I have to say is that Mr. Drew is gone and I would like to see his works follow after him."

An impartial observer who in the course of his work spent many hours in the gallery of the Legislature remarked that it was wonderful to see how cabinet ministers squirmed when Agnes Macphail rose to speak, how they behaved like schoolboys conscious of misdemeanour, hoping Teacher would not point them out to the class.

Mr. Daley, Minister of Labour, on March 12 introduced a Bill entitled "An Act to Ensure Fair Remuneration for Female Employees". This was apparently some progress along the lines Agnes and Eamon Park had started during the last session. But Agnes pointed out that the title was not as good as "Equal Pay for Equal Work". She began her speech with the usual sweetness: "Mr. Speaker, I am glad indeed that our gracious and good-looking and affable and suave Prime Minister has made a gesture towards justice for women. I appreciate even a gesture."

She then proceeded to tear the Bill apart, finishing with a motion to refer the subject matter to the Select Standing Committee on Labour, "with instructions to hear evidence, etc. from qualified experts and interested organizations and draw up for presentation to this House a Bill that truly expresses the principle of equal pay for equal work."

Park spoke eloquently, reviewing the history of the Bill. Frost remarked rather sourly that he did not believe Agnes' heart was in her amendment, she was just trying to kill the Bill. The amendment was lost, and the C.C.F., on the half-a-loaf principle, voted for the Bill as it stood.

In the matter of reform institutions, Agnes at last thought she saw the approach of genuine progress. John Foote, V.C., was made Minister of Reform Institutions. She was delighted and lost no time in going to him to get started on her projects. He was friendly and co-operative. He sent Agnes and Mrs. Burrows, her choice for a successor to Miss Milne at Mercer, on a trip to a model women's reformatory at Alderston, West Virginia. It did not occur to him to ask Agnes to keep this expedition a secret, and it did not occur to her that discretion might be desirable.

In the debate on the committee of supply, she rose to praise the improvements in reform institutions that had already taken place, mentioning the boys' school at Brampton and pointing out some things that still needed doing. Foote thanked her for her "gracious and instructive remarks" and for the co-operation and help he had had from her.

Then Agnes launched into a detailed description of the things that were wrong with the women's institution, Mercer, and an even more detailed account of the way the reformatory at Alderston was run. She spoke glowingly of the Minister sending her to West Virginia, and told the House all about it, even down to the subjects that were taught in classes there, and the handicrafts and games that kept the girls busy and content.

Mr. Foote was disconcerted. It had been unusual and indiscreet of him to send a member of the Opposition on such a mission. It was disquieting to have pointed out to his party how closely he was working with that member. He made the best of it. He announced that Miss Milne had retired and he had appointed Mrs. Burrows in her place. "I did not tell anybody about the Virginia trip, but now that it is out I am sure all hon. members would be very much in favour of it." A public-school course was being put in at Mercer, business courses, classes in beauty culture, a gymnasium, a library were planned. "I think we can do a great deal for the girls."

The last battle

The honourable members of his party were by no means in favour of the trip taken by Agnes Macphail on what amounted to government business, especially when it had such immediate results. And Mr. Foote was by no means the only embarrassed member of the House. Agnes had accepted the payment of her expenses for the trip. By law, a member of the Legislature can accept payment for a very restricted number of actions, one of them being work on select committees, but none of them covering this type of jaunt. Mr. Frost went to Mr. Jolliffe about it, and pointed out that Agnes had automatically forfeited her seat by her action. However, Mr. Frost said, he considered that the fault lay with the responsible Minister, and he would not mention the matter, nor would he allow it to be brought up by his own party members.

This was a generous gesture which put Jolliffe in an uncomfortable position, and he pointed it out to Agnes. She dismissed it as nonsense—why in the world would anyone expect her to pay her own expenses? Or alternatively, why would anyone expect her to reject a mission so dear to her heart and so important to the welfare of Ontario? She was entirely unrepentant, considered the law, in the classic phrase "an ass", and remarked that Mr. Frost had behaved very sensibly, which indeed he had. The incident, however, evidently gave Mr. Foote such a bad time that he was unwilling to buck the Cabinet on her behalf later on.

The West Virginia trip produced an important by-product. Agnes was invited to speak to a group of women in the Unitarian Church in Toronto shortly after her return. She was still full of her experience and made that the subject of her speech. She spoke so eloquently, so persuasively, that she fired her audience with her own enthusiasm. They set to work at once to form a society to work closely with the women's reformatory, to help rehabilitate the girls when they were freed, to be friends and advisers to them while they were incarcerated.

This was no fleeting enthusiasm. It took a full year to organize and get started, and Agnes did all she could to help. The women had decided to call their group the Elizabeth Fry

Society. But there was already an Elizabeth Fry Society, a group of Quakers who had every right to the name, and who had nothing to do with this new movement. Agnes went to them and explained the project, persuading them to make no protest over the use of their name. With Mrs. Burrows as matron of Mercer, the women had no initial difficulty in getting access to the building and to the girls. The Society was a source of great pride and satisfaction to Agnes.

In the fall of 1951, there was a special short session of the Legislature. The Speech from the Throne announced an agreement with the Federal Government to provide old-age pensions without a means test for everyone of seventy years and over; and an eligibility test from sixty-five to sixty-nine. There was also to be an extension of certain health services, and a provincial staff of field workers to assist the Federal Department of Welfare.

Mr. Frost announced that this was the outcome of a successful federal-provincial conference, that while it might not be perfect, some compromise had been necessary to get agreement among eleven governments—one federal and ten provincial. The House sat for little more than an hour.

The next day the Bill came up for second reading. Agnes arose in her wrath. "Yesterday I thought—although I may be wrong—that the Hon. Prime Minister was taking a great deal of credit, as he is in the habit of doing, for his party and throwing what was left over to the Liberals. I just did not like that, because it happens I was in the House of Commons when the first Old Age Pension Bill was passed, and now it happens that I am here when we are making it a bit better, so there are some things about the ancient history which I want to say."

She reviewed the history of the struggle for old-age pensions, and her recurring taunt was that both Liberals and Conservatives had fought against it every step of the way. "All the social legislation I have watched during the last thirty years . . . almost all of it has come down because a party was seeking power and made definite promises which they kept in this case, or they were shoved into that position by a desire to stay in power. . . . From now on we will go on improving the legislation little by little, but again we will get the improvements only at the time it suits the government, because of pressure or because of a desire to attain power or stay in power, to give it. We in the C.C.F. are going to vote for this Bill. It represents an important step towards the goal of social justice for which some of us have been talking and fighting for the last thirty years. Of course we will vote for it. It is our baby. . . . But just because you have taken one step toward doing something about it, I hope you will not go out and say that the millenium has come, and you brought it in yourselves. It has not come, in the first place, and secondly, you did not bring it in."

She found the pension of $40 a month inadequate, the restrictions on the earnings of people between sixty-five and sixty-nine too harsh, the health care too meagre. She ended her remarks: "I want to see . . . complete health service, medical care paid for at a decent rate, hospital care, dental care, and whatever else they need."

It was her last speech as an elected representative of the people.

Twenty-seven

Finale

The Ontario provincial election in October 1951 finished Agnes Macphail's political career for good. There would be no comeback, no other chance. The C.C.F. official opposition, including Ted Jolliffe, was defeated, only two members being re-elected. The newspapers printed editorials deploring the loss of these two able people in particular, but Agnes was dismayed at the rejection of what she had considered an exceptionally able group as a whole.

For a little while she thought her years of experience in penal reform were going to be used for the public good. Mr. Foote, Minister of Reform Institutions, told her she could expect a position in his department, probably as inspector of women's reformatories. This prospect buoyed Agnes up for a time. It was work she would enjoy doing, work that needed doing. From the first sight of him in the Legislature she had had a high opinion of Foote, and was convinced that together they could make genuine headway in the field of reform. It was so important that she was willing to renounce party politics and become a civil servant.

Time dragged on and no word came from the Department. She was unable to get in touch with Mr. Foote by telephone. Finally she went to his office and stayed until he saw her. He told her that he had been unable to get Cabinet consent to her appointment.

This was a terrible blow. She had counted on the post, not only to give her an opportunity to earn her living, but to provide a continuum in penal reform. No one understood better than Agnes Macphail the need for constant work and endless vigilance in that field. It is altogether unlike such reforms as old-age pensions, in which, once the public has accepted the principle of the thing, the amount of the pension is fixed by statute and revisions can be made steadily upward. People have a feeling of personal involvement in such welfare measures, as well as a sense of guilt when they know old people are being neglected.

There is no such emotional involvement in dealing with criminals, not even with young delinquents. They are stowed away, out of sight, and the public is willing to keep them out of mind as well. Administration is all-important in this field, and unless there is someone intensely concerned, patiently observant and untiringly vocal, the public is more than willing to accept official statements of reforms on paper, assurances that all is well, and to leave this difficult and unpleasant problem to somebody—anybody—else.

A memorial dinner was held in Windsor in honour of the founder of the C.C.F., J. S. Woodsworth, and Agnes went there to speak. She had a severe attack of cerebral thrombosis and was rushed to the hospital. She never recovered completely from this attack, and it left her sadly changed. Her doctors were explicit in their warnings. She must be quiet, she must not strain herself physically or mentally, she must diet severely to reduce the strain on her heart.

She hated being careful as much as she hated feeling useless, with so much to be done in the world. She hated the way her sturdy body had betrayed her. The illness had left her uncertain in her balance. "I stagger around like a drunk!" she said indignantly. She was reduced to wearing sensible footwear—no more elegant shoes for Agnes. She made jokes about it to her friends. But her restlessness was dreadful.

She talked about her poverty, and dreamed of some kind of part-time job, but her physical condition precluded anyone being interested in employing her. People tried to help her with suggestions of things she might do—her old plea for voluntary visitors to the aged came back and camped on her doorstep when she was asked to become one. This was not the sort of thing she had in mind.

Her sister, Mrs. Bailey, was in daily touch with her by telephone, as well as through frequent visits back and forth, and she had Ruby Campbell living with her. Ruby was teaching, and it bothered Agnes to see her leave for work every day and come home again at the end of it, while she, Agnes, stayed behind like the housewife she had never wanted to be. She was proud of her competence in the house and enjoyed having friends in for nicely served meals, but occasionally she would decide she was being treated like a housekeeper, and explode. It was difficult for her companion, and her tantrums were extremely dangerous to herself and resulted invariably in her having to stay in bed for a day. She could not even afford her temper any more.

She played with the idea of putting a second mortgage on her house and getting into speculative real estate to make money, and Ted Jolliffe patiently came to talk these proposals over with her and persuade her to keep what she had.

She was encouraging and helping the Elizabeth Fry Society, taking part in some C.C.F. functions, and acting as guest speaker at church services. But she had always done these things as accompaniments to her main work, not as her principal interests.

Her obsession with financial security cast a shadow over her life and led to some unfortunate misunderstandings. This obsession was not, of course, entirely what it appeared to be. Agnes had always soaked up love and admiration like a thirsty plant, and like a plant deprived of moisture, she suffered without it. A fixed income from the public treasury would be a recurring recognition of her services to Canada, a reassurance that she was valued.

The campaign to get her into the Senate was in full swing. Women's organizations, newspapers, magazines, individuals, all were urging the Prime Minister to make the appointment. A poll early in June of 1952, conducted by the Canadian Institute of Public Opinion, showed that a majority of the people of

Canada knew her and wanted her in the Senate. This could be construed as a genuine, general opinion, not as a statement of pressure groups. Still Mr. St. Laurent promised vaguely to look into it.

Meanwhile Agnes was on the trail of something much more desirable from her point of view. The House of Commons was studying a bill that would set up a superannuation fund for Members who had served for a long time. Agnes put on pressure in all directions. She even wrote George Drew, her old enemy. Mr. Drew must have been astonished, but he replied in a very courteous letter, promising to bring the matter up in the appropriate committee.

Agnes' earlier illness had cut her attendance at the House of Commons by a session. This was just enough to exclude her from the category of pensioner when the final bill was passed. She, and many others, felt that she should have been included, that there were so few people in her particular situation that it would have cost the country very little to recognize their services in this very sensible form. She was aware that women who had done nothing but background work for the major parties had been provided for in sinecures of one kind or another. There was some talk of an arrangement being made to get her in, but this would involve paying a sum of some thousands of dollars into the fund, and she could not do it.

She wrote a letter to the papers about her plight, in an effort to arouse public opinion in getting her the Commons pension. This unfortunate epistle sounded not at all like Agnes, but like a petulant, forlorn old woman. It alarmed her acquaintances and well-wishers and appalled her friends and relatives. A move began at once to take up a collection throughout the C.C.F. in Canada, through the women's groups. When Agnes learned of this, it was her turn to be appalled. She begged the women to do nothing of the sort. This was not at all what she had meant, and she disliked people taking literally her statements that she was poor.

A pleasant interlude brightened her life in 1952. She had bought a ticket from her paper boy on a car draw. The draw took place at a street festival in Leaside, and Agnes Macphail's name was on the winning ticket. The paper boy ran all the way to her house to tell her the good news, and Agnes lunched out with him, enormously pleased.

She already owned a little English car, so she took the cash value instead, something over two thousand dollars. To reporters who asked what she intended to do with it she said primly that she would pay it on her mortgage. She did pay some of it on her mortgage; she also trudged down to the C.C.F. office and made a generous contribution to the party. But the bulk of it went on a trip. "Here am I," she said, "named Agnes Campbell Macphail, and I have never been to Scotland!" So she went to Scotland.

Her travelling companion on this trip was a very old friend, Mrs. W. H. Wilmott. They had met when Agnes was teaching at the East Gwillimbury school near Sharon just before Agnes' political career began, and they had never lost touch. Mrs. Wilmott and Agnes sailed for the British Isles on the *Empress of France* on July 17 and stayed away until the first of October. It was a delightful trip, and although Agnes sometimes got dreadfully tired, she enjoyed it thoroughly. The return passage was very rough, and Agnes sought out the captain as they neared Quebec, to thank him for bringing them through turbulent waters.

The campaign for the Senate went rolling on. Agnes' former secretary, Lilla B. Bell, wrote eloquently to many organizations and kept the support steady. It is impossible not to recall Agnes' own words early in her career when she remarked on the obstinacy of the Government in the face of things that were necessary and right.

She was resigned to the fact that she could never fight another election campaign. Her riding of East York had been divided so that it was, at that time, smaller and more manageable than it had been, but at suggestions that she might have another try, she replied that she would rather stay alive. She had sold her house in Ceylon, but she enjoyed going back to the

Finale

neighbourhood and dropping in unexpectedly on friends and relatives, sure of a warm welcome.

Ted Jolliffe resigned as Ontario leader of the C.C.F. Agnes wrote Miss Bell : "Resignation of Jolliffe breaks my heart, but four children cannot be raised on air . . . would have come sooner but Ruth was willing to make every possible sacrifice." Only the "Lovingly" at the end and her signature were written, the rest of the note was printed.

She attended the convention to elect a new provincial leader and received a courtesy nomination. This gave her an opportunity to make a speech, a moving tribute to Ted Jolliffe and an amusing series of suggestions about the requirements for a new leader.

She paid a visit to Ottawa, where her friends were dismayed at her changed appearance—in the House of Commons, where she went to visit Elmore Philpott, some old acquaintances literally did not recognize her.

Under pressure from all directions, the Prime Minister decided to give Agnes Macphail a Senate appointment. He assured Elmore Philpott of this in a reply to a letter. But he moved slowly, very slowly, too slowly. He told Philpott verbally, in the presence of Miss Bell, that the appointment would be announced in the spring of 1954, along with several others.

Agnes had spent her life as she spent her money, generously and impulsively, pausing occasionally to tot up her resources and decide to be more careful, but quite unable to be parsimonious. On one occasion she asked Ruby Campbell to draw up a budget for her, so she could live within her income. Ruby did so, and when Agnes examined the careful allotment, she said, "But there's nothing left for Agnes!" and put it aside.

By February of 1954 there was nothing left for Agnes in the budget of life. Her body could not wait for the slow process that would give her public honour while she was alive to enjoy it. She had a heart attack on Thursday, February 11, and died in the Wellesley Hospital, Toronto, on February 13.

Three funeral services honoured her, one in Toronto on the following Monday morning, one in Flesherton on the same evening, and the final burial service at Priceville on Tuesday afternoon. Jolliffe wrote about it: "When we stood beside her grave, the swift driving snow was lashing the Grey County hills all around us and so fierce was the wind that the voice of the minister could scarcely be heard. Agnes Macphail had left the storm-troubled world in which she had done so much for peace and justice."

Men and women all over Canada mourned her, privately and in print. The newspapers carried tributes to her work and her personality. Her sisters were moved to find, among the hundreds of floral gifts, a wreath from the Inmates' Welfare Committee of Kingston Penitentiary.

The four women Senators and the five women Members of Parliament, whose entry into public life had been eased by Agnes years before, formed a committee to arrange a memorial to her. Her sisters had a bust of her that had been made some time earlier, and allowed this to be used as a model. The sculptor, Felix de Weldon, contributed a silver plaque for the pedestal.

A year after her death, in March, 1955, an impressive ceremony took place in the House of Commons. The Hon. C. G. Power for the Liberals, Hon. Earl Rowe for the Progressive Conservatives, Angus MacInnis for the C.C.F., and J. H. Blackmore of the Social Credit party, made the formal short speeches. These were all men who had known Agnes—the deans of their parties. MacInnis said: "She was a person of warm human sympathies. She was anxious that everyone should have the opportunity to make the best of his or her life."

Power quoted Agnes' opening speech in Parliament: "Mr. Speaker, I want at the outset of my remarks to assume full responsibility for what I am about to say; I do not want anyone else to have to bear that responsibility with me except my constituency." Mr. Power went on to say, "To that proposition, namely her sole responsibility for the attitudes which she assumed, she adhered during the whole of the nineteen years of her career in the House; and neither cajolery nor flattery nor intimidation would change her point of view in support of or opposition to the legislation which came before her for consideration. She co-operated with others as individuals or groups, but she was ever a coequal ally, never a subservient follower."

The bust, standing in the north-west corridor of the House of Commons, was unveiled by her sisters, Mrs. Bailey and Mrs. Reany. The inscription is perfectly simple :

Agnes Campbell Macphail, M.P.
First woman elected to the House of Commons
1921–1940

Meanwhile the Elizabeth Fry Society that she had founded in Canada began collecting, from all across the country, money for a memorial fund. This takes the form of a scholarship fund to assist social-service students who are interested in the probation and rehabilitation of women prisoners.

Agnes Macphail's own summary of her life is contained in a form letter. The Canadian Encyclopaedia, gathering information, had sent it to her to fill out. It was found and mailed from the hospital two days after her death. In difficult, scratchy printing, it read : "Went to League of Nations with Canadian delegation 1929 . . . went to Northern Europe, Sweden, Denmark and Russia with McGill group in 1937 . . . Spoke from Atlantic to Pacific in U.S.A. and in Canada, and also made speeches in London, England . . ." Under "Special Honours or Other Important Facts", she printed, "No special honours except the love of the people, which I value more than any other."

There is no doubt that the tribute she would have valued most came from Kingston Penitentiary, in an article called "In Memoriam" carried in the *K.P. Telescope* :

"Imprisonment at its best is distasteful and degrading, yet conditions today in Canadian penitentiaries are far better than they were in the 1930's when Agnes Macphail set foot within the old North Gate. The changes wrought within these cold grey walls were her handiwork ; to her must go our tribute."

303

Index

Addams, Jane, 145, 147
Anderson, Harry, 187, 198, 210–211
Archambault Commission, 182–183, 190, 201, 203–204, 211
Archambault, Justice Joseph, 210–212
Astor, Lady, 71–72

Bailey, Hugh, 55, 259, 283
Bailey, Lilly (Macphail), 32, 35, 55, 283, 299, 303
Baynes, Charles, 185, 187–196
Beaudoin, Gerard, 195–196
Bell, Lilla B., 80, 212–213, 242, 259–261, 300–301
Bennett, R. B., 62, 112, 116, 152–153, 155–161, 166, 206, 208,
    210, 213, 215, 219–220, 226
Bisaillon, J. E., 108–109
Black, Martha Louise, 234–235
Borden, Sir Robert, 16, 46, 48, 58
Boxer Rebellion, 130–131
Bracken, John, 229, 244
Brewin, Andrew, 266
Buck, Tim, 207
Byng, Lord, 14, 103, 115

Cadets, 87–90, 129, 140
Campbell, Jean, 23–25, 32, 53–54
Campbell, John, 23, 25
Campbell, Ruby, 284, 298, 301

Campbells, 19, 21–23
Canadian Club, 131, 135, 227
Canadian Council of Agriculture, 46, 75, 81
Canadian Prohibition Bureau, 139
Casgrain, Thérèse, 48, 232–233
Ceylon, Ont., 28, 52, 59, 74, 97, 136, 174, 218, 238, 243, 257, 262, 275–276, 300
Chautauqua, 142, 144–145
Church, Tommy, 130
Coldwell, M. J., 128, 162, 215, 231, 258
Conscription, 46
Conservatives (Progressive Conservatives), 16, 37–38, 46, 50, 58, 103–110, 113–115, 122, 153, 181, 189, 220, 253–254, 269, 294
Co-operative Commonwealth Federation (C.C.F.), 85, 106, 156, 163, 165–179, 215–222, 228, 231–232, 249, 260, 266–267, 270, 272, 276–277, 281, 283, 292, 295–296, 298–300
Craig, R. W., 210
Crerar, T. A., 16, 46, 63, 65, 67, 75, 80, 125, 233
Customs scandal, 108–109, 110, 112

Dawson, J. D., 190–193, 195–198, 203, 209
Drayton, Sir Henry, 53
Drew, George, 263, 269–270, 273, 275, 278, 281, 291, 299
Drury, E. C., 44, 47, 50–51, 66, 81
Dunbar, George, 279
Durham, Ont., 55–56, 58–59, 98, 118, 120–123, 154, 219

Eggleston, Wilfrid, 72
Elliott, Preston, 81–82
Equal pay for equal work, 282
Euler, W. D., 148–149

Farmer's Sun, 43, 47, 105, 166
Ferguson, G. Howard, 131–132

Foote, John, 280, 285, 290, 292–293, 296
Ford, Henry, 145
Forke, Robert, 79–81, 103, 125
Foster, Sir George, 149–150
Frost, Leslie, 284–285, 287, 291, 293–294
Fry, Elizabeth, 31 ; Elizabeth Fry Society, 293, 298, 303

Gardiner, Robert, 40, 66, 81–82, 160, 162, 165, 170, 220, 241–
    242
"Ginger Group", 81–82
Glace Bay, N. S., 91–92, 217
Good, W. C., 44, 47, 81, 164
Gouin, Sir Lomer, 63
Gowanlocks, Ont., 35–36
Graham, George P., 64
Grange, The (farm organization), 44–45
Grey County, Ont., 17, 19, 22
Group government, 45, 66
Grube, George, 266
Guthrie, Hugh, 68–69, 123, 176, 186–190, 193–198, 204, 206,
    208–210

Hall, Alfred, 191–195, 197–198
Hannam, H. H., 51, 168, 174, 176, 259
Harris, Walter, 253–254
Heaps, A. A., 111, 177, 215, 217, 231
Hearst, Sir William, 50
Hepburn, Mitchell, 126, 172, 221–222, 268

Irvine, William, 50, 57, 66–67, 69, 82, 163, 165

Jamieson, Dr. David, 54, 124, 181
Jamieson, Laura, 145–146
Jolliffe, E. B., 200, 266–267, 269–270, 275–277, 282, 287, 293,
    296, 298, 301–302

Kennedy, Tom, 271, 273, 278, 281–282, 287, 290
King, Mackenzie, 15–16, 50, 62, 67, 69–70, 80, 102–120, 123,
    127–128, 135, 145, 152, 157, 161, 210, 217, 219, 220, 226,
    246, 251–253, 258, 260–261, 289
Kinloss, Ont., 36–38, 40
Knowles, R. E., 72, 173

Labour, 16, 50, 69, 111, 125, 128, 157, 159, 162, 168, 172,
    175–178, 291
Lapointe Ernest, 64, 108, 110–112, 134, 203, 210, 233, 261
Latter Day Saints, 23, 34, 58
Laurier, Sir Wilfrid, 38, 44, 46
League for Social Reconstruction, 168
League of Nations, 139, 145, 149–151, 180, 246
LeBourdais, D. M., 171–172, 174, 176–177
Lemieux, Rodolphe, 18
Lewis, David, 232
Liberals, 15–16, 37–38, 46, 50, 75, 80, 102, 105, 107–108, 110,
    113–114, 117–119, 122, 125, 127, 161, 172, 179, 220–222,
    253–254, 262, 270, 294
Long, Huey, 240
Luckock, Rae, 270, 273

McClung, Nellie, 239
McCullagh, George, 218, 261–263
MacDonald, Ramsay, 148–149
MacInnis, Angus, 169–170, 175, 217, 231, 250, 302
MacInnis, Grace (Woodsworth), 276–277
Macphail, Alexander, 20, 22, 25
Macphail, Dougal, 22, 25, 28–29, 32, 35, 52, 58, 97, 136
Macphail, Henrietta (Campbell), 22, 25–26, 32, 238
Macphail, Jean, 21
Macphails, 19–20, 24
McRuer, J. C., 195–197, 211
Megloughlin, Col. W. B., 196–198, 208

Meighen, Arthur, 15, 58, 63, 65, 67, 103–107, 109–110, 112,
    115–118, 123
Mitchell, Humphrey, 168, 176

Neilson, Dorise, 259–260
No-More-War Society, 140–141

Old age pensions, 106–107, 109, 114, 126, 223, 279–282, 287,
    290, 294–295
Oliver, Farquhar, 29, 32, 58, 96, 101, 122, 124, 154, 181, 221–
    222, 270, 290
Ormond, D. M., 190, 198, 202–204, 208–209
Ottawa Citizen, 72
Ottawa Journal, 71–72, 127–128
Owen Sound, Ont., 22, 32, 121–122, 135, 181, 222
Oyen, Alta., 40, 172

Park, Eamon, 282, 291
Patrons of Industry, 44
Peate Bureau, 145, 237, 240
Penal reform, 91, 111, 133, 179, 182, 200–205, 272, 288, 292
Philpott, Elmore, 57, 172–174, 176, 178, 222, 261, 301
Pouliot, Jean-François, 65, 132
Power, C. G., 115, 302
Progressives, 16, 60, 62, 65–66, 68–69, 75, 80–82, 98–99, 102–
    107, 109–111, 114, 118, 125, 220, 257
Proton Twp., Ont., 19, 21–22, 24, 28, 54–56, 122

Quay, Mrs., 70, 78, 80, 107, 239, 276

Reany, Gertha (Macphail), 35–36, 55, 283, 303
Recall, Power of, 45, 66

Reconstruction Party, 218
Regina Manifesto, 168–170
Robinson, Judith, 242, 255, 268
Rowe, Alvin, 275–276
Royal Empire Society, 236
Ryan, "Red", 213–214

St. Laurent, Louis, 268–269, 290, 299
Scott, Frank R., 232
Senate, 73, 78, 132, 289–290, 301
Sharon, Ont., 41–42, 51, 58
South-East Grey, 17, 59, 61, 67, 74, 95, 104, 122, 124, 135, 153, 173, 180
Stevens, H. H., 108–109, 113–114, 131, 218–219

Tariffs, 37, 45, 53, 58, 67, 70, 126, 132
Toronto *Globe,* 130, 186–187, 198
Toronto *Globe and Mail,* 261–263
Toronto *Mail and Empire,* 37
Toronto Star, 60, 166, 173, 218, 226
Toronto *Telegram,* 71, 123, 140–141, 268–269

Underhill, Frank, 171, 174
Unemployed, 67, 156, 160, 164, 285
Union Government, 46
United Farmers, 46, 81, 140, 159, 162
United Farmers of Alberta (U.F.A.), 66, 104, 125, 157, 162, 220, 242
United Farmers of Ontario (U.F.O.), 44–45, 47, 49–54, 56, 60, 72, 75, 81, 85, 103, 122, 153, 155, 157, 163–166, 168, 172–173, 175, 177–179, 220, 226, 253, 283
United Reform Party (Unity Party), 259, 261

Votes for Women, 38, 47–48, 68

Wilkinson, Ellen, 147–148
Willingdon, Lady, 135
Women's International League for Peace and Freedom, 111, 140–141
Wood, Henry Wise, 45, 162
Woodsworth, J. S., 17, 66–67, 74, 77, 81–82, 87, 106–107, 111–115, 123, 130–131, 133, 159–160, 163, 166, 171, 175–178, 208, 216, 231, 249–251, 258, 297